# Coping with Learning Disabilities

*A Book for Parents*

Alan Balter Ph.D.

**KENDALL/HUNT PUBLISHING COMPANY**
4050 Westmark Drive    Dubuque, Iowa 52002

Copyright © 1996 by Kendall/Hunt Publishing Company

ISBN 0-7872-1356-X

All rights reserved. No part of this publication may be reproduced, stored in a retrieval system, or transmitted, in any form or by any means, electronic, mechanical, photocopying, recording, or otherwise, without the prior written permission of the copyright owner.

Printed in the United States of America
10  9  8  7  6  5  4  3  2  1

For
my sister Abby
who might not have
been our parents' favorite
but has always been
mine

# Contents

| | | |
|---|---|---|
| Introduction | | 1 |
| Chapter 1 | *Family Reactions* | 5 |
| Chapter 2 | *Learning Disability: What Is It?* | 37 |
| Chapter 3 | *The Prevalence of Learning Disability* | 61 |
| Chapter 4 | *The Parent-School Partnership* | 73 |
| Chapter 5 | *Outside of School: Diet, Vision, and Learning Centers* | 95 |
| Chapter 6 | *Outside of School: Medication* | 127 |
| Chapter 7 | *Into Adolescence* | 143 |
| Chapter 8 | *Adults at Last* | 163 |
| Chapter 9 | *Bringing It All Home* | 179 |
| Epilogue | | 193 |
| References | | 195 |
| Appendix I | *Individualized Educational Plan (IEP)* | 197 |
| Appendix II | *Addresses of Organizations* | 213 |

# Introduction

Not long ago, I was having a leisurely lunch with an old, fat friend. He is a person who has lost and regained almost a ton during his personal, 40 year "Battle of the Bulge". When it comes to eating, moderation has never been his style. Instead, he has alternated between the deprivation of crash dieting and the gluttony of feeding frenzies. Now, he weighs more than ever. With resignation and a hint of sadness, he said, "You know, I think I've finally come to grips with it; I guess I'll always be fat, but I really hate that word". I asked him what he would use in its place. His jowls shook as he answered. He told me that in the future, he would prefer to be called "calorically indulged". We laughed and then he shoveled in another substantial mound of banana cream pie.

My friend's choice of words is an example of how our language changes. Words are constantly being added and dropped, or they are used differently. Sometimes it's an invention like computers that stimulates change. Nobody talked about floppy discs, software, word processing, CD Roms, or modems a generation ago. A hacker was someone who drove a taxicab, and a hard drive was a difficult golf shot. In other instances, existing terms became offensive and were replaced in the spirit of political correctness. So a chairman is now a "chairperson"; a stewardess is a "flight attendant"; waiters and waitresses are "waitstaff"; a short person is "vertically challenged"; and a dead person is "terminally inconvenienced"!

The language used in certain professions changes too. Consider special education, for example. Each generation proposes a new set of terms. Children who were once called "feebleminded" became "educable mentally handicapped", and recently evolved into "cognitively delayed". Similarly, deaf children are now "auditorilly impaired", bad kids are "behavior disordered", children who don't sit still are "hyperactive", children who don't listen have an "attention deficit disorder", and those who stutter have a "fluency disorder". Furthermore, institutions have become "residential facilities", and talking with another teacher is now "collaborative consultation". It's not that changes in terminology are necessarily bad or never needed; it might be better, though, if more of the energy devoted to thinking up new words to call children with disabilities would be spent in figuring out new and more effective ways to teach them.

Some new terms aren't derivatives of older ones. They just spring up and suddenly gain widespread acceptance and usage. "Learning disabilities" is one of those. It wasn't until thirty years ago that the term appeared in textbooks, professional journals, and the popular press. Shortly thereafter, the public schools began to offer special programs for students with learning disabilities. Growth has been so extensive that at the present time, there are more children attending learning disability classes than any other type of special education program.

During the same time that learning disability services have expanded so rapidly, there has been a lot of controversy over the most basic issues. Experts in the field continue to disagree about definition. Similar debate goes on with respect to the causes of learning disability and the prevalence of the problem. How to identify children with learning disabilities in school, whether they should be separated from their classmates for special instruction, and how to teach them are questions that are likely to lead to heated arguments.

While these controversies are being debated, there are people awaiting guidance and counsel. They are parents of children with learning disabilities. With the exception of their children, they are closest to the problem. Every day, they see the impact that learning disability has on the academic, social, and emotional development of their children in school. They live with the problem after school and on vacations, and they struggle with its effects on their families. Given their close, continuous, and often painful involvement with learning disability, parents are less interested in the results of scholarly debates than in immediate, practical suggestions for dealing with the problem.

Much could be learned by inviting about 50 parents to meet for informal talks about learning disabilities in their children. In their discussions, they would probably discover they have a lot in common. It would not be surprising to hear recurrent themes and similar episodes as they shared accounts of past and present problems. In fact, what often brings a real sense of relief to people is the realization that others are wrestling with issues that are very much the same as their own. It is also quite likely that many of these parents would have concerns about the future that were similar. It would be interesting to ask them, "In the years ahead, what is it that you want most for your children?"

Those of us who have children can guess what their answers would be. With hardly an exception, parents would reply, "We want out children to grow up to be self-supporting, healthy and happy, independent adults." Naturally, there would be some variation in the exact wording of their answers, but the message would be essentially the same.

Of course, this answer is no different than the parents of any child would give to such a question. That's because children with learning disabilities are children *first* and learning disabled somewhere after that. Their learning disabilities are only one part of them; in other important areas of development, they may have above average or even quite superior abilities.

So, as troublesome as they may be during the school years, learning disabilities are not sufficient reason to accept lower expectations for students. Parents of children with learning disabilities must not settle for anything less than the same outcomes that are valued for all other students. However, while the end results being sought may be the same, almost certainly, learning disabilities will make it more difficult to achieve them.

As time has passed and more knowledge has accumulated, we have learned that learning disabilities in children often turn out to be persistent. They are present throughout childhood and adolescence and remain to have an effect upon adjustment during the adult years. The idea is to work around them, to compensate and cope. The goal for families is to identify and apply specific means that boost the probability for children to make successful adjustments *despite* the continuing presence of learning disability. Parents would welcome an answer to the following question: "OK, we understand that this problem may not go away, but what can we do anyway that will help our children grow into well-adjusted adults?"

It can happen. The current opinion of most teachers, counselors, and other professionals in the field is that there is room for some optimism. This opinion gains support from the results of a few recent research studies that describe a small group of adults with learning disabilities who are nevertheless successful in all aspects of their lives. They have families of their own, satisfying social lives, financial security, and eminence in their professions. The passion they have for their work shows up in other areas too. They participate in a wide variety of leisure time activities and have become leaders in their communities. These are people with learning disabilities who have still managed to achieve at the highest levels.

But, there is room for some pessimism too. The superior levels of achievement described above remain the exception. For most adults who are learning disabled, satisfactory adjustment has proven to be very elusive. Those learning disabled adults who are unemployed or underemployed, who have limited social lives, who enjoy fewer leisure time activities, who make minimal contributions to the community, and who, in general, have a hard time functioning independently make up the larger group.

The objective is to increase the size of that smaller group of adults with learning disabilities who excel. Perhaps what follows will help parents and children make decisions and pursue courses of action that minimize the negative effects learning disabilities can have during childhood and, at the same time, lay the groundwork for an easier passage from adolescence that culminates with a full and productive adult life. It's an important objective, so let's get started.

# Chapter 1

# Family Reactions

*If the child is yours, the percentage is one hundred.*

There is little agreement on the number of children with learning disabilities. Some authorities say it is as low as one or two percent of the children in school, and others contend it may be as high as forty percent. These differing opinions are due to the fact that the same authorities have yet to agree upon a definition of learning disability. With no clear definition, it is hard to know exactly who to count, so estimates of the number of children involved continue to vary widely. While the debates are lively and the arguments are interesting, to the parent, they are largely irrelevant. For if the child is yours, the percentage is one hundred.

There is no universal response from parents when they first learn of disability in their children. On the contrary, many different reactions are seen from one family to the next. Some parents feel relieved to finally have their vague suspicions and concerns confirmed. More often, there will be some initial shock followed by a period of anger. This anger may fuel a need to blame, perhaps the child's teachers or even one's spouse. Sometimes there are feelings of guilt that cause parents to think back and wonder what they might have done wrong. Or, they may think forward with real anxiety about what the future will bring for their child. Parents may initially deny that a problem exists and travel from one professional to another, searching for a diagnosis that confirms their denial. Almost certainly there will be disappointment and sadness. Some parents speak of deep depression, even a period of "mourning" as they struggle to come to grips with the realization that the perfection they had hoped for in their child has been lost forever.

None of these reactions is unusual, and none of them is "bad". Each of them is understandable, and becomes increasingly so, with the realization of how devastating it can be when hopes are dashed and dreams are shattered.

It may be that you are reading this because you are a sad and disappointed parent. Perhaps, a while ago, a child was born into your family, and things have not turned out exactly as you had hoped. Certainly you must know that you are not alone. Other families like yours are experiencing similar kinds of problems as they struggle with learning disabilities in their children.

Before speculating any further about your current dilemma, let's take a close look at one of those other families. What follows is one mother's story of the first nine years of her son's life. As you're reading about these people, it might be interesting and useful for you to compare their feelings and experiences to your own.

## There Are No Guarantees

*I am the mother of a disabled child.*

I never thought those words would apply to me. This is something that happens to other people, in other families. Some mornings I wake up thinking it's just been a bad dream and that everything will be OK again. But, it doesn't go away, and there have been more than a few very difficult days and nights. During the last year or so, I have cried a lot. My husband and I have been on an emotional roller coaster; at times, we think we're beginning to adjust to the problem, but at other times we're not even sure we know what the problem is.

The paragraph you have just read comes from a journal that I've kept since our son Billy was born. Writing in this journal was something I did sporadically. Sometimes I would write things every day; other times, several weeks or even a month would pass without an entry. Some of the material in the journal is hard to read, even for me. It was written late at night, and it's difficult to write legibly when you're so tired. Legible or not, the journal material is a mirror of my emotions. My writing clearly reflects the depression, hope, or optimism I was feeling at the time. It has been interesting for me to look back at the journal, because in many ways, it is a history of our family. Perhaps what I have written will be interesting for you. I think it will be if you are the parent of a disabled child. I think it will be if you are a parent.

Our son Billy recently had his ninth birthday. He has fair skin, blue eyes, a shock of unruly blond hair, and a wide smile just like his dad's. He is our first born child, the older brother of twin sisters, four years younger than he. It's fair to say that from the very beginning, Billy hasn't been easy. My pregnancy didn't seem difficult, although I had nothing to compare it with. At birth, however, Billy didn't follow the rules. He decided he would be different and stubborn, and instead of presenting himself in the usual way, head first and face down, he was in the breech position. The doctor assured me, after a period of long, hard labor, that everything was fine and we had a good healthy son. My husband told our parents that Billy had given his first opinion of the world. Indeed, our son might have established a record for the earliest "mooning" in recorded history.

About half way into my pregnancy, I decided that when our child was born, I would breast feed. This did not turn out to be easy. Billy was very active; it was hard to keep him still long enough in a position that would allow me to finish feeding him. Sometimes he would stiffen, arch his back, and spit like a cat. He seemed to startle very easily; it was like he was overly responsive to everything around him, including me. After a while, I worried that Billy wasn't getting enough nourishment. Our pediatrician didn't seem overly concerned. He pointed out that Billy was gaining weight and that he was well within the normal range for children his age. He agreed, though, that if I were uneasy about the situation, switching to a formula would be the thing to do. After another week or so, that's what I did.

The first few months were hectic. In fact, they were closer to exhausting. Billy was very irritable much of the time. He cried an awful lot, and it was very difficult to get him to go to sleep. There was seldom a night when I wasn't up holding him for long periods of time, alternating between the rocking chair and walking a path around the dining room table. My husband was very good about it, laughing one day when the afternoon sun struck our dining room carpet and clearly revealed the route of our night time hikes. On a few occasions, we noticed that Billy would fall asleep in the car on short trips to visit relatives. Apparently, the motion soothed him. One early morning, at about four, bleary eyed and tired of holding Billy, I packed him into his car seat and drove him around the neighborhood hoping he would fall asleep. It worked like a charm. Instead of tracks around the dining room, we made tracks around the block.

As Billy got older, he seemed to calm down a bit. Or perhaps we did. We began to enjoy each other. There were actually a few times when we slept through the night. Drives through the neighborhood in the wee hours stopped. My husband and I were new to the business of child rearing, so much of what unfolded before us was amazing. We were thrilled at our son's development. While changing him one morning, I noticed an unmistakable smile. Soon after, I found that he had rolled over on a blanket on the floor, Then he sat up and began to creep and crawl.

When I was around Billy, I always talked to him. I don't have a degree in child psychology, and I certainly don't qualify as an expert in language development, but I knew that children learn to talk by hearing the speech of other people near them. Billy always made a lot of noise. Not just wails in the middle of the night, but cooing and throaty noises during quieter times. I guess this is called babbling. As he got a little older, it was exciting to hear him begin to repeat some of the sounds we were making. Then, like a miracle, he began to use words in a meaningful way. He was truly talking. My husband, always the jokester, tells people that the first words Billy said were "Lord, I'm so tired". He says that Billy heard those words at our house more than any others.

We discovered, as first time parents, that it is impossible not to compare the development of your child to other children. Next door, my girlfriend had a little girl two months after Billy was born. Alicia slept through the night when she was six weeks old, walked a month before our son, and was talking a few months before Billy. My friend, as kind and perceptive a woman as I have ever known, refused to make comparisons beyond saying things like "girls are usually faster" and "Billy is all boy; give him time, you'll see what he can do". I wanted to believe her, but I had some gnawing doubts. Billy seemed so immature next to Alicia. He still cried a lot more, and his speech was infantile compared to hers. Billy seldom spoke in full sentences, and sometimes his articulation was so poor that it was hard to understand him. Once, after I had expressed some of my concerns to my husband, we had a rare argument. He lost his temper and claimed that I was behaving like an overly concerned, "neurotic" mother. Later, when we talked about it again, he admitted that he had overreacted, probably because he had some of the same kinds of concerns that I had and didn't want to hear them.

We spoke about our concerns with the pediatrician. He was reassuring. He told us there was no question that Billy's infancy and early childhood hadn't been easy. He reminded us that children come into the world with a large variety of temperaments, and that ours had one that was unusual. He told us that Billy was obviously healthy and that his development was within normal limits. He agreed that Billy's speech development was a little immature and delayed, but he was optimistic that he would catch up. He suggested that we consider enrolling Billy in a preschool the following fall. We all agreed that Billy was ready for some time out of the nest and would benefit from being around some other children and adults. I, too, would benefit, because I was pregnant.

A church in the neighborhood sponsored a nursery school and day care center for children between three and five years old. My husband and I visited, met the director, and talked with the teachers. It was a cheerful place, clean and well-decorated, and everyone seemed very enthused and happy to be there. The rooms were filled with educational toys and games, and student art projects had been tacked to the bulletin boards. It was clear to my husband and me that this was indeed a school, not just a facility that provided safe care and custody for children while their parents worked during the day.

The director spent a full hour with us. She was warm and friendly and gave us the feeling that she would be happy to give us as much time as we needed to learn about the preschool. She explained her views on early childhood education and told us how important she felt it was for later academic success in school. She said that at the preschool, teachers followed a daily schedule, prepared lesson plans, and were expected to keep in close contact with parents. She went on to explain that she and the teachers had developed what she felt was an excellent curriculum that emphasized language development, the development of children's perceptual and motor skills, and provided a lot of opportunity for children to socialize, to play, to share, and learn to get along with others. She told us that, above all, her staff were committed to the importance of self-esteem in children. "What we care about the most", she said, "is that children leave us feeling good about themselves, feeling happy and secure, with a positive attitude toward school and confidence in their ability to succeed".

On the walk home, my husband and I agreed that this seemed like a fine place for Billy. In fact, my husband was so impressed that he joked about signing up himself. "I could use a good jolt of self-esteem", he said. We decided to enroll Billy in a morning program that he would attend three days a week. In the fall, our little guy would go to school.

The next two years were OK. After a brief period of resistance, when Billy didn't want me to leave him, he adjusted to the preschool and was happy to go. He made some new little friends and brought home some of his "work" which he showed off proudly. Happily, I taped his efforts to the refrigerator door.

I grew incredibly large, of course. The twins were born, easily and without incident. There was no question that during their infancy, the two of them together were easier to manage than Billy had been alone. For a while, I thought things were going smoother only because I was experienced now; after all, I had been through all of this before. Later, I came to understand that it was more than my veteran status. The doctor had been correct. Babies come into the world with different temperaments. The girls were so much easier; they were quieter, more relaxed, less prone to be bothered by things going on around them. In the language of the day, Billy was "wired", and the twins were "laid back".

The director at the preschool hadn't exaggerated when she told us the teachers were expected to keep in touch with parents. We heard from them on a weekly basis and attended conferences almost every month. The teachers never failed to begin these meetings by saying something good about Billy. We were told that he was bright and curious, that he especially liked his arts and crafts projects, that he was an affectionate child, and that he loved to feed and otherwise take care of the hamsters. It is also true that the teachers never failed to conclude these conferences without expressing some of their concerns about our son. We heard that he was immature compared to many of his classmates, that his speech and language development were a little behind, and that he was clumsy with motor skills, particularly things like finger dexterity and eye-hand coordination. They were most concerned with Billy's short attention span. They described him as "somewhat driven". The teachers told us that sometimes he would flit around the room, going from one activity to the next, without finishing anything. One teacher said, "It's almost as if Billy sees and hears too well; he is so easily distracted by all of the sights and sounds in the room; many times he doesn't hear what I say, because he's exploring something else."

Naturally, I preferred hearing the good comments about Billy over the concerns of his teachers. I knew they were right, though. In fact, they had come to know our son very well. Their descriptions were right on the money; they had discovered things about him that we had seen at home since his infancy. The least they could have done was shown up a few years ago when I desperately needed someone to drive him around in the middle of the night.

Billy completed his two year hitch at the preschool with 15 little classmates. There was a "graduation" ceremony, and I don't know for sure, but I suspected that at least some of the teachers breathed a huge sigh of relief when it occurred to them that our bundle of energy would be off to the local public school in the fall.

All in all, my husband and I were pleased with the preschool. We felt they had offered our son a well-rounded program from which he had benefitted and made some progress. Despite worrying about certain areas of development, we felt our son was certainly normal, not much different from a whole lot of other boys his age. The summer passed uneventfully, and Billy began kindergarten in the fall.

The first year in the "major leagues" was less than OK. Billy was not at all resistant toward going to kindergarten, and many of the activities were about the same as those in the preschool. He seemed happy and brought home a rather constant flow of material for the door on the fridge. The kindergarten teacher was a kindly, soft-spoken woman who had been teaching for over twenty-five years. At an open house at school in September, she told us that she had a few children whose parents had come through her kindergarten. She also said she hoped to "get out of the business" before the grandchildren got there.

My husband and I went to a parent conference in November. What we heard from the kindergarten teacher was strikingly similar to what we had heard from the teachers at the preschool. "Billy is bright", we were told, "but some of his behaviors are still a little bit young". We were told that his articulation of certain speech sounds was still unclear, that he was clumsy in movements requiring both fine and gross motor skills, and that his activity level was very high. "I'm so concerned about his short attention span and his impulsiveness", teacher said. "Sometimes Billy has to get up and move around the room".

The teacher assured us that our son's behaviors were not unique. She had seen them often in her kindergarten. She did say, however, that these behaviors could become more of a problem if they were still present when Billy got to first grade. "At that level", she reminded us, "learning to read and write and do numbers is expected of children, and they are required to sit still and concentrate for longer periods of time". Cheerfully, she concluded the conference and told us we should feel free to come in at any time, and she would see us for sure at our parent conference in the spring. Before my husband hurried off to work, he asked me if I thought "having a high activity level" meant about the same thing as being a pain in the butt?

With all that was happening, the year moved along very swiftly. The twins, although easy to manage, still required a lot of attention. Despite their being identical, each was developing a unique personality. Billy loved his little sisters; he liked to be around them, and the "big brother" role was something he enjoyed. I envisioned him being their protector from neighborhood bullies and flirts when they got older.

Shortly after Easter, it was back to the school for another conference with the teacher. Billy's dad was away on a business trip and unable to attend. As it turned out, I could have used him. In a gentle way, but at the same time firmly, the kindergarten teacher told me she now felt more serious concerns about Billy's development and behavior. She told me that Billy's speech and coordination had improved a little, but his ability to control himself, to sit still and pay attention, really hadn't. She said that the previous week, when she was trying to read a story to the children, Billy wouldn't listen and left the group. He had gone to the back of the classroom where he alternated between talking to the gerbils, rapping on the windows to get the attention of some children on the playground, and humming the song "Bingo Is His Name O". Of course, Billy's young classmates found his behavior more interesting than the story that teacher was reading, and the lesson was ruined.

Billy's teacher had good reason to be angry, especially when he would not respond to her requests to return to his seat. Finally, she had to go to him and forcibly escort him back to the group. "His whole body stiffened, and he arched his back", she said. "Tears came to his eyes, and for a second I thought he was going to have a temper tantrum. Of course, I tried to comfort him, and when he quieted down, I knew in my heart that Billy really couldn't help it. I don't think he can control his behavior; right now, he doesn't seem to have any choice in the matter".

Naturally, I was upset. I knew the teacher was correct. She had noticed behaviors that were identical to those that I had seen during our son's earliest days. I couldn't help it as my mind wandered back to those first days during infancy when my attempts to get Billy to behave correctly and nurse had been no more successful than his teacher's attempts to get him to comply with the rules of behavior that she had established for her classroom. It was depressing, and I wondered if anything had really changed.

Billy's teacher asked if I had talked with our pediatrician recently. She urged me to make an appointment soon and to talk with the doctor about what she called the "attention deficit disorder". These words were new to me, and I didn't like the sound of them. Disorders and deficits are certainly not things that parents want for their children. The conference ended, and I assured the teacher that I would make an appointment the next day.

Billy was due for a physical examination anyway, so during the routine visit to the pediatrician, I told him about my talks with Billy's teacher and his problems in school. The doctor explained this attention deficit disorder, gave me some pamphlets to read, and told me that it was something he was seeing more of in his patients. He said he would be happy to give me the names of some other parents who were having similar problems and who had formed a group that met regularly to discuss issues, hear speakers, and provide mutual support. The doctor said there were certain kinds of medications available that were beneficial in some cases. However, he felt that since the school year was almost over and Billy would soon be free to enjoy his summer vacation without the rules and restraints of a classroom, the question of prescribing such medication for Billy should be deferred until the fall. Doctor also suggested having Billy participate in a summer day camp sponsored by our community YMCA. He felt it would be a good idea for Billy to continue to have experience with other children his age in group activities.

The school year ended, and Billy was chosen to have the "honor" of taking care of the gerbils over the summer. He was thrilled. I wasn't but I said it would be OK. Feeding them and cleaning the cage were things that he managed to do in a reasonably quiet way for 10 or 15 minutes at a time. He enjoyed the animals, and we enjoyed the relative quiet, although I resolved to teach him a tune other that BINGO to sing.

The following week, we walked Billy over to the Y for his first day at camp. Some of the kids in his group were classmates from kindergarten, and some were children he didn't know. The counselors were energetic and enthusiastic college students, home for the summer, most of whom were preparing to be teachers or recreation specialists. Billy and his group of nine others were assigned to Tony and Lisa, a truly dynamic duo who outlined the summer activities for the parents. Swimming every day, field trips to interesting places in the community, relay races and other sports and games, time for quiet play and rest, arts, crafts, treasure hunts, and good lunches. Billy, his dad, and I thought it would a terrific experience and a great way to spend the summer. But, it really wasn't. Camp wasn't a total disaster, but there were some obvious trouble spots. It seemed that nothing ever went smoothly for Billy.

At special days set aside for parents to visit, we noticed how inattentive and impulsive Billy was. He knew the daily routine, but he didn't listen to his counselors as they talked to the group. Sometimes he wouldn't stay with the group at all, choosing instead to wander off on his own around the camp grounds. He chased butterflies, threw stones, splashed water from the drinking fountain, made siren noises whenever a fire truck passed, rolled in the dirt, made mud pies, and picked weeds, flowers, and his nose. Tony and Lisa tried their best. As Billy's counselors, they were very patient with him. Often, one of them had to stop an activity to go off and find Billy. On a few rare occasions when he stayed with the group for an activity, he wouldn't wait his turn, or he blurted out silly things that were not related to what the group was doing. I found myself getting angry, and I would feel guilty afterward when I would think that maybe his teacher had been correct. Perhaps he really couldn't help himself.

In sports and games, Billy was very inept. It was clear that the other boys noticed his clumsiness, and a few even groaned when they discovered that Billy was on their team. I knew how painful this was for Billy's dad. My husband had been quite an athlete in his younger days. He had earned letters in two sports in high school, and he even played basketball at the college level. He still spoke of his victories and the great camaraderie he had shared with his teammates, many of whom were still close friends. These men had shared a special bond in their youth that is reserved for a talented few, and I knew how important it was to all of them.

Like most other fathers, Billy's dad looked forward to participating in sports with his son. He had been a wonderful helper when Billy was an infant, doing his share of diapering, feeding, and bathing. I knew these were things that he didn't enjoy, but he did them anyway, biding his time, waiting for his son to grow, waiting for the time to put up a basket in the driveway and "shoot some hoops" with his boy. Now, seeing how poorly coordinated Billy was and hearing the teasing of other boys his age was heartbreaking. My husband maintained a brave exterior, but I knew how disappointed he was. Inside, a little bit of him broke when he realized that his athletic prowess was something that he hadn't passed down to Billy. With a weak smile on his lips and the hint of a tear in his eye, he looked at me and said, "Well, maybe we'll try fishing together". I will never love anyone more than this man.

As always, summer flew by. Camp ended and there were a couple of weeks before school would start in the fall. I remembered this time of the year during my own childhood. Around the middle of August, on an atypically cool day when the first few leaves would fall to the grass, I would feel a twinge of apprehension. School would be starting soon. I would get up early and stay up as late as my parents would allow, trying to prolong the freedom and fun of summer vacation. But, of course, the carefree mood of the Fourth of July would finally be replaced by the anxiety and gloom of Labor Day. Beginning the next day, there would be new teachers, new routines, and new things to learn. As an adult, I had long since forgotten those feelings, but now, as my son approached first grade, they flooded back to me. I was nervous for him, and for me. I guess there is some truth to the idea that we never really forget anything. Even memories from our early days remain, waiting to pop out when something in the present triggers them.

It may be vulgar, but there is no better way to say it. In first grade, the stuff hit the fan. It was a disaster. Within two weeks, Billy was no longer eager to get up and trot off to school. In fact, he actively resisted. One morning, about 15 minutes before his alarm was set to go off, he padded into our bedroom, sucking his blanket, and complaining about a head ache, stomach ache, "dye a rear", ear ache, sprained ankle, and slivers. These symptoms persisted throughout the week, but only in the morning. By three o'clock, when Billy got home from school, he had miraculously recovered, at least to the extent that he was able to go out and play.

And, by Friday afternoon, he would become a picture of good health, a perfect specimen of wellness. Of course, his remission would come to an abrupt end on Monday morning.

It was time for a visit to the school and another one of those conferences that I was coming to dread. I needed to see what was going on that had caused Billy's negativism toward school. On the morning of the conference, I woke up with a head ache and an upset stomach. I didn't fret for long, however, because I just knew I would be better by lunchtime, when I came home from school. My mood was also buoyed by the fact that I didn't have any slivers.

I met with Billy's teacher for a half hour before school. She told me she was glad I had come in and that she had been planning to call me to talk about first grade and some of the problems Billy was having. By this time, I qualified as a veteran at parent-teacher conferences. I knew that somewhere during their training programs, prospective teachers are taught to begin a conference by saying something good about a child. So when Billy's teacher began by telling me she thought he was curious and bright, I was not surprised. I also knew that the boom was about to be lowered. The good comments are used to fatten one for the kill.

Billy's teacher was very concerned about him and stressed how his behavior was disrupting her class. She told me he didn't follow directions, wouldn't sit still, would seldom wait his turn during group activities, wandered around the classroom, daydreamed, and would not concentrate on his lessons for more than 10 or 15 seconds. She showed me some of the children's work that had been displayed on the class bulletin boards. I had to admit that the differences were obvious. In contrast to many of the children, whose printing was neat and clean, Billy's efforts were an illegible scrawl that wandered all over the paper. He couldn't stay between the lines, and his papers had dark smudges and even some holes from rigorous attempts at erasing with a wet eraser. I knew that Billy liked to suck the end of his pencil. In school, it took the place of his blanket.

Teacher continued with her report telling me that Billy was nowhere close to being ready to learn to read. She had him in a small reading group with three other boys who she felt were also a "little delayed". She said they were reviewing readiness activities—things like identifying similarities and differences between objects in a series of pictures and listening for the differences between sounds. These activities were identical to what Billy had done in kindergarten and even in preschool. The material being hung on the refrigerator door hadn't changed much in three years.

Finally, our conference ended. Billy's teacher told me she would keep a close eye on him and try to give him some extra attention. "You might want to talk with your pediatrician about his attention deficit", she said. "He might have some suggestions".

That evening I discussed the conference with Billy's dad. There was little that teacher had said that we didn't already know and hadn't heard before. Naturally, we were concerned that our son's behavior in school and his slow academic progress had set him apart from his classmates. We were very discouraged and tried to tell each other that maybe this was just a phase that Billy was going through, something that he would grow out of. I don't really think either of us believed that, though.

What concerned us the most was the obvious change in how Billy felt about himself. What a far way he was from what his preschool teacher had hoped for. In contrast to feeling good about himself, feeling happy and secure, positive and confident in his ability to succeed, Billy wasn't happy at all. He was resisting going to school, because he knew that school was a place where the comparisons were. Every day, his performance was stacked against that of the other kids, and he had already perceived that he didn't measure up. Sadly, at this young age, Billy, our bright and curious son, was well on his way to believing that he was a loser.

The next morning I made another appointment with the doctor. I wanted my husband to be there, and there was an appointment open the following week when we could all go together. In the interim, we reread some of the literature that we had collected about the attention deficit disorder. Billy's kindergarten and first grade teachers had both mentioned this problem to us, and Billy's doctor had told me he was seeing more of it recently. I wondered where all these children with attention deficits had been when I was in school? Was this a new problem that was an epidemic, sweeping the nation, and distracting thousands of children? What were these drugs that we had heard about? Did they really work and what were the side effects? These were all questions I would ask the doctor.

At the pediatricians's office, the doctor was generous with his time. He spoke with my husband and me for the better part of an hour while Billy played with some other children in the outer office. They pulled apart wooden toys and watched the tropical fish in the aquarium. Or maybe they watched the wooden toys while pulling apart the fish. Both possibilities were equally likely.

We did learn a good deal more about attention deficit disorder, its probable causes, and some of the treatments that are available. For example, we learned that Billy's behavior was indeed outside of his control. The doctor explained that the latest thinking was that certain chemicals in the brain are responsible for helping children screen out distractions. When these chemicals aren't used enough, it seems that the brain is literally bombarded with more transmissions than it can handle. The doctor compared Billy's brain to a switchboard that was being overwhelmed with too large a quantity of incoming calls. With no effective way of filtering out the unnecessary messages, Billy's "switchboard" became overloaded, and he was forced to respond in a haphazard and seemingly random way.

The doctor went on to tell us that there are medications available that stimulate the appropriate chemicals in the brain to do their job of slowing down and filtering the number of messages. He said that in most cases, the right medication and dosage result in a very quick change in a child's behavior. He had seen children in his practice become quieter, less impulsive and distractible, and more able to sit still and pay attention for longer periods of time. "Sometimes their teachers are so overjoyed, they can hardly contain themselves", he said.

My husband and I are both very conservative when it comes to treating our illnesses with drugs. Neither of us likes to take medication, we don't like the way it makes us feel, and we have tried to avoid it whenever possible. It's not that we have any religious or moral opposition to prescription drugs; it's just that we've always felt that the body, given a chance, will heal itself in a more natural way. Also, we both knew that any time medication is taken, even supposedly harmless, over the counter drugs, there are going to be some side effects. With these feelings, we were very hesitant when the doctor suggested we medicate Billy.

So, we asked the doctor questions about the frequency of dosage and likely side effects. He told us there were newer drugs available that required only one dose a day, in the morning, before a child left for school. He also explained that research findings had documented a number of side effects. He told us that some children lose their appetite and may have a hard time falling asleep. He said that these problems were fairly common, but they usually disappeared after a few weeks on the medication. He went on to say that in a very small percentage of children, the medicine caused head aches and stomach aches. "A few children have become depressed", he said, "and some doctors feel that the drugs may cause irregular heart rhythms and may temporarily interfere with a child's growth".

The doctor saw our obvious concern and reassured us that these side effects were really quite rare. He ended the discussion by suggesting we do some more reading, think about if for awhile, and understand that if we did decide to try the medication, he would watch Billy very carefully to check on the development of any harmful effects. We gathered up our son in the outer office, thanked the receptionist who had been keeping an eye on him and his companions, and took a couple of minutes to straighten the mess on the waiting room floor. I wondered how long it would take before someone noticed the two small wooden trucks that were floating in the fish tank.

For the next week or so, my husband and I debated the issue. If anything, Billy's negativism toward school had increased. It was becoming a real chore to get him ready in the morning. The endless physical complaints increased along with his sucking on his blanket. There was no question that Billy was very unhappy, as we all were. I called a couple of women who were members of a parents' group for attention deficit disorder. They were both very supportive and sympathetic. They told me they knew exactly what was happening in our family, and they encouraged me to go ahead with the medication. "Why allow your family to suffer any longer, when appropriate treatment is available", they said.

I decided to go along with trying the medication before my husband did. He remained worried about the question of side effects, but he had another concern also. "What kind of lesson will we be teaching Billy?", he asked me. "Even if we're all fortunate and there are no physical side effects, Billy might learn that the way to deal with problems is to take pills."

Certainly, my husband had a very valid point. What parents hope for, what we want to see develop in our children is their ability to take responsibility for themselves. They show us a sign of their maturity and independence when they are able to admit that their own individual efforts, or lack thereof, account for their successes and failures. Wasn't it possible that Billy would come to learn that his accomplishments were dependent not so much upon his own efforts as they were upon chemicals in a small bottle?

It was an event at school that finally helped us reach a decision about the medication. The principal called me at home one morning at about ten. She said there was a problem with Billy at school and asked that I please come over. I left the twins with my girlfriend next door and got over to the school very quickly. I found Billy in the office where he was sitting with the school nurse in a corner, quietly sobbing. His cheeks were stained with tears, his eyes were red, and his nose was running. When I asked him to tell me what had happened, he didn't say much. He put his little arms around my neck and whispered, "Mommy, I don't yike it here. Please take me home". Clearly, Billy was not one of those happy children "in their places with bright shiny faces". Quite the contrary, he was one very miserable guy.

After comforting Billy as best I could, I went into the principal's inner office to talk with her. Billy's teacher was there too, and she was obviously upset. She explained that Billy had been unable to behave acceptably from the moment he had arrived at school this day. He hadn't stood during the Pledge of Allegiance, he picked at Lizzy McNamara's pigtails and made growling noises during the Star Spangled Banner, he had asked no less than six times if he could go to the bathroom (two requests being made after he had returned), he couldn't find his pencils or paper for the morning lesson in printing, and he had strewn the contents of his desk all over the floor in his attempt to find them.

All of this had happened during the first ten minutes of the day. And, things didn't get any better. In reading group, Billy wouldn't wait his turn, he shouted out words that weren't even on the page, and when it was his turn, he couldn't keep his place. He poked the kids on either side of him, rustled the pages in the book, and hummed his favorite tune, BINGO, of course. He didn't stop fidgeting, he swung his feet, and he fell off his chair, much to the amusement of his classmates. He picked himself up, wandered around the room, and stopped to whistle and click at the gerbils.

When teacher insisted that he rejoin the group and pay attention, he did so reluctantly, but his behavior continued to be inappropriate, almost "bizarre", his teacher said. "I thought he might calm down if he were actively involved in the lesson", she went on, "so I insisted that he read". Teacher explained that when Billy came to the first few words and he couldn't read them, he tore the pages from the book, threw the book down, turned over his chair and had a violent temper tantrum, crying, screaming, and jerking his arms and legs while rolling around on the floor. Finally, he quieted down and went to his desk where he put his head down, apparently exhausted.

I excused myself and returned to the outer office to see Billy. I sat next to him, softly stroked his hair, and tried to reassure him that everything would be OK. As we sat there, Billy softly weeping and me softly stroking, I really wasn't sure what to do next. So I just asked Billy, as gently as I could, what the matter was. He said, "Mommy, I just can't help it".

With those words, in that simple sentence, I learned a lesson. Sometimes we need to listen to our children. Even when they are little, and we don't think they know very much, we need to listen. The doctors and other experts, as knowledgeable and caring as they may be, can only view the problem from afar. They may know about brain chemicals and neurotransmitters, but they cannot get inside a child's head.

With his own words, Billy had revealed the truth to me. Our son was ill. This child, who had grown within me, and who in seven years had shown me and his dad the joys and trials of parenthood, was ill. For me or his teachers to say, "Sit still and pay attention" was as futile as telling a child with leukemia to sit still and get better. Billy was sick and he needed treatment.

Later that evening, when I reviewed the day's events with my husband, we agreed that we needed to try a more vigorous approach to help Billy. The next morning I would call the doctor for a prescription.

Billy began taking his medicine the following day. Resistance had become part of our morning routine. Now, in addition to resisting going to school, we had the daily battle of the pill. Billy thought it was the same as any other medicine, and he didn't want to take it. Being bigger and stronger, my husband and I won these morning battles, and Billy grudgingly went to school.

Almost immediately, we noticed some very obvious changes. Our son, who had always had a voracious appetite, suddenly had very little interest in food. And, when we reminded him that it was bedtime, he would tell us that he wasn't sleepy. On more than a few occasions, I found him playing in his room at three in the morning or wandering around the house. The doctor had alerted us to the possibility of these side effects and told us they would diminish as Billy's system got used to the medication.

At the end of a couple of weeks, it seemed to me that Billy was really quieter and less impulsive in his actions. One evening he sat by himself for 40 minutes sorting a deck of playing cards into suits and trying to build the cards into houses. I couldn't remember another time or episode in Billy's life when he had done anything for 40 minutes without being distracted at least 8 times.

My husband also noticed what he thought was a significant change. He had taken Billy along on a trip to the local supermarket while I attended to the twins. In the past, we had learned to avoid taking Billy to "high energy" places like supermarkets and pharmacies whenever possible. So many things on so many shelves in so many colors, smells, and sizes were just too much for him. Unless restrained, he would run up and down the aisles touching, smelling, and once even tasting some fruit in the produce department. On this trip, though, Billy was able to restrain himself. "He stayed at my side, pushed the cart in a straight line, didn't touch anything on the shelves, and didn't lick a single apple", my husband said.

We were guardedly optimistic about what we had perceived as changes in Billy's behavior. We knew that we really wanted his behavior to change, and perhaps we were looking for changes and exaggerating what had happened. Our confidence soared, however, when we received a note from Billy's teacher the following week. She, too, had seen real changes in Billy and told us that he was concentrating better, sitting still for longer periods of time, less distracted by irrelevant things going on around him, and less impulsive in his behavior.

As usual, events did not proceed as perfectly as we would have liked. Billy began to complain of frequent headaches and stomach pains. These happened at all times of the day and did not seem to be attempts to avoid going to school. We spoke with the doctor, he changed the dosage, and Billy's symptoms disappeared. Quietly, we hoped and prayed that perhaps we had turned a corner and that things would start to improve for our son in school.

In many ways, things did get better at school. Billy was less stubborn about getting up and going in the morning. His ability to control himself improved, and I never got another note or phone call to come in for an emergency regarding any disruptive behavior. Once Billy even told me that he liked his teacher and most of the other kinds in "fust gwade". But, with these good changes, we also noticed that he wasn't making any noticeable progress in learning to read.

At home, Billy had a few favorite story books that he liked us to read to him, and one evening, at bedtime, he "read" one of these books to me. It was obvious that he was just saying words that he had memorized from hearing the story repeated so many times. Sometimes, he and the author of the book weren't even on the same page. Naturally, I praised him for his effort, but I knew that he had not yet even begun the process of actually learning to read. He could recognize a few words at sight, but it seemed to me that he had a real difficult time attaching sounds to the letters he saw in words he didn't know. With the exception of an "m" or "b" at the beginning of a word, he couldn't come up with any other sounds. The vowels were a mystery to him, and blending two or three sounds into a word was out of the question. I was also concerned about his printing. It wasn't just that almost every word was misspelled, even those he copied from the board, or that he couldn't seem to stay between the lines. What seemed strange to me was that letters were sometimes omitted entirely or printed in reverse order. He even messed up the letters in his own name, and more than once I saw him printing from the right side of his paper to the left.

At the regularly scheduled parent conference toward the end of the school year, I mentioned these concerns to Billy's teacher. Of course, she had seen the same problems. She said that the kinds of things Billy was doing were not all that unusual in first graders, but she felt that in Billy's case, the symptoms were a little more severe. When I heard the word "symptoms", a red flag went up in my mind. "Here we go again", I thought. "I'm going to hear about another disorder or deficit". I wasn't wrong.

As our conference continued, teacher mentioned the possibility of dyslexia. I had heard the term before, and I'd seen a documentary on television that addressed the problem. Although I was anything but well-versed on the subject, I remembered that dyslexia was a medical term that meant about the same thing as "severe reading problem". I thought people were dyslexic if they were bright enough and had sufficient opportunity to learn to read, but remained unable to do so.

Billy's teacher agreed with my thinking. She suggested that if Billy's problems persisted into second grade, we should consider getting him evaluated by someone who was expert in the area. She stressed the importance of early diagnosis, because the chances of fixing the problem would be best when Billy was still young.

Teacher concluded the conference by telling me that Billy would be promoted to second grade. She encouraged us to continue to read to him over the summer and gave me some books to take home. I dutifully carried them out to the car, along with the gerbils. Once again, Billy was given the honor. He was a two summer gerbil man. Oh, joy!

This summer, instead of enrolling Billy in the day camp, we decided to take out a family membership in a community swim club. The twins were old enough to venture into the kiddie pool, and Billy had become a pretty good swimmer. In this sport, eye-hand coordination wasn't important, and he seemed to have enough natural ability to hold his own with other children around his age. In fact, Billy always seemed to come in first in their informal races. His dad tried not to make a big thing of it, but I knew his competitive juices were flowing again, and he enjoyed seeing Billy win something, no matter how insignificant it might have been.

I can't honestly say that we spent a whole lot of time reading during the summer. We opened a book a few times early on, but it was clear that this was something that Billy didn't want to do. He knew he wasn't good at it, he would avoid books whenever he could, and with all the unpleasant episodes and resistance to school during the year, I felt we all needed a vacation. Especially me.

The doctor thought it would be OK for Billy to have some time off from his medicine, so we declared the month of August a "drug free zone". We did notice some slight increase in Billy's activity level, but it was hard to tell if it was due to his being off the pills or simply the natural excitement and exuberance he was feeling. Billy and his dad would be going on a five day white water rafting and fishing trip. Just the two of them. They were both excited; in fact, as their day of departure grew near, it was easy to detect an obvious increase in my husband's activity level too. I told my husband how "hyper" he seemed and asked him if he'd like to take one or two of Billy's pills, I'm not sure he appreciated my humor.

The trip was a smashing success. My guys had five wonderful days roughing it together. They camped out, cooked some of the fish they caught, rode the rapids, hiked the trails, and did what dads and sons do. They came home exhausted, happy, and smelly. It was good. I heard the inevitable story about the "one that got away". Billy said, "Mom, ya shudda seen it, it was a weal monstew". My husband told me that he had never seen Billy so relaxed and happy. For the rest of the summer, we all were. Then school started. The house was empty. Billy began second grade, and the twins went to preschool.

With very little trouble, Billy resumed his routine on the medication. He got his dose each morning. But, I know in our hearts, my husband and I didn't want our son taking pills. There was no question that the medication altered his behavior; we worried, though, whether the drugs were also altering him. We wondered how the drugs actually worked and what they were doing to our son as they daily bathed his brain in powerful chemicals.

We understood the school's point of view. Billy's behavior had not been acceptable. He interfered with the teachers' plans, and he made it more difficult for other children to learn. In a room with a couple of dozen children, all of whom are young and eager to learn, the negative influence of one inattentive and disruptive child cannot be allowed to delay the progress of the rest. So, Billy and thousands of others like him across the country, begin their day with a pill that makes it possible for them to arrive at school in a suitable state of attentiveness. Or, might it be a suitable state of submission?

As second grade proceeded, it was clear that as quiet and attentive as Billy was, he still wasn't learning to read. It was obvious to me, my husband, Billy's teacher, and Billy that he was not making any progress at all. Reading was something that the other kids had learned rather easily; it was something most of them were now using to learn about other things, but to Billy, it seemed like an impossible task. There had been some progress, however. In place of a disruptive, impulsive, and uncontrollable child who couldn't read, we now had a quiet, subdued, and manageable child who couldn't read. Maybe I should have been thankful, but I wasn't.

Just before Thanksgiving, we received a letter from school. It came on official school stationery, and even before I opened it, I had a bad feeling. I just knew that this correspondence hadn't been sent to inform us that Billy had been selected for the honor roll. There is something to the notion of mothers' intuition.

On letterhead stationery, and in very formal language, we were told that Billy's slow academic progress had become a "source of serious concern" to his teacher and others. The school wanted our permission to conduct a "comprehensive evaluation of cognitive and academic functioning". They wanted to test Billy to see if he would qualify for a special program for children with learning disabilities. We were asked to come in to discuss the situation with the principal, Billy's teacher, a psychologist who worked for the district, a social worker, a speech and language therapist, and a teacher from the special education department who was an expert in learning disability.

There was a chance that a third dimension was compounding our son's problem. In living color, up close and personal, we were now in 3D. In addition to Billy's previous deficit and disorder, there was a good chance of a disability.

Of course, my husband and I kept the appointment. We got to school and were ushered into the principal's conference room where everyone was waiting for us. It was clear that the two unoccupied chairs were for us. The principal chaired the meeting and began by introducing everyone present. Billy's teacher was called on to give her opinion of the problem and to summarize his performance in her class. She spoke of his improved behavior and his slow acquisition of academic skills, particularly in reading, writing, and spelling. She had a folder of Billy's work, and she talked about how little it had changed since the beginning of the year. She concluded her presentation by emphasizing how bright she thought our son was and how she felt he would benefit from placement in a program where he could receive more individualized help from a person with special training in teaching children with learning disabilities.

The school psychologist was next up. He explained that before the school could make any recommendation for placement in a program for children with learning disabilities, a complete battery of psychological and educational tests would have to be administered. He said he would need to give Billy an intelligence test, an achievement test that would pinpoint the level Billy had reached in his school subjects, tests of his perceptual and motor functioning, and tests that assessed his personality traits. The psychologist went on to say that he would be observing Billy in his classroom, in the lunchroom, and at recess in order to determine how he related to the other children in informal, everyday situations outside of the testing office. The speech and language therapist said that she too would be required to do some testing. She said she would need "to assess Billy's receptive and expressive communication skills in order to determine his level of overall language development".

During all this time, neither my husband or I had said a word. We just sat, turning politely from one expert to the next, listening to the litany of tests they had planned for our son. Finally, they finished and we were asked if we had any questions. My husband, direct and forthright as usual, said, "I have just two. What if we don't want you to test our son? And, if we decide to give you our permission and Billy does poorly on your tests, what will your recommendations be?"

There was an awkward pause. It seemed as if the questions caught our hosts by surprise. I think they had assumed we would be easy, cooperative parents who would quickly "sign on the dotted line" and tell them to go ahead and do whatever they thought was best. Finally, after several of the participants looked at each other, apparently to see who would take the lead, the principal responded and told us that Billy could not be tested without our consent, and that if we wanted to, we could seek professionals working outside of the school district and have the testing done privately.

The learning disabilities teacher spoke up and explained that if the results of testing indeed showed that Billy might benefit from placement in a program for children with learning disabilities, the school might recommend anything from a part-time, pull-out program, to a full-time special classroom, or even a special school. She told us that the type of program depends on the results of all the testing and observations, and the school could not place any child in a special program without first getting the consent of the parents. She concluded by saying, "We have learned that the children who benefit the most from our special programs are the ones whose parents are enthusiastic supporters of such programs. So, if our evaluations and assessments indicated that Billy would be eligible for such placement, we would only do so after both of you agreed and were in favor of the decision".

My husband said we would need a couple of weeks to discuss the issue and get some input from other people. We were given the names of people to talk with who belonged to a parent group for children with learning disabilities. We were also furnished with a list of people in private practice who were qualified to do the kind of testing the school was planning. We left the meeting after thanking the participants and assuring the principal we would inform her of our decision within two weeks.

It wasn't an easy ride home for my husband and me. "Don't you remember those special classes when we were in grade school", he asked? "We teased those kids, called them weirdos, dummies, and losers. And now, they want our son to be in one of them. Do you ever get the feeling we're being paid back?" I told him how ridiculous I thought that was, but inside I, too, was feeling very sorry for us. "Why us", I thought? "What did we do wrong to deserve this?"

Feeling sorry for myself wasn't the only feeling I had. There was a combination of sadness and disappointment, and a real sense of loss. Mothers have hopes and dreams for their sons. Mine began very early. Many times toward the end of my pregnancy, in the middle of the night when I was too uncomfortable to sleep, I would imagine what Billy would be, 25 years in the future. I saw a brilliant scientist investigating the nature of matter, a lawyer defending the rights of the indigent, and a neurosurgeon removing a child's brain tumor. I saw an architect planning cities and a senator on the floor of Congress. I didn't aim low. These glorious maternal fantasies would come to an abrupt end, replaced by the reality of my yet unborn son as he vigorously kicked and struggled. Now, I mourned those memories. I mourned the loss of perfection that would never be. Those fading recollections had been replaced by tears in the middle of the night, in the same bed.

Our bout with self pity passed, at least enough that we were able to move on to a more productive use of time. At the local library, I found some books and pamphlets on dyslexia and checked them out. My husband and I had to agree that what we were reading described our son almost perfectly. The way he approached reading, the kinds of errors he would make, his reversals in reading and writing, the bizarre combinations of letters when he tried to spell, his immature speech and language development, the distractibility and impulsiveness, his at least average intelligence—all these were characteristics we had seen in Billy. In fact, the authors could have used him for a model.

From our reading we learned some good news and some bad news. For example, it was encouraging to find out that some very famous, successful people were dyslexic. Former Vice President Nelson Rockefeller, Tom Cruise and Cher, the movie stars, and Bruce Jenner, the one time Olympic decathlon champion all had the same problem as Billy. One of the books even suggested that Albert Einstein and Thomas Edison, both of whom had learning problems in school, might have been dyslexic. We also learned that more and more universities were recognizing that learning problems, even dyslexia, should not disqualify students from pursuing higher education. Colleges across the country were starting special programs, admitting students who were learning disabled, and making special provisions for them after they arrived. All of this was heartening.

The bad news was that the research and follow up study that had been done on dyslexia indicated that it was a very persistent problem, particularly if it weren't remedied during the early years in school. Many dyslexic children grew up to be dyslexic adults, even some whose problem had been identified early and for whom special, remedial work had been prescribed. So, it looked as if we had something here that wasn't going to go away. We were in this for the long haul.

During the two week period, we also talked with members of the parent group. We found them to be honest and realistic in their appraisal of how the school had handled their children's problems. They believed the school district had a corps of special personnel who were extremely competent and really concerned about the welfare of children who were learning disabled. They encouraged us to have the people at the school do the testing rather than seek an outside evaluation. They felt it was important for Billy to be evaluated by people, "insiders", they called them, who had thorough knowledge of how the school worked, who knew and trusted each other, and who would be there to follow up on Billy's progress. They also pointed out that the kind of extensive evaluation that the school was offering would be free, but might run over a thousand dollars if we chose private practitioners. They reminded us that the results of testing are open to parents, but confidential with respect to everyone else. Finally, they told us that giving our consent to the school to have Billy tested in no way obligated us to give our consent for placement in a special program, should such placement be the recommendation of the team who had tested our son.

After a week of discussion, debate, and reading, my husband and I decided that it might be a good idea to include Billy in the deliberation. After all, he was the one who would be having his "brain picked". After dinner one night, we tried to ask him how he felt he was doing in school. The topic was not one he wished to discuss at any length; however, we discovered he did have some pretty accurate insights into the problem. He said school was OK and he didn't mind going, but he concluded his comments by telling us, "I don't wead vewy good"; (The "r" sound was still hard for him.)

We asked him how he would feel about getting some special help at school. He said that would be OK too, although we weren't sure if he really meant it or just said it to end the conversation. We told Billy that some people who wanted to help him in school would probably want to give him some tests. He shrugged his shoulders on the way to his room and his collection of trading cards.

I think at least trying to include Billy in the decision was a good idea. We had been leaning toward giving the school our permission to test him, and the fact that he didn't really resist the idea might have helped us make up our minds. The next morning I stopped off at school and signed the necessary papers.

Within three weeks, all the testing and observing had been completed. Billy would tell us about the testing on days that he had been called out of his classroom. When we asked him if he remembered any of the things he had to do, he told us about putting puzzles together, copying designs, having to remember a series of numbers and words, and telling the meanings of some words. He seemed very impressed with the people who gave him the tests. "They're nice to me, and fun too", he said. "Most of the stuff they asked me to do was easy, and the man with the moustache (we knew he was talking about the psychologist) pulled a dime out of my ear. He told me when I get older, I should look for quarters".

Of course, my husband and I were pleased that the testing hadn't been unpleasant for Billy. Now, we were hoping that hearing the results wouldn't be unpleasant for us. The following Monday we attended a meeting called a "multidisciplinary staff conference". The same people who had been present at the earlier meeting were also here at this one. The purpose of the meeting was to present the results of the testing and to determine what to recommend for Billy. Again, there was good news and bad news.

The people who had tested Billy presented their findings. We learned that all of our son's previous teachers, those who had worked with him from preschool through second grade and who had referred to him as bright, had indeed been correct. On the intelligence test, Billy's overall performance was better than 90% of the children his age. The psychologist explained that although Billy's overall score was very good, his performance had been uneven. Along with some strong areas, there were a few obvious weaknesses. Among other things, Billy had a real problem on some of the tests that required him to think about and remember things presented in a series. It was hard for him to solve problems when he had to proceed through a number of small steps with each successive step being dependent upon the preceding information. Billy had also had a difficult time on test items where he needed to coordinate something he saw with a movement he had to make.

The psychologist continued his summary by saying that our son's uneven development and the difficult time he had thinking through a series of facts were very typical of children with reading disabilities. He told us that on the school achievement test that tells the grade level children are working at in their basic school subjects, Billy was still at the very beginning of the first grade in reading and spelling. His achievement in math was higher, at grade level, in fact. This was understandable, we were told, because the calculation of math problems did not require Billy to read.

The psychologist explained that given Billy's above average intelligence, it was reasonable to assume that he had the ability to be reading at the third grade level. He was already two years behind where he should have been. He concluded his summary by telling us that Billy was quite aware of his problems in school.

Our son had already perceived that many of his classmates were capable of doing things that he couldn't do, and these unfavorable comparisons had affected his self-esteem in a negative way. We agreed when the psychologist said, "We must take immediate steps to help Billy start to like himself again".

The summaries from the other people who had tested Billy continued. I must say that after an hour or so, it got to be confusing and somewhat overwhelming. The people were not the problem. They were kind, patient, and obviously cared a great deal about us and our son. Much of the problem had to do with the language. We heard terms like "visual-motor integration", "word finding disorder", "auditory sequential memory", "full scale IQ", and "simultaneous processing". It may not be possible to translate this lingo into language suitable for parents; what I do know for sure is that, for the most part, my husband and I didn't know what the hell they were talking about. Finally, I think because she sensed we were becoming antsy, the principal asked the group for their recommendation.

The opinions of the participants were unanimous. They all felt that Billy was learning disabled and was eligible for special education services offered at the school. The consensus of everyone present, all these people who had either taught or tested our son, was that Billy's learning problems were severe enough to require full time attention in a special class for children with similar problems. This placement would mean that Billy would be removed from his teacher and his friends in second grade and go to another room down the hall. I caught my husband's eye, and each of us knew what the other was thinking, without having to say the words: "weirdos, dummies, and losers".

My husband, who stands and whose voice softens to an almost inaudible level when he gets angry, rose and said, very quietly, "We gave you permission to test our son and you poked at him, prodded, and probed him for many hours. You have told us many things about our son, most of which we already knew, and some things that we didn't. You have described a few things that he is good at and a lot of things that he is not so good at. You have been patient with us, and it is obvious that you care about our son and our family, But, with all of this information, the one thing nobody has explained to me or my wife is the cause of Billy's learning disability. Please, could one of you tell us, as specifically as you can, just what it is that is causing our son's learning disability, because until we know what the cause is, it will be very difficult for us to give you our permission to treat him".

My husband's question met with silence. To use an overworked term, there was a real pregnant pause, accompanied by some throat clearing and paper shuffling. Finally, the psychologist, who had been smoothing his moustache, spoke up. "Folks", he said, "that's a real good and fair question. I know how difficult this is for you, and I know you are entitled to an answer. The problem is that no one knows for sure what causes dyslexia or other kinds of learning disabilities". He continued by telling us that many people, perhaps even a majority of those who had studied the problem, felt that the cause was in the child's brain. He told us that in some cases there may actually be damage to certain areas of the brain, but in others it's probably just a question of slow development, a "maturational lag", he called it. He ended his explanation by saying, "I wish I could be more precise, but if I told you that the exact cause of learning disability were known, I wouldn't be telling the truth."

My husband told the group that we were very hesitant about removing Billy from his class and his friends. We were afraid of his being further singled out and labeled in a negative way. We were concerned about the possible permanence of this placement and its effect on his self-esteem, which everybody agreed had already suffered. In a hushed tone, my husband said, "We went along with you and put our son on drugs, because you couldn't tolerate his behavior, and now you're asking us to move him to a class for disabled children, and you can't even tell us the cause of his problem. If this is truly a maturational lag, as you suggest, why don't we just leave Billy where he is and give him more time to mature?" When nobody answered him, my husband sat down.

Next, the principal rose. She told us that she and her husband had three children, each of whom had done well in school and earned college degrees. "Although I am a parent, just like you", she said, "I can only imagine, from afar, how sad, disappointed, and frightened you must be. I think there can be nothing worse than learning that all is not right with a child". She continued and told us that it was true that the exact cause of learning disability remained unknown, but she felt that even without that knowledge, the special program in her school had helped children whose problems were similar to Billy's.

The principal suggested that we at least delay our decision. "Come and visit the class, see the other children, meet the teacher and her assistant before you make up your mind", she said. She told us we didn't have to hurry; there was no emergency, and Billy would stay where he was until we felt we had sufficient time to come to a decision. It seemed reasonable for us to take a closer look at the option the school was offering.

At last, the meeting ended. We agreed with the principal and made arrangements to visit the class they had recommended for Billy. We planned to go there one morning, the following week. I think one of the factors that convinced us even to consider the placement was reassurance from everyone that if we decided to go ahead with this move, it would be temporary. We were told that our son would be watched very carefully. He would get individualized attention, he would be reevaluated periodically, and everyone would be working toward the most important goal of returning Billy to his class in the standard education program.

During the time prior to our visit, we spent more than a few hours discussing the decision. Nothing seemed clear cut. For every positive of the special program, there was a negative. The advantage of individualized instruction was offset by the disadvantage of being singled out. The advantage of a special teacher using special techniques was offset by the disadvantage of going to the "dummy room" down the hall.

One thing did emerge clearly from our discussions. Our decision needed to be based solely on what we thought was best for Billy, and not upon issues that had to do with our own self-esteem. That was easier said than done. I think my husband and I were both surprised at the degree to which our egos had become involved in the question. I guess we shouldn't have been surprised. After all, we had produced Billy, and try as we might, it was impossible for us to ignore the idea that his flaws were ours. We had become all wrapped up in his learning disability, and as his feelings toward himself had diminished, so had ours. It almost seemed to us as if we had failed and would be going to a special class too. Kind of like a dummy room for parents.

We spent more than two hours visiting the special class. We arrived not knowing what to expect and trying our best to be neutral. We were very pleasantly surprised and impressed with everything we saw. We sat in the back of the room and tried to be inconspicuous. Of course, that was impossible. The children came over to us, introduced themselves, and welcomed us to their room. There were eight children in the class, six boys and two girls, and they all looked just as normal as Billy. There were no big heads, no children in wheelchairs, and no one who looked retarded. Of course, I had learned from my reading that learning disability is not accompanied by visible characteristics, and I should have known better, but, I must admit, I was still happy to see all this "normalcy".

The teacher and her assistant had things well under control. Each child knew his or her routine and exactly what was expected. When individual children or small groups of children were working with the teacher, the others were working with the assistant or completing assignments on their own. The room was filled with all sorts of equipment and materials including tape recorders, typewriters, and two modern, Apple computers. Each child had time at the computer every day, and they were learning the keyboard and the basics of word processing. No matter how poor a child's printing, the Hewlett Packard Desk Writer printers would make the work legible and something to be proud of.

Walls were covered with student work. My husband and I were both impressed with the fact that the marks on the papers were next to right answers rather than errors. Even if a child had spelled only three of his ten spelling words correctly, the "good" three were attended to rather than the seven that were wrong. Across one wall, there was a series of "private offices" where children could go if they felt distracted and needed some time to complete an assignment away from the others. Children were free to get up and move around, and they did so, but their movement in the classroom always seemed to be purposeful; that is, it related to a lesson or getting information needed to complete an assignment.

About half way into our visit, the teacher began to work individually with one of the boys in the class. She motioned to us to come up and sit with them at the table so we could get a better look at what they were doing. I could tell that the activity was a reading lesson, but the methods were different that I had ever remembered. First, she sat behind her young student and had him close his eyes while she printed some letters on his back. She encouraged him to see the letters in his mind. Each time he was able to identify a letter correctly, she had him say the sound that it made. She was very patient, firm in her expectations, and generous with her praise. When the student was able to identify seven letters and say their sounds with perfect accuracy, she began to print two and three letter combinations on his back. Then he blended these sounds into syllables and words. The boy was really pleased with his efforts and was happy to continue. Next, the teacher showed him cards with the syllables and short words that he had been able to identify. The letters were made of sandpaper, and he slowly felt each letter as he read the words. Finally, teacher spent the last five minutes of the lesson dictating the words to her student and having him write them on a piece of spelling paper. He kept a collection of cards called "words I know". When he could read a word quickly, at a glance, he got to add it to his collection. His stack had grown to over 50 words, and he was very proud of that.

After the lesson, the class went to gym, and teacher was available to talk with us for about 20 minutes. My husband and I both commented on the techniques she had used during her reading lesson. We felt they were really unusual and fascinating. She told us that with children who had severe reading disabilities, special methods were required. She said, "I've learned that the usual methods of instruction really don't work. It doesn't matter how slowly I go or how small the group is, even one on one, unless I use very different ways of teaching, I don't see much progress." She described what she called a "multisensory approach" to teaching reading. In this way, children get to see, hear, feel, and write words as they are learning them. The information travels over the different senses on the way to a child's brain.

When my husband mentioned our feelings about special classes and the stigma that could be associated with them, the teacher didn't disagree or become defensive. She explained that all her students spent some time out of her special class during the day, participating in activities with everyone else in the school. "Mainstreaming", she called it. She also told us that she had initiated a project where bright and capable eighth grade boys and girls came into the class to help by doing some tutoring and just assisting in general. We appreciated her candor when she said, "Despite these efforts at integration, I can't honestly tell you that being a member of this class is ever going to be considered a privilege to be shown off as a badge of distinction".

We stayed a little longer, and as we left, I asked the teacher how many of her students left her program and went back to their regular classes. She told us that it was her goal for everyone to return, and that in her five years at the school, just more than half her children had done so. It was her opinion that the children who made it back tended to be the ones whose overall intelligence was high, despite their learning problems. She felt that even if their learning disabilities were stubborn and persisted, the bright ones were able to develop ways to work around them, ways to cope. This was encouraging to us.

We stopped at the office to thank the principal for arranging our observation. We told her what an informative visit it was, how much we had learned, and how impressed we were with the teacher and the children. My husband told her we would be discussing the issue and would get back to her with our decision within the week. On the way out of school, the principal walked us past her conference room where we saw a familiar group of people—the psychologist, social worker, school nurse, speech and language therapist, and learning disability teacher-meeting with another set of parents. Mom and dad didn't look too happy. Obviously, we weren't alone; the learning disability business seemed to be thriving.

It's hard to pinpoint any one factor that ultimately helped us make a decision. We tried our best to be objective and dispassionate. We went so far as to make lists of advantages and disadvantages of placement in the special class, sometimes supporting and sometimes rebutting each other's arguments. We tried to include Billy in the process, but, for the most part, he was noncommittal. He seemed most concerned about having to go to another school, and when we assured him that the special class was right down the corridor, he didn't voice any serious objection to it.

Finally, I think mostly due to our observation of the special class and our very positive impression of the teacher, we decided to give it a try. I can't say that it was a decision that was made enthusiastically or confidently. We came to understand that there would be no magic flash of insight that would guide us in making our decision. We felt that we would always have some doubts, no matter what we did. About all we did know for sure was that Billy was not doing well in his current situation, and there was no prospect that it would be getting better. It may be that we simply realized that we had to provide something different for Billy, and this change to the special class would be the lesser of two evils.

Billy has been in his special class for about a year now. He made the adjustment easily, and never once has he complained about going to school. There has been some teasing from other children on occasion, but I guess that's inevitable, and Billy has handled it well. As bright as he is, he has a good understanding of his problem. He considers the special class temporary, as we all do, and he talks about improving his reading, spelling, and writing so he can go back to "regular".

There have been some signs of growth and development that have pleased us. Billy has learned some computer skills. He knows the keyboard and can do some simple word processing. His achievement in math is above grade level, and at the school science fair, his project won a third place ribbon. By using hamsters running on a wheel that he had attached to a series of gears, a small container of light weights was lifted from the bottom of the cage to the top. He called his project "Hamster Power: A New Source of Energy".

Billy has also continued to improve in swimming. He tried out and was accepted on the YMCA swim team, and in competition with other teams from the area, he has won several trophies. He has a new interest in wrestling, and he wants to compete when he gets older. Naturally, this interest and achievement in sports has been great for Billy's dad. He's the one who screams the loudest at swimming meets.

My husband and I have become active in the local parent association for children with learning disabilities. We attend the monthly meetings, and there is usually a speaker, most often a doctor or professor from the state university. One of the things we've noticed, from reading pertinent literature and from hearing lectures, is that almost every recognized authority in the field stresses the importance of "acceptance" when talking about the problems that parents have in adjusting to disability in their children. It may be a question of semantics, but I think that "acceptance" is one of those words that is used so often, usually by "experts" who aren't parents themselves, that most people just automatically go along with it, without even questioning it. I know that my husband and I will never fully accept Billy's dyslexia. We wish it would go away; we wish it were never there in the first place, we don't like what it has meant for our son in school; we don't like what it has meant for our family. The fact is we don't accept Billy's learning disability any more than we would accept hemophilia or drug addiction. We will all live with this problem and do the best we can with it, but I will never go along with those authorities, far removed from first hand contact with the problem, who tell us we must learn to accept this. "Walk a mile in our moccasins, people".

For the most part, the membership in the parent association has been useful; at the very least it keeps us abreast of new developments in the field and new approaches to teaching children who are learning disabled. It has also been nice to know other parents who have had similar experiences and are available for mutual support.

As for the future, of course, it is difficult to know what to expect. But I suppose that's no different than it is in any other family. No set of parents can ever know how things will turn out for their children. Billy has made some progress in reading, spelling, and written composition, but I don't think it would be realistic to think that these are areas that will ever be strengths for him. It may be that his overall intelligence is high enough that he will be able to work around his dyslexia. After all, in spite of his learning disability, he has still managed to learn a lot of things; he has just had to do it differently. We are always hopeful that new developments in the field will make the process of learning easier for him.

As we look back at nine years, there is much that we have learned. The denial, guilt, sadness, disappointment, sense of loss, and self-pity we felt are normal, common reactions. Almost all of the parents we've talked with have had similar feelings. These feelings are mostly behind us now, although once in a while, on down days, I will still feel an ache or twinge.

We have learned that in our typical community, and in most others, there are professional people—teachers, doctors, social workers, psychologists, school administrators, and others—who sincerely care about children and try their best to counsel parents and help them make the correct decisions. Sometimes, though, the input coming from so many different sources is confusing and even contradictory; and it would have been easier had there been one person or one source to whom we could have turned for consistent advice and answers to our questions. I think it's very important for parents to have one trusted confidante, someone knowledgeable and skillful enough to integrate diverse opinions, translate professional jargon, and just be there as an advocate and friend to support them during the many times they need it. Perhaps it's too much to ask for such a person; maybe they don't even exist. It sure would have been easier though, even for parents like us who are supportive of each other, had there been someone else to lean on.

We have learned that there are very few easy decisions regarding the welfare of a child. Instead, what usually prevails is agonizing uncertainty. Most often, we had to carefully consider each move to make, looking at advantages and disadvantages, weighing possible alternatives. This constant need for careful deliberation can be exhausting and incredibly stressful. Some might say it's the same in any other family. Being a parent is exhausting and stressful whether a child is disabled or not. It's part of the package. The difference has to do with the light at the end of the tunnel. For most parents, the period of time when their children are dependent upon them is relatively brief. Childhood passes, school is remembered as the "good old days", and parents can turn their attention to worrying about other matters like retirement, weddings, and grandchildren. They exit the tunnel. For us, however, it seems as if Billy's dependence might last longer. Or, at the very least, we will have to be concerned about certain areas of his development long after other parents have turned their attention to other matters. Parents of 18 year old students usually do not have to think about their children's reading levels as they happily help them select a college and send them off. We may still be.

We have learned that learning disability is a tough test for every member of the family. Billy has been fortunate. His father and I have become stronger, more devoted, and more loving as we have both dealt with this problem together. Other marriages suffer; in fact, almost every study indicates that the divorce rate is significantly higher than average in families where a child with a disability is present. It may be that energy which is normally available for working on the marriage and satisfying each others' needs is drained away by the stress and demands of learning disability in the child.

Finally, we have come to learn the wisdom of our own parents. Isn't it amazing how much wiser, more perceptive, and tolerant our parents become as *we* get older? The fact is, of course, they always were; it just takes us a while to grow up and recognize it. It also takes us a while to recognize that when it becomes our turn to "buy the package" of parenthood, all the little pieces require considerable assembly, and, if everything doesn't fit just exactly right, there are no guarantees.

---

This mother's story is an accurate and very moving description of some of the kinds of reactions in families where there is a child with a learning disability. It is easy to feel their anguish and frustration and to share their disappointment and hope. We understand when they have bouts with self-pity and when they question whether their own shortcomings are somehow responsible for problems their son has. It would be interesting to revisit them in one year or maybe even five or ten years to see how things have turned out for Billy and his parents.

These parents have done very well. They have worked together in what is obviously a mutually supportive and loving relationship. They have been active in dealing with the problem. They have sought out appropriate information, they have weighed their decisions carefully, they have good insight into their own emotions, they have acted in the best interest of their son, and they realize there is much that remains to do ahead of them. While mother claims they will never accept Billy's disability, at least they have made an adjustment to it and are progressing forward as a healthy family unit.

Other families do not do as well. It is true that there is no universal reaction that all families exhibit when a child is learning disabled. Families are made up of unique individuals with entirely different experiences, temperaments, and personalities; therefore, it would be foolish to expect them to react in exactly the same way to something as complex and difficult as childhood learning disability. Nevertheless, perhaps there are certain elements in this family's story with which you can identify. Maybe some of your experiences are similar to things that happened to them.

Let us assume that in your case, at least some of the story applies. Yours is an unhappy family. For reasons that you may not fully understand, your child's progress in school has not been satisfactory. You are probably confused, maybe a little embarrassed, frightened or angry. There may be a lot of tension and stress in your home; this isn't what you expected; this is not the way it was supposed to be.

Perhaps you too have already been to many conferences at school, heard the teachers' concerns with growing frequency, tried to help at home, debated and argued with your spouse, and talked with your family doctor seeking suggestions and reassurance. You might have already been to a psychologist or educational specialist to find out what was wrong, and maybe you have hired a private tutor for extra help during the week.

Indeed, you may be bewildered by all of the suggestions that various experts are asking you to consider. You've heard about the medication that was prescribed for Billy and how it supposed to lengthen attention span and lessen the amount of impulsive, distractible behavior. You've been told about special diets that minimize the effects of allergic reactions that may be interfering with your child's learning. You might have seen television documentaries about treatments for learning problems that range from taking massive doses of vitamins to wearing glasses with different colored lenses. You've heard about special education classes, with limited enrollment, that have been established for children with problems similar to your child's. You know there are private schools with specially trained teachers who use remedial teaching techniques designed to help children with learning disabilities. You're aware of all these things, and of course you are bewildered. You might even feel overwhelmed.

Adding to the problem, you may be growing increasingly uneasy because you have seen a transformation in your child. A happy little person entering an important new phase of life has changed to a sad child, disliking school, who may be starting to believe that somehow the other kids are different, more capable, better. The free and easy time of childhood has become difficult.

If any or all of the above seems familiar, please continue reading. This is a book for you, parents who need some help, just as their children do. You need to learn about learning disability. You need answers to many questions. For example, what is learning disability? What causes it? How many children are there with these kinds of problems? Do children grow out of this, or is it a permanent problem? What special services are children with learning disabilities entitled to at school? Is higher education something that can be realistically considered? What kinds of adjustment problems are there for adults with learning disabilities? Are there support groups for you? What are your legal rights?

All of these are important questions. You are entitled to the best answers that are currently available; answers that are straightforward and free of professional jargon; answers that will help you adjust to this problem and will help your student move through school in as normal a way as possible. In the long run, it is answers to the above questions that will help regain and preserve what is most precious of all: your child's self-esteem. Read on and learn.

# Chapter 2

# *Learning Disability: What Is It?*

Watching a young child learn can be a wondrous thing to see. Often, learning takes place so easily that it seems to be automatic, as if no effort were required at all. As an example, think about learning to speak. As long as children have reasonably normal intelligence, the ability to hear, people near them who surround them with appropriate speech to imitate, and some encouragement for their efforts, they will learn to speak. Children come into the world with no knowledge of speech, and, in the short span of 36 months, they reach a level of relative mastery of their native language.

Usually, by twelve months of age, they begin to use words correctly; that is, they attach appropriate meanings to sounds. "Mama" is no longer a meaningless, vocal parroting of two syllables they have heard; it is now a word used with correct reference to one older female in the child's life. By two years of age, children begin to string words into simple two and three word sentences, and by their third birthdays, they have learned hundreds of words, they can construct complex sentences, and they understand rules of grammar and usage including plurality and tense.

Amazingly, all this learning takes place without any formal instruction. A young child masters the uniquely human ability to communicate through speech, and no lessons are required. It is almost like a miracle, and as more is being learned about how the brains of young children work, indeed the word "miraculous" seems increasingly appropriate. Later, in this chapter, we'll take a look at some recent discoveries about our brains.

A few years later, young children come to school. Most are successful. The natural ease with which they learned to speak continues in evidence as they learn other language skills including reading and written expression. With these tools, their passage through school proceeds without much difficulty. They are able learners. A percentage of children, however, do not make it through school smoothly. For them, learning is not easy; on the contrary, it requires tremendous effort. More and more, the term "learning disability" has been applied to these children. Our purpose here is to examine that term and reduce the confusion associated with it.

## Learning disability: What is it?

Some children have problems in school that are easier to understand. If a child is obviously mentally retarded, for example, people are not surprised when learning is slow and academic progress is limited. Similarly, if a child has a sensory handicap such as deafness or blindness or is severely emotionally disturbed, people expect that learning will be more difficult and progress through school may be delayed. On the other hand, there are problems in school that are not so easy to understand. Learning disability is one of those.

Sometimes it is easier to understand the present after a brief look at the past. The term "learning disability" did not exist before 1963. At that time, Dr. Samuel Kirk, a leader in the field of special education, first used it while speaking to a convention of educators and parents who were meeting to learn more about learning problems in children. Dr. Kirk spoke about some children who were not mentally retarded, deaf, blind, or emotionally disturbed; but still, they did not learn satisfactorily in school. He told his audience that these children had ample opportunity to learn; they were not lazy, they had been in regular attendance at school, they had the advantage of able and conscientious teachers, and yet, they did not make normal progress. He described children who were intact in many important ways, who were "put together well". They were children who had many strengths along side of their weaknesses; but still, they lagged progressively further behind their classmates. He said these were children who were learning disabled.

Soon, a number of formal definitions of learning disability were proposed. One of these evolved into the current federal definition of learning disability. It is part of the Education of All Handicapped Children Law (Public Law 94-142), enacted in 1975, which made it mandatory for all public school districts to provide appropriate educational services for disabled children of school age. This definition appears below:

> Specific learning disability means a disorder in one or more of the basic psychological processes involved in understanding or in using language, spoken or written, which may manifest itself in an imperfect ability to listen, think, speak, read, write, spell, or to do mathematical calculations. The term includes such conditions as perceptual handicaps, brain injury, minimal brain dysfunction, dyslexia, and developmental aphasia. The term does not include children who have learning problems which are primarily the result of visual, hearing, or motor handicaps, of mental retardation, of emotional disturbance, or of environmental, cultural, or economic disadvantage.

"Wow!", you may be saying. "That's some fancy definition". It's filled with terms like "dyslexia", "developmental aphasia", "minimal brain dysfunction", and "psychological processes". The problem is that most parents (and perhaps some teachers) have a very hard time understanding such language. For example, just what are the basic psychological processes anyway? They seem to be a very important part of the definition, but there is no clue to their meaning. Furthermore, can a brain dysfunction really be *minimal* any more that a woman can be a little bit pregnant? And, if learning problems are **not** the result of so many things, then what are they the result of?

All of these are quite legitimate questions. The federal definition is difficult to interpret; it confuses rather than explains. It leaves parents in the dark when they really need to be enlightened, and, to make matters worse, later definitions didn't clarify things much.

Dissatisfied with the federal definition, a group of six professional associations came together in 1981 and formed the National Joint Committee for Learning Disabilities (NJCLD). This organization proposed the following definition:

> Learning disabilities is a generic term that refers to a heterogeneous group of disorders manifested by significant difficulties in the acquisition and use of listening, speaking, reading, writing, reasoning, or mathematical abilities. These disorders are intrinsic to the individual and presumed to be due to central nervous system dysfunction. Even though a learning disability may occur concomitantly with other handicapping conditions (e.g., sensory impairment, mental retardation, social and emotional disturbance) or environmental influences (e.g., cultural differences, insufficient/inappropriate instruction, psychogenic factors), it is not the direct result of those conditions or influences.

Either you're impressed with the language or you're about to close the book in disgust and turn on the television. Probably the latter. No one would blame you if your choice were Letterman or As the World Turns over the NJCLD definition of learning disability. Like the federal definition, this one is also a large mouthful. I've had graduate students tell me that after reading it the first time, they began to suspect *they* were manifesting intrinsic disorders that were due to their own central nervous system dysfunction. In short, they didn't get it. It's also true that a few admirably honest college professors would not be ashamed to admit they're not always sure either.

If you can get past the verbiage, there are some important changes in the NJCLD definition. One of these is the absence of the word "children". This is the first definition that did not limit the problem to the school age population. It recognized the potential longevity of learning disabilities. More recent study has confirmed their permanence. In many cases, learning disabilities do not go away; on the contrary, they require a series of adjustments throughout life. Obviously, the sometimes persistent nature of learning disabilities is reason for concern in parents; it is a concern to which we shall return later in a discussion of LD in adolescents and adults.

The NJCLD definition gets closer to telling us what learning disability **is** caused by, although it does waffle a bit with its use of the word "presumed" in front of "central nervous system dysfunction". We want to pin them down and ask, "Is it a brain problem or isn't it people?" This definition also tells us that learning disability may occur in combination with, but not be caused by, other handicapping conditions such as blindness, deafness, mental retardation, and emotional disturbance. Finally, and to the relief of many teachers, it lets us off the hook by stating that learning disability is not due to poor teaching.

One of the six associations that made up the National Joint Committee for Learning Disabilities took exception to their definition. The Association for Children with Learning Disabilities (ACLD) proposed their own definition in 1984:

> Specific Learning Disabilities is a chronic condition of presumed neurological origin which selectively interferes with the development, integration, and/or demonstration of verbal and/or nonverbal abilities. Specific Learning Disabilities exists as a distinct handicapping condition in the presence of average to superior intelligence, adequate sensory and motor systems, and adequate learning opportunities. The condition varies in its manifestations and in degree of severity. Throughout life the condition can affect self-esteem, education, vocation, socialization, and/or daily living activities.

Quite significantly, the ACLD definition tells us that learning disability is a handicapping condition which may be found in people who have superior intelligence. It reinforces the idea that learning disability may be a lifelong problem. It includes more areas of functioning that may be affected. In addition to academic achievement, it mentions vocational and social adjustment and the transition to independent living. The reference to self-esteem is a good thing, for in the final analysis, during all of the years after we leave school, a positive set of feelings about ourselves is much more important in determining our ultimate levels of adjustment that our reading and math scores.

The three definitions of learning disability presented thus far are not inaccurate. They represent the best thinking of recognized authorities in the field at the time they were written, and they continue to be widely quoted today. For us, their primary problem is that they are not "parent friendly".

We could go on and take a look at many other definitions. Since, 1963, more than two dozen have been submitted by various individuals, professional groups, and associations. However, it is clear that these definitions, too, were not written with parents in mind as the primary audience. The language is tedious, repetitive, and, worst of all, not easy to comprehend. There is no easy definition, free of professional jargon, that just "tells it like it is".

Instead of further attempts to translate any more scholarly sounding, textbook definitions and additional debates on their advantages and disadvantages, what is needed are straightforward answers to questions that are important for parents. Questions like:

- What is learning disability?
- What do we know about it?
- What can we tell parents that will help them understand it better?

Let's get on with the business of answering these questions.

There is no doubt that learning disability is a difficult concept. In trying to clarify ideas which are hard to get a handle on, it is sometimes useful to start by listing things that everyone agrees with. We can call these "basic truths", "universally held beliefs", or "things which are certainly true". Having identified these things, the next step toward clarification is to describe things about the concept that a majority of people would consider true but about which there is some disagreement. Finally, it is useful to compare and contrast the concept to other ideas that are related to it but different. These are the steps we will take in an attempt to understand learning disability.

We'll begin with some things about learning disability that we know for sure. These are things that every teacher and counselor of children with learning disabilities would agree with. Then we'll continue with some things we think are true but can't say with one hundred percent certainty. Finally, we'll conclude by comparing learning disability to some other disabilities. With this information, you will have more of what you need to answer the questions that are asked above.

For sure, we know that children with learning disabilities are not doing well in school. Their problems in learning to read, to do math, and to write are what bring them to the attention of their teachers in the first place. It is universally held that children with learning disabilities have average or above average intelligence. Teachers and other professionals who work at schools use the term "underachiever" when talking about the LD child. This means that children have the capacity or potential to be achieving at a satisfactory level in school, but aren't. You might think of children with learning disabilities as students with gaps between their "ought to" and their "really are". Up here is where they ought to be achieving in school and down here is where they really are.

Furthermore, we know for sure that certain things are **not** causes of learning disability. Defective vision or hearing, emotional and behavioral disorders, lack of opportunity to learn, poor teaching, language differences between school and home—all of these factors are excluded; they are ruled out as causes. These things may go along with learning disability, and they may make the problem more difficult to remedy; however, they are not the primary causes.

We can also say, with certainty, that children who are learning disabled have areas of strength; that is, in many types of learning they will do just fine. Their problems show up in a few specific areas rather than appearing generally, across the board, in all areas of learning. Think of their development as uneven, out of balance. So, they may be very poor in reading but good in math. They may learn and remember things they hear much better than things they see. Or, they may be excellent at oral expression but unable to express themselves in writing.

Finally, there is now unanimous agreement that learning disabilities have long-term effects on many important areas of functioning. As the field has developed and more information has accumulated, it has become clear that beyond the relatively narrow and short-term influence upon academic achievement, there are, in many cases, persistent difficulties in socialization, vocational adjustment, and skills necessary for independent living. Thus, it can be said, for sure, that learning disabilities have negative effects upon all important areas of human development, and these effects may be present throughout the life span.

Now, given these basic truths, let's turn to another aspect of learning disability for which agreement is *less* than unanimous, a topic about which there is still a lot of controversy. There is a good deal of uncertainty about the question of causation. If certain factors have been ruled out or excluded as causes of learning disability, it is quite correct to wonder what has been ruled in.

Every semester, at Chicago State University, I teach a course to groups of graduate students who are preparing to teach children with learning disabilities in the public schools. When I come to the section of the course that deals with causation, I tell my students that they are really in a good position, because if I examine them on causes of learning disability, any answer they write in their exam booklets will be correct. They can't be wrong! Within the bounds of common sense, no matter what cause they list, it would be possible to find support for it somewhere from an authority in the field. (Of course, I go on to tell my students that it's always a good idea to remember that none of those authorities will be grading their exams.)

Consider the following list; at one time or another, everything on it has been suggested as a possible cause of learning disability:

1. neurological impairment; that is, damage, dysfunction, structural irregularity, or chemical imbalance in the brain*
2. heredity
3. food additives including artificial colorings, flavorings, and preservatives
4. allergic reactions to sugar or caffeine
5. weak eye muscles
6. excessive amounts of trace elements like zinc, chromium, or magnesium in the body
7. fluorescent lights in the classroom
8. vitamin deficiencies
9. glandular disorders
10. visual hypersensitivity to black print on white paper

Given the scope of the above list, graduate students are indeed in an enviable position at examination time. If they don't know the answer, just about anything will do, although they would probably get the highest grade if they stressed the first entry on the list. Most authorities in learning disability now believe that the cause of learning disability is within the child. They speak of *intrinsic neurological factors*. We need to look at this probable cause in more detail.

Think back to your own early years in elementary school. Chances are you moved through the grades with 30 or 40 classmates, all of whom got to know each other pretty well. After all, a classroom is a fairly intimate place, and given almost 10 months of close encounter, by year's end, there are very few strangers or secrets. You could point out the teachers's pets and the obnoxious trouble makers. You knew who the good athletes were and who the nerdy kids were. You could name who bathed regularly and who was prone to lice, ringworm, and blackheads. You also came to know who was good at school and who wasn't, who was bright and who was dull, who was grouped with the Eagles and who was a Crow. Some of the Crows, the slower learners, didn't read very well. At the time, you didn't think much about all of the different reasons for not being a good reader;

---

*Reread this entry carefully. Underline or highlight it. There's always the possibility of a quiz.

instead, you probably just lumped poor readers into one category: kids not as smart as you.

Now, years later, you are more discriminating, older and wiser, so you understand there are other factors, besides intelligence, that determine how well or poorly children learn to read. For example, children may have poor vision or hearing that goes unnoticed during their early years in school. They may have chronic illnesses which cause them to be absent from school for long periods of time, thus limiting their opportunity to learn. Family problems including divorce or death of a parent may cause emotional disturbances that affect concentration and learning. Parental job requirements may necessitate excessive family mobility and subsequent transfer from one school to another. Children may come from homes where the primary language is not the same as the one used at school. There is even the possibility that some children do not learn to read well, because they have not been taught well. (Shhh, don't spread this one around, it makes some teachers nervous.)

We could continue, but the conclusion would be the same. The truth is there are many factors that are important in learning to read. Some of these factors have their impact from outside of the child. They are called extrinsic factors. Poor teaching, lack of opportunity to learn, and family dysfunction would be examples. Other factors come from inside the child, and these, of course, are called intrinsic factors. Vision and hearing problems, emotional disturbance, limited proficiency in English, and chronic physical illness would fit here.

Although certainly not unanimous, the opinion of the majority of those who have studied learning disability in children and who have worked as teachers and counselors for these children is that the core of learning disability is within the learner. In fact, most people in the field now believe that learning disability is caused by what has to be the most intrinsic factor of all—a brain that is not working in the usual way. It would be hard to imagine getting any further inside a child than that. Remember, this is not to suggest that factors outside of the child, things like inappropriate instruction and lack of opportunity to learn, may not contribute to the problem. However, these extrinsic factors are considered secondary; they are seen as aggravators that make the basic problem worse. The basic problem is inside the child, *a central processing disorder*, a brain that does not process information in the normal way.

At this point, if we were at my college class on learning disability, there would probably be some hands in the air. At least a few of the students (former Eagles, no doubt) would have some questions. "What do you mean professor, by a central processing disorder"? "If you are saying that the primary problem is *abnormal* processing by the brain, then shouldn't you be telling us how the brain processes information normally"? "Why not just get on with it Doc; cut out the fancy lingo and tell us how the brain is supposed to work?"

Professors have a choice when bold students dare to ask hard questions like these. They can try their best to answer the questions, or they can tell those who ask them that class time is precious and require that they write a term paper on the topic to enlighten themselves. Students soon learn the penalty involved in asking hard questions and stop doing it. Of course, you don't have to worry about self-enlightenment. As bold as you may be, I have no choice in this instance but to go ahead and try to answer the questions myself.

To know what is meant by a central processing disorder, it is first necessary to understand how the brain functions without disorder. The question is: How does the brain work when everything is operating as it should? If we can answer that one, it will be easier to appreciate what may be happening when things go wrong.

We know the brain is an incredibly capable organ. It is the primary control mechanism for everything that we do from before we are born until we die. It allows us to think in abstract terms, to contemplate the future and reflect upon the past, and to develop a sense of self. It enables us to attend to what is happening around us; it warns us of danger, makes it possible for us to speak with others, and it helps us remember our multiplication tables, spelling words, and the faces of old friends we haven't seen in years. It causes us to salivate when we are hungry, and it stirs us at the sight of a painting or the sound of music. It discharges chemicals that control our moods and can cause us to be aggressive, even violent, depressed, or passionate. It stores everything that we have ever learned, long after that learning has left our consciousness. It enables us to record the history of our society and to read the histories of others. Deep within this small space is a repository for the imagination out of which has sprung a range of exquisite creative expression from primitive drawings on the walls of caves to the Mona Lisa, to the wheel, manned flight, and vehicles that land on other planets.

The brain never rests, even when we sleep, and it hardly ever breaks down, although the probability of such a dire outcome increases to the extent that we continue to abuse it with toxins like alcohol, drugs, and environmental pollutants. In the long run, the ravages of time, strokes, and Alzheimer's ultimately win, but until then it serves us mightily. When the service ends, so do we.

Given the diverse and magnificent capabilities of the human brain described thus far, we are still left with the problem of understanding how it actually works. Exactly how does it do all of those things? Precisely what's happening up there between our ears? Recent and ongoing research is beginning to provide some answers to these questions.

Prior to the last decade, very little was known about how the brain functioned during the process of learning. There was no direct way of observing what was going on internally as learning was taking place, so the brain was thought of as a kind of mysterious, isolated and unapproachable black box. Stuff from the outside world called sensory stimuli (things we see, hear, touch, smell and taste) traveled over the senses and entered the box. Other stuff, called responses, came out in the form of observable behavior like moving or talking. But what occurred inside the black box between entry and exit was not very well understood. This intermediate process was vaguely described as "the internal manipulation of ideas", more fancy words that gave a label to the process but didn't really describe what was going on inside.

Even today, complete understanding about the inner workings of the brain is a long way off, but more has been learned about it in the last ten years than in the rest of our prior history. Some recent discoveries have resulted in totally new thinking about the brain. Instead of being an organ encapsulated within the skull that functions in ways somewhat isolated from external reality, we now understand that the brain is always active in its pursuit of sensory stimulation. There is a constant, dynamic interplay between the brain and the outside world.

Think of your senses as avenues to the brain. The stimuli that flow along these avenues are analogous to food for a starving man. The brain requires and therefore welcomes sensory stimulation; it seeks it, because without such nourishment it will wither and die. The very structure and functioning of the brain are dependent upon environmental events. In fact, our experiences determine how our brains are shaped and ultimately how efficiently they operate during learning and remembering. Let's take a peek inside to see how this interplay between the brain and environmental events takes place.

If it were actually possible to get in there and take a walk around, the first thing that would astound you would be the crowded conditions. It is estimated that our brains consist of approximately one hundred billion cells! That's a big bunch, folks. To get some idea of how much a billion is, consider the fact that a million seconds are 12 days, but a billion seconds are 32 years.

Brain cells are called neurons. If you had previously walked through the brains of other animals, this stroll through a human one would impress you even more. A common house fly probably has about 100,000 neurons, a rat has maybe 5 million, and our closest relatives, the apes, have around 10 billion. Clearly, we've got it all over them, but you already knew that. The point is that within your skull, there are a lot of residents crammed into relatively tight quarters.

Continuing with your walk, you would notice that individual neurons are connected to others. These connections between brain cells are called synapses, and there may be as many as 15,000 of them branching out from each cell. When you consider 100 billion individual cells, each of which is linked with so many others, the total number of possible connections and combinations between and among them is so huge that it's impossible to envision. Certainly, it is well up into the hundreds of trillions. One estimate tells us that the number of connections that could possibly exist between all these brain cells is greater than the number of atoms in the universe!

Once you came to grips with this staggering quantity of brain matter and got some elbow room, you would begin to notice how things are arranged in there. There is nothing haphazard or slipshod about the construction of the brain; on the contrary, everything is well-organized. There is an efficient architectural plan, if you will; a plan which results in different parts of the brain being responsible for different things like vision, hearing, language, and movement.

Now, with this brief description of some of the structure of the brain, let's turn to a description of how it functions. Assume that the brain you've been walking through is that of a young child who is at the stage of his development when he's learning to talk. While you're inside, the child's mother happens to speak to him. Sound vibrations are carried by his ear drum over three small bones in the middle ear. The vibrations cause fluid to stimulate tiny hair cells on the cochlea, the organ of hearing, in the inner ear. In turn, these hair cells stimulate a set of auditory nerves which send messages to the portion of the brain responsible for helping the child interpret his mother's words. That's where you are, at the hearing center, within the temporal lobe, of this child's brain.

When the message arrived at the hearing center of the brain, you would notice an amazing thing. Millions of language cells would stand at attention and instantly swing into action. New synapses would form. More connections between neurons would develop. The more speech the child heard, the more new connections he would have. Right before your eyes, you would see this child's brain grow and become more powerful. Exposure to an environmental event (a mother's voice) has actually shaped and modified the structure of the child's brain. What you would have observed is but one example of the dynamic interplay between the brain and this child's environment.

Consider another example that has to do with the sense of smell. One of a child's most important bits of learning takes place right after birth. An infant first relates to its mother by smelling. This initial contact has been called bonding. Scientists who study the brain have discovered that within seconds of the first time that a baby smells its mother, new connections quickly form in the brain. Again, we see how an environmental event modifies the structure of the brain. It grows and becomes more powerful.

These two examples of the interaction between the brain and the environment are instances that resulted in positive outcomes. In the first case, a child's language development was enhanced, and in the second he learned to identify his mother. There are other instances, however, from which a negative outcome occurs as a result of contact between a brain and the environment. Exposure to bad experiences associated with high levels of environmental stress, either during the prenatal period or early childhood, have been shown to have a harmful effect on brain development.

Ordinarily, when we find ourselves in a stressful environment, hormones like adrenaline are released to help us respond to what we perceive as a dangerous or unpleasant situation. Our hormones prepare us to handle the situation by either sticking around and dealing with it or by getting the heck away as soon as we can. It is fight or flight, and in either case, we get back to a balanced state, an even keel, when the stress ends.

Some neurologists have suggested, though, that when hormones must be consistently overactive because of *persistent* stress upon the fetus or young child, atypical or unusual connections between neurons develop. The brain mislearns and becomes less stable. This leads children to overrespond in subsequently stressful situations. They have a harder time getting back on balance. They may become depressed instead of happy or aggressive and violent. Persistent stress has caused them to become less efficient neurologically, and, of course, this lowers their capacity to learn.

So it is that the brain learns and remembers by a process of constant modification. The network consisting of trillions of connections between cells increases and becomes more or less efficient as a result of positive or negative stimulation from the environment. Far from being a static organ that simply sits around and waits to interpret stimuli that are carried to it by our senses, the brain dynamically modifies its structure in response to these environmental events. The brain does indeed use the outside world to shape itself; the environment is the source of nourishment that stimulates its growth.

There are other fascinating discoveries about the brain that have been made in the last decade. It appears that the brain does not grow at a constant pace; instead there are periods of very rapid growth and periods of slower growth. These are followed by times when brain cells die, resulting in a lessening of their total number. During the very earliest part of the life cycle, in the first few months of the prenatal period, the fetus is a neuron maker performing at peak capacity. The brain produces an extravagant excess of cells, fully twice the number it will ever need. It's as if the brain wants to make sure it's got everything covered, enough to provide for any contingency. "Hit me with anything; I can handle it", the brain says, as it swaggers in abundance.

With this exorbitant excess of neurons in the fetal brain, an economic system flourishes. "Neurological capitalism" develops as brain cells engage in competition to produce a better product. Cells vie for jobs. They attempt to hook up to some part of the body, and those that lose; that is, those that find no useful employment for themselves, do not receive the chemical nourishment they need to survive and quickly die off before a child is born.

After birth, brain development increases at a steady, quick pace. This is when the division of labor takes place and different parts of the brain assume responsibility for different functions. Toward the back of the brain, the occipital lobe handles vision. The temporal lobe in the middle takes care of hearing, and the frontal lobe (straight in from the forehead) is in charge of things like problem solving, planning, and concentration.

Beginning at about age four and through age ten or eleven, brain development takes off again. In fact, it goes wild. New tests that make it possible for neurologists to measure the activity level of the brain show a tremendous energy spurt during these years. When learning occurs during childhood, the brain reorganizes itself, and new connections are formed as new things are learned. Finally, at around age twelve, the brain quiets down. There is another die off as cells that are not strengthened by stimulation from the environment have no use and perish.

Happily, as we get older, the brain can still be shaped by exposure to environmental events. This makes it possible for us to continue learning throughout our adult lives and even into old age. As adults, there is good reason to believe that the harder we exercise our brains, the more fit they will remain. Autopsies of university graduates who remained mentally active throughout their lives have shown up to 40 percent more connections than the brains of high school dropouts. There is some recent evidence that suggests that a robust, active pursuit of intellectual stimulation can even forestall the development of Alzheimer's disease. So, the ball game is not over when we hit middle age, it's just that we have to play harder in order to keep winning.

As flexible as the brain is and as easily as it responds to sensory stimulation, it does have a few rigid rules of its own. It is downright stubborn when it comes to timing, for example. The brain prefers that we learn certain things at specific times, and should learning not occur at those times, it may not occur at all, or, at best, it will be very difficult. These crucial times during which learning must take place are called critical periods.

The discovery of critical periods began with research on animals. Newborn kittens were deprived of a normal amount of sensory stimulation by having one eye sewn shut. A couple of weeks later, when those eyes were opened, they could not see. The eyes were blind, despite the fact that there had been no physiological damage to them. And, the eyes that had remained open could see better than normal eyes. In kittens, the critical period for visual stimulation is the first few weeks of life. If the brain cells responsible for receiving visual information are not nourished during this crucial time, they stop working and take their business elsewhere, where they are wanted.

Critical periods operate with respect to the functioning of human brains too. For infants born with cataracts, the practice used to be to delay surgery until two or three years of age. These children grew up blind, because they missed the critical period for visual experience. Their opaque lenses prevented visual stimulation from reaching the brain when it was supposed to, so the cells that normally handle vision either perished or moved away to do other jobs. Now, cataracts are removed early, and blindness is prevented.

Think also of language development and how it relates to critical periods. It has been noted that children learn their language with amazing ease. No lessons are required. They will learn two or three languages just as naturally if they are fortunate enough to be exposed to them early in life. On the other hand, if, as an adult, you have ever attempted to learn a second language, you know how very difficult it can be. Even if you acquire a rudimentary vocabulary and grammar, your accent is probably awful. The reason it is so easy for children and so hard for us is that they are still within the critical period when the brain is so receptive to learning language. Our older brains have turned to other things. The most dramatic evidence of the relationship between learning to speak and critical periods shows up in the cases of children who have been locked away and experience severe sensory deprivation. If they have not heard speech by ten years of age, no effort after that point will help them learn a language.

Thus, the brain is a real stickler for time. The foundations for everything that the brain regulates—our emotions, reactions to stress, memory, learning, and all the rest of it—are built in our early years when the brain is most flexible and subject to change. Give it stimulation when you're supposed to, essentially between birth and 12 years of age, and it will soak up information like the most efficient sponge. But, if you miss the right time, it becomes increasingly stingy with second chances. We have learned that the brain, more so than any other organ in the body, operates according to the dictum: **use it or lose it.**

The implications of these new discoveries about brain functioning are vitally important for learning disorders in children. Our approach to problems like mental retardation and learning disability has always been after the fact. We wait for these crises to happen, and then we attempt to deal with them. If, as current investigations of brain functioning suggest, a stimulating environment helps the brain become a more efficient learning machine, and the best time to supply the stimulation is early in life, then it is but a short leap in logic to the realization that learning problems can be prevented. Stimulating environmental intervention in the form of infant and early childhood education programs would be the mechanism for stopping learning problems before they begin.

This is not science fiction. Several experimental programs have already shown that with very early exposure to stimulating environmental experiences, children born into poverty, even those whose mothers have marginal intelligence, gain 15 to 20 IQ points compared to children from similar backgrounds who do not have the benefit of such intervention. What these programs have demonstrated, in fact, is the prevention of mental retardation. And, if it works for mental retardation, there is every reason to believe it will work for learning disability too.

Until such time in the future when there is a fuller understanding of brain functioning and we are more willing to spend money to fund infant and early childhood education programs, the best we can do is attempt to understand learning disability and remediate those problems that children already have. But, nowhere is the adage "an ounce of prevention worth a pound of cure" more appropriate than it is here. For every dollar not spent on programs to prevent learning problems in early childhood, at least three dollars will be spent on remedial programs later on.

Now, we can return to the probable cause of learning disabilities in children. Remember, the majority opinion is that neurological factors; that is, central processing disorders, constitute the core of the problem. The preceding discussion of the brain was a description of how the brain usually works. With some knowledge of normal brain functioning, it should now be easier to understand one that isn't working normally. Therefore, we are ready to go ahead and look at examples of central processing disorders and how they interfere with learning.

The senses have been described as avenues to the brain. During the process of receiving information from the senses, the brain helps us do some things which are very significant, in fact vital, in the process of learning. These functions include attention, perception, and memory; things which along with language development and concept formation, are referred to as "basic psychological processes" in the federal definition of learning disability.

It is important that you know what these psychological processes are and what purpose they have. Think of them as *prerequisites* that are essential for academic learning. They are abilities that supply the foundation for future success in reading, math, and written expression. For a child who is deficient in one or more of these psychological processes, the risk of learning disability increases. We'll take a closer look at some of these prerequisites in order to see how they are involved in learning and learning disability.

Psychologists use the term "perception" when referring to the brain's task of helping us *interpret* visual and auditory events around us. (Of course, perception is involved in the interpretation of input from the other senses as well, but smell, touch, and taste are not as important for learning in school.) These events, stimuli, they have been called, surround us in large numbers and constantly compete for our attention. In the classroom, a place which is rich in stimulation, children are literally bombarded with a profusion of sights and sounds all day long. They rely on perception to sort out, to filter, to make sense out of all the stimuli flowing over their sensory avenues into their brains. The eyes see and the ears hear, but the brain has the crucial responsibility of interpretation.

Children with learning disabilities have been called "perceptually handicapped". Here, then, is a clue to what is meant by a brain that is not working normally; that is, one that is not processing information in the usual way. The eyes may see and the ears may hear with perfect acuity, but the information they send along their respective avenues to the brain may not be interpreted correctly. When incoming messages from the eyes and ears are garbled, when the signals are confused, when they are not interpreted appropriately, the brain is not working normally. It isn't processing information correctly. The child has a central processing disorder.

I can remember my first visit to an optometrist. I was about eight or nine years old; I couldn't see the blackboard or clock in class, and I was always squinting. The doctor had me look into a device, and he proceeded to drop a series of lenses, correcting for varying degrees of nearsightedness, in front of my eyes. I was amazed at the change in my vision. I didn't believe that it was possible for people to see so clearly. For me, the tops of trees had always been big globs of green rather than a collection of individually defined leaves. I had always assumed that friends' faces were supposed to be blurred until they got as close as a foot or two away from mine. My assumptions were understandable. How could I know what normal eyesight was, since I had never experienced it? Clearly, I had no way of knowing what I was missing.

Something similar is true with respect to learning disability. How can you, even as a parent who knows your child better than anyone else, begin to understand perceptual handicap or learning disability if you have never experienced it directly? Your brain is working normally, so you can't know what you child is missing. Perhaps an example will help.

Assume that you are back in school. Your teacher has given you an assignment. By next week, you are required to hand in a five page written composition. Your topic is "Learning Disabilities in the Elementary School Child". This will be a snap, you think. You are highly motivated, because the topic is something that has interested you for a long time. With this degree of motivation and interest, you are confident that you will write a well-organized, concise, factually correct paper that will be deserving of the highest grade.

Early Saturday morning you go to your local public library where a kind and friendly librarian helps you do a computer search for everything that has been written about your topic in the last ten years. With the help of modern technology, in just 15 minutes, you have a list of books, magazines, and pamphlets specifically related to your topic. Equipped with freshly sharpened pencils and a stack of note cards, you find an empty table in a corner of the library and get to work. You open your first book, and to your great puzzlement and dismay, you are confronted with the following passage:

*Learning Disability: What Is It?* 53

> **Learuiug bisadility**
>
> It has deeu snggesteb that as wauy as 10% ofthe qrodlews qnqils have iu school cau de dlaweb nqou qerceqtnal haubicaqs. Mom! Me're sqeakiug adont wauy, wauy, chilbreu mho ueeb rewebial helq. Mhere areallthe bebicateb qeoqle tohelqthew?
>
> Thesitnatiou isu't fnuuy. There is uosolntiou iu sight. Cau yon iwagiue the qrodlew for the teachers aubqareuts? Hom monlb yon like to de resqousidle for iustrnctiug qnqils mhoare hyqeractive, bistractidle, mith atteutiou beficits, audmho cau't keeq their qlace in their dooks mheu
> t
>   h
>     e
>
>                           y wnst reab?

What in the world is going on here? You rub your eyes, take out a tissue to clean your glasses, and start over. But, it's no different the second time. You can see all right, but you can't seem to understand much of the reading passage at all. Your eyes are OK, but your brain isn't. It can't process the information. No matter how hard you try, your reading is laborious, and you just can't seem to grasp the author's meaning. Your puzzlement is replaced by panic as you think back to what you had to drink last night and even consider the possibility of a stroke.

Of course, you needn't call for help or hurry over for a visit to a neurologist. It's only a simulation. The problem is not real, there is nothing wrong with you; the reading passage itself has been tampered with. In the above passage, pairs of letters with similar shapes like *b* and *d*, *p* and *q*, *m* and *w*, and *n* and *u* have been reversed, rotated, or placed upside down. Whole words like *on* and *no* have been reversed. Spaces between words have been omitted, and words "jump around" on the page.

This simulation may approximate some of the perceptual problems that children with learning disabilities face as they attempt to learn to read. To bring you back to the present, a translation of the passage follows on the next page.

That's better. Your ability to interpret the passage was impaired only very briefly, because your experience with perceptual handicap was just temporary. Isn't it nice to be functioning normally again? For your child, however, the problem will certainly not be as transient. In fact, it may not go away at all. Even as an adult, long after the completion of formal education, there may still be residual learning problems present. That's why it is so important to learn about learning disability now.

> **Learning disability**
>
> It has been estimated that as many as 10% of the problems that pupils have in school can be blamed upon perceptual handicaps. Wow! We're speaking about many, many children who need remedial help. Where are all the dedicated people to help them?
>
> The situation isn't funny. There is no solution in sight. Can you imagine the problem for the teachers and parents? How would you like to be responsible for instructing pupils who are hyperactive, distractible, with attention deficits, and who can't keep their place in their books when they must read?

Remember, perception, this ability to interpret what is seen and heard, is only one of a number of basic psychological processes important for learning. Now, let's examine memory, another of these prerequisites. Perhaps you know someone who has experienced an obvious memory loss. For that person, things don't "click in" as easily and rapidly as they used to. He may have to struggle to remember a phone number or the name of a friend. He finds himself relying on written lists more than he used to. Strangely, he has a vivid recollection of things that happened 30 years ago, but he can't remember what he had for breakfast. Maybe you know someone like that. Maybe it's you.

It's true that our memories, like so many of our other skills, deteriorate with age; the good news, however, is that surrounding ourselves with stimulating activities and keeping mentally alert and active seem to slow the decline. So, let's get you active here, because as you already know, if you don't use it, you lose it.

Psychologists who have studied memory distinguish between short term, or immediate recall, and long term memory. Although the distinction may be somewhat arbitrary, it's probably correct to say that anything requiring recall more than a few seconds after first being exposed to the information involves long term memory. Since we don't have a whole lot of time, we'll try a short term memory task. Your cooperation is required; that is, I'm expecting you to uphold the honor code. In other words: No Cheating!

Do the following things:

1. Study this list of 4 words for about 5 seconds: House, Apple, Wagon, Shoe

2. Now, close your eyes and say them aloud, in *reverse* order.

That shouldn't have been too difficult. Let's make it just a little harder by trying a list with 5 words. Do the following things:

1. Study this list of 5 words for about 10 seconds: Heart, Bus, Shirt, Orange, Camel
2. Close you eyes and say them aloud, in *reverse* order.

---

That may have been a little more difficult, but you were probably still able to do it. Now, let's try one more list. Do the following things:

1. Study this list of words for 10 seconds: Circle, Scarf, Plane, Horse, Peach
2. As quickly as you can, name colors that start with these letters: O, P, B, Y, G, R, B, P, G, T
3. Now, without looking up, close your eyes and say the list of 5 words in *reverse* order.

---

That was probably considerably more difficult. Most people can only remember one or two of the words. This final short term memory task was harder, because you were forced to attend to information, the names of colors, in between initial exposure to the words and the test of recall. Your concentration was interrupted; you were distracted. Your attention deficit interfered with your memory. For a moment, you were just like Billy.

Do you see, now, how problems with basic psychological processes like perception, memory, and attention can interfere with learning? Given such problems, the likelihood for reading and other academic disabilities to develop increases, and such likelihood will be the case even in children whose overall level of intelligence may be quite high. Let's try a few more examples.

Language is another of the psychological processes that is considered an important prerequisite for learning in school. In fact, those children who are skilled at using language tend to be the ones who do the best in school. One of the language problems that children with reading disabilities often have is called a "word finding disorder". When speaking, even in casual conversation with no apparent reason to be anxious, they will pause for a long time between words. They use fillers such as "uh", "y'know", or "like", and they often choose the wrong word, pick another word from the same category, or talk around a topic as they struggle to speak. It's not that they don't have ideas; instead, it seems as if they are slow to retrieve words to express those ideas.

Children with this type of language problem are likely to have a hard time recalling letter names and the sounds that go with each letter. Their attempts at decoding or sounding out new words will be so slow and arduous that by the time they get to the end of a sentence, they will have forgotten the beginning. Naturally, subsequent comprehension of what they have read will suffer.

To give you an idea of what a word finding problem may be like, try the following exercise. All you need to do is come up with words for each of the initials. The first two are done to get your thinking on the right track.

1. 365 D. in a Y.                365 Days in a Year
2. 12 E. in a D.                 12 Eggs in a Dozen
3. 88 K. on a P.                 _____
4. 32 D.F. and which W.F.        _____
5. 366 D. in a L.Y.              _____
6. 54 C. in a D. including the J. _____
7. 3 B.M. See H.T.R.             _____
8. 200 D. for P.G. in M.         _____
9. 76 T. in the B.P.             _____
10. 1L. 2L. 3L.I.                _____

You are familiar with each of the above. They are common, everyday things that you have heard and seen, and it is probable that you have said them a lot too. If you had any problem coming up with answers for these things that you certainly know, what you experienced was probably similar to the struggle that learning disabled children with language problems have in retrieving words. (By the way, you can find the answers at the end of this chapter.)

Just one more activity follows to see if you have a latent learning problem that has been lying dormant in you for all these years. Concept formation is a very important prerequisite for successful learning. It makes it possible for the learner to classify individual ideas into larger, unified wholes. Without the ability to form concepts, it would be impossible to cluster single things into categories, and the learner would be overwhelmed by too many things to learn and remember. It would then be very difficult to engage in higher level thought processes like comparing and contrasting or evaluating.

As an example of how concept formation works, if you heard the words "rocking", "easy", "recliner", "wingback", and "folding", you would have no problem recognizing that each word is a member of the larger concept of "chair". Similarly, the words "koala", "Qantas", "kangaroo", and "down under" are all representative members of the concept "Australia". Easy, right?

Now, you try it. Below, there are ten sets of three words each. In each instance, your task is to think of the fourth word that goes with the first three. Again, the first two are done for you to get you started, and the answers, should you need them, (hah!) are at the end of the chapter.

| | | | | |
|---|---|---|---|---|
| 1. | stool | powder | ball | foot |
| 2. | blue | cake | cottage | cheese |
| 3. | finger | rose | toilet | _____ |
| 4. | high | start | broad | _____ |
| 5. | plan | show | walker | _____ |
| 6. | puff | foot | gun | _____ |
| 7. | club | race | tender | _____ |
| 8. | news | doll | tiger | _____ |
| 9. | hop | cow | liberty | _____ |
| 10. | made | cuff | left | _____ |

Did you do well on these simulations? Or, perhaps your self-esteem is suffering, because your spouse did better than you. In either case, the idea was for you to get a better understanding of how difficulties in processing information relate to learning disability. Always remember that deficiencies in these prerequisites for learning are independent of overall level of intelligence; that is, there are some very bright people who have problems with perception, memory, attending, language, or concept formation.

Continuing with our attempt to better understand learning disability, let's briefly consider some other disabilities. One child, due to complications during birth, was deprived of oxygen for too long and suffered serious brain damage. Cerebral palsy was the result. This child cannot move smoothly. He has very limited use of his legs, and when he tries to move his arms and hands, the results are abrupt, spasmodic, and jerky movements that he cannot control with any degree of accuracy. He needs help to feed himself and in toileting, and he spends most of his time during the day in a wheel chair. His voice is unpleasant, and his articulation is so poor that his speech is very difficult to understand.

Another child hardly speaks at all. On occasion, when someone asks him a direct question, he will repeat the question instead of answering it. For the most part, he has withdrawn so far into himself that he doesn't really relate to other people. It's as if he doesn't recognize the boundary that exists between the internal fantasy world where he is and the external world of reality where the other people are. His movements are often repetitive and mechanical, and he will sometimes even do self-destructive things. He will rock, wave his hands in front of his eyes, gouge his fingers into his eyes or bang his head on the wall or floor. He likes to play with small, metallic objects and will do so for hours if allowed. The diagnosis is infantile autism, and his doctors now believe it's due to a chemical imbalance in his brain.

A third child has been blind since shortly after birth. Hospital records indicate that exposure to oxygen while in an incubator caused scar tissue to form behind the lenses of her eyes. This girl is very bright and has good language skills. She has learned to read and write with Braille, she has excellent listening skills, and she knows a lot about her academic subjects and current events. She gets excellent grades in school and goes to a special training facility every afternoon where she is learning to get around in her community with the assistance of a guide dog. She is an accomplished guitarist and enjoys both classical and folk music. She speaks of going to college and studying law when she gets older.

Clearly, there is much that is different about these children. Their disabilities come from different causes and have many different effects. The ability to communicate, mobility in the community, the degree of dependence upon others, potential for academic achievement, interests, hobbies, and capacity for creative expression—all these things vary according to the nature of the problem.

It is also true, however, that these disabilities have something in common. They are all highly visible. Problems like cerebral palsy, autism, and blindness are obvious. They are apparent to anyone, even people who have no training or expertise in special education, medicine, or related fields. Therefore, they tend to evoke feelings of tolerance. Think of it. We would not be critical of a child who was crippled with cerebral palsy for not wanting to go to gym class. Nor would we say that a child who was autistic and didn't say "good morning" had an attitude problem. We don't hesitate for a second when it comes time to provide a blind child with assistance.

With all these disabilities, there is understanding rather than blame. Moreover, the visibility of these disabilities has led to the relatively quick provision of special educational services in school, speech and language therapy, physical and occupational therapy, and vocational rehabilitation services thereafter. With learning disability, however, things are different.

The difference with learning disability, and another thing that has made it so puzzling and hard to understand, is that it is an invisible disability. It is not possible to see the neurological impairments that are interfering with learning. There is nothing about the appearance or overt behavior of children with learning disabilities that immediately suggests the possibility of problems learning in school. So, when they have failed, there has been the tendency to consider them lazy and unmotivated, to think of them as children with negative attitudes toward school. Tolerance and understanding are not as forthcoming as they have been in the cases of more visible disabilities. Blame is.

"He just isn't interested", "she won't put forth the effort", all he needs to do is try harder at school", "he's just lazy"—these are all statements heard regularly when children with learning disabilities are the topic of discussion. They are statements that place the responsibility for the problem squarely on the shoulders of the child. Very often, children who are learning disabled feel frustrated and angry, because they know they are being blamed for failure when they have no control over the matter. And, if their problems in school are indeed caused by neurological impairment, certainly their feelings are justified. As Billy said, so correctly, "Mommy, I just can't help it".

We need to remember that children with learning disabilities are entitled to just as much understanding as other, more visibly disabled children. Subtle neurological impairment, invisible though it may be, can be debilitating just like crippled legs or sightless eyes. With acceptance of that fact, an important first hurdle will have been crossed. Blame, frustration, and anger will diminish, and the energies of all those involved—children, teachers, and parents—will be used more productively. Full effort could be directed to helping students overcome, or at the very least, learn to cope with what are very real disabilities.

Simulations such as the reading passage, the memory exercise, and the others with which you might have had trouble before may be somewhat helpful. They may shed some light on what it is like to have an intrinsic neurological problem resulting in processing difficulties and learning disability. But they are probably only rough approximations of the actual problems that are experienced by children who are learning disabled.

Complete understanding of learning disability, by those who aren't disabled themselves, remains difficult, because the brain does not yield its secrets easily. Even with the development of technologically advanced, highly sophisticated diagnostic tools like positron emission tomography (Pet Scans) and magnetic resonance imaging (MRI), complete knowledge of how the brain works in the process of learning is still in the future. Until the time that such knowledge is available, it would do us all well to at least remember that children who are learning disabled are not lazy, disinterested, or undermotivated in school. Those are children who **won't** learn satisfactorily. It is a true neurological difference in children who are learning disabled that makes academic achievement so difficult. Therefore, your child is a student who would be more accurately described as someone who **can't** learn satisfactorily. Your child did not bring laziness or a negative attitude to school on the first day. No indeed. What came was a neurological impairment that has made learning the way most kids do very hard.

The distinction between "won't learners" and "can't learners" is a crucial one, because in the latter case, a child is as much entitled to special consideration and service in school as a blind child is entitled to Braille, a crippled child is entitled to ramps, and an autistic child is entitled to therapy. In fact, this entitlement has been recognized and is guaranteed by the law. Since 1975, it has been mandatory for every school district in the country to provide special educational services for children with learning disabilities until they graduate from high school. Important details of this law are explained in Chapter IV.

The purpose of this chapter has been to help you understand learning disability. To summarize what has been said, there are some things about learning disability that people in the field believe to be true with certainty: 1) Children with learning disabilities are underachievers in school; they are not doing as well as they should. 2) Their learning problems show up in a few specific areas rather than having a general effect on learning in all areas. 3) Factors such as sensory impairment, ineffective teaching, and bilingualism are ruled out as causes of the problem. And, 4) Children who have these problems in school often grow up to be adults who have these problems in life. These are things we know for sure.

Regarding the question of causation, there is less certainty, although most authorities are now maintaining that learning disability is due to things within the learner. These are neurological factors affecting children's ability to process information; for example, to attend, to perceive, to remember, to use language, and to form concepts about material during the process of learning. These factors make normal rates of academic achievement very difficult, even for children who are not visibly handicapped and whose overall aptitude for learning in school is average or above.

Along with some lack of agreement on what may be causing learning disability, no one is sure about how common the problem is either. We'll discuss the prevalence of learning disabilities in the next chapter. In the meantime, you may be looking for answers to the simulations appearing earlier in this chapter. I hope you haven't looked at them until now. We have talked about the honor code, haven't we?

*For the word finding simulation*

3. Keys on a Piano
4. Degrees Fahrenheit at which Water Freezes
5. Days in a Leap Year
6. Cards in a Deck (including the Jokers)
7. Blind Mice How They Run
8. Dollars for Passing Go in Monopoly
9. Trombones in the Big Parade
10. Little, Little, Little Indians

*For the concept formation simulation*

3. bowl
4. jump
5. floor
6. powder
7. foot
8. paper
9. bell
10. hand

# Chapter 3

# *The Prevalence of Learning Disability*

The question is easy. How many children have learning disabilities? Answering it isn't easy at all. Just as people in the field continue to have different opinions about the causes of learning disability, they also disagree on the prevalence of the problem. The disagreement is striking. Authorities in the field give estimates that vary from as low as one percent of the children in school to as high as forty percent. Actually, the wide range of figures should not be surprising; in large part, it is due to the confusion that still exists about the definition of learning disability. It will continue to be difficult for authorities to agree on **how many** children with learning disabilities there are until they agree on **who** they are.

Although there is a lot of disagreement over the estimated percentage of children with learning disabilities in the total school population, there is no arguing that the actual number participating in special education programs across the country has increased dramatically in recent years. Remember that the term "learning disability" didn't even exist until 1963. By 1969, just six years later, more than 120,000 children had been identified and placed in special programs in school. Fourteen years later, in 1983, the figure had mushroomed to 1,700,000 children.[1] At the present time, growth has slowed somewhat, but it is estimated that in school districts across the United States, more than 2 million children participate in special programs for children with learning disabilities. Thus, in the span of just one generation, the number of children who are being called "learning disabled" has increased by almost 17 times!

For an idea of the prevalence of the problem in one metropolitan area, consider the Chicago Public Schools. In Chicago, there are special programs for students with learning disabilities in almost every one of the 600 elementary and high schools. Students who qualify for placement in these programs are provided

---

[1] Chalfant, J.C. Identifying disabled students: A summary of the National Task Force report." *Learning Disabilities Focus*, Vol. 1, 1985, pp. 9-20.

with either part time or full time assistance depending upon the severity of the disability. About 18,000 children and adolescents are currently enrolled in these programs. They represent almost five percent of the total number of students in school. And, these figures do not include those children with learning disabilities who haven't yet been identified as such or those who have been identified but haven't yet been placed in special programs. If these "children in waiting" are added, it would not be unreasonable to arrive at an estimate of somewhere between 5-10% of the total school population.

After all the statistics are digested, it would be hard to deny that learning disability is a high incidence problem. In today's public schools, it has become alarmingly common. Cynics have said that it's almost considered fashionable to have an LD child. You know you've "arrived" when you can afford a home in the suburbs, a Mercedes, and you have a dyslexic son. Such glib cynics may have none of these, but they do have a point.

The point is there are more children participating in special education programs for learning disabilities than in any other type of program, and, if the present trend continues, it will soon be correct to say that there are more children in learning disability programs than in the rest of special education put together. In the very near future, the total of all children enrolled in special school programs for the mentally retarded, deaf, hard of hearing, blind, partially sighted, orthopedically handicapped, communication disordered, chronic medical problems, and behavior disordered/emotionally disturbed will be less than those who have been placed in programs for the learning disabled. And, all this growth has occurred in just thirty years. Here is a problem that has assumed truly epidemic proportions, and just one generation ago, there wasn't even a name for it.

One needn't be a cynic to question what has happened. Any reasonable person would have to wonder where all these children with learning disabilities were before 1963. This reasonable person believes two things about the explosive growth of learning disabilities. First, some of it is real; there has been an actual increase in learning disability. But second, some of it isn't. A portion of the increase is unreal. There have been some factors that have created the illusion that learning disability is more common than it is. Let's look at these illusory factors first.

Shortly before the good doctor died, someone asked Albert Einstein what factors he thought were responsible for the frightening outbreak of cancer. The questioner wondered why it had become so common when 50 years earlier, hardly anyone had ever heard about it. Although Einstein will always be remembered best for his revolutionary theory of relativity, he was no slouch in other more practical areas either. In his wisdom, he pointed out that cancer is indeed frightening but had always been prevalent. It had just seemed to have become more common, because more had been learned about it, and, with advances in medical treatment more people were living long enough to be counted.

Similar reasoning may be applied to learning disability. Some of the apparent growth isn't real. Children with subtle neurological impairments and learning disabilities have always been there, but since we gave it a name and learned more about it, we have become much more aggressive in our attempts to identify "new" cases. It is also true that a generation ago there were no laws mandating schools to locate and provide for children with learning disabilities. Many of these children left school very early and weren't counted. Educationally, children with learning problems are now "living longer"; that is, they are still in school when the administration goes about the business of quantifying the population of children who are learning disabled. Again, they were always there; the current prevalence seems so much greater, because they're present in school where they can be counted.

There is a second reason that has led to an exaggerated estimate of the prevalence of learning disability. Special education has not always been diligent in developing and monitoring satisfactory procedures for the identification and placement of children in learning disability programs. In fact, some practices within the field are downright sloppy. The issue has to do with the steps that are taken to get children into programs for children with learning disabilities in the first place.

The process involving entry to special education typically begins with a classroom teacher. The teacher, concerned about a student's academic difficulties, refers that child for evaluation. A team of experts made up of a school psychologist, social worker, school nurse, guidance counselor, and teacher with advanced training in learning disability administer a number of psychological and educational tests. After the evaluation, the team and the student's parents meet to discuss the results and determine if the student meets the requirements for placement in a special program.

On paper, the process appears to be efficient and equitable. All concerned know exactly what their professional responsibilities are, time lines have been written in to assure the rapid disposition of cases, and, very importantly, no decisions involving placement of a child in a special program can be made without permission from the parents. In fact, however, there is reason to believe that what looks good on paper does not always translate to good and fair practice in the real world.

For example, during the same time that the population of children participating in special programs for learning disabilities has increased, the number of children who have been placed in programs for the mentally retarded has decreased. Labeling in special education has become a fact of life. None of the labels is particularly prestigious, but given their choice, most parents would certainly choose to have their child called "learning disabled" rather than "mentally retarded". It's possible, therefore, that at least some of the apparent growth in prevalence of learning disability is due to the fact that many children, who were previously called something else, are currently being misplaced in learning disability programs. This has happened despite the fact that totally different sets of requirements are needed to make children eligible for placement in these two very different categories of special education.

It is also true that in public education, like many other fields of human endeavor, money may be the root of some evil. When learning disability paraded into the public schools, monetary incentives marched right alongside. The bandwagon provided a stirring beat. Federal and state governmental grants were made available to school districts. Dollars were provided for in-service training, a percentage of teachers' salaries, psychological and social work services, and the purchase of equipment and materials. However, in order to get the goodies, children with learning disabilities had to be identified quickly and programs had to be kept full. It may be, that in their haste to cash in on these incentives, at least some school districts have been less than precise in determining which students were learning disabled. They might have even gone out of their way to keep classes "fully stocked"; a practice, which, of course, leads to an inflated estimate of prevalence.

School personnel haven't always been appropriately selective in determining which children to include. Too often, instead, they have indiscriminately put all children having problems in school, for any reason, into programs for the learning disabled. This wholesale misplacement (some have called it "dumping") of children may make things easier for some teachers, and it may bring some funds into the district, but it certainly doesn't help those children who have been correctly diagnosed as learning disabled and therefore require truly specialized teaching techniques in school.

We have considered some factors that have led to an exaggerated estimate of the prevalence of learning disability. More knowledge about learning disability, children with learning disabilities staying in school longer, and questionable identification and placement practices in special education have been discussed. The point has also been made, however, that the growth in learning disabilities has been more than illusory. Indeed, some of it has been very real.

In the last generation, we have seen unprecedented changes in our country. Many of these changes have been suggested as reasons for, or at least factors related to, the increase in the numbers of children with learning disabilities. One authority in the field tells us what some of these changes are:

> The challenges for the next generation of educators who would deal with learning disabilities include accommodating *even greater numbers of children.* (Emphasis mine) It would appear that ever increasing pollution of the earth, the widespread continuing abuse of drugs and alcohol, the lack of prenatal care in this country, increasing numbers of children raised in poverty, and the appalling decline in the quality of American education, to mention only a few factors, will insure a rising number of children with learning disabilities in the near future.[2]

The author of this quote, Dr. Barbara Bateman, contends that we can expect the number of children with learning disabilities to continue increasing. She believes that the epidemic has not yet peaked. And, it is easy to find plenty of evidence to support her contention. Let's look at poverty first.

Our country is the most affluent in the world. Still, many people live in poverty, and recent figures indicate that the problem is worsening. For example, between 1979 and 1986, there was a 17% increase in the total number of poor people. Of significance, during the same period of time, the degree that poverty increased in children was even higher at 23%.[3] Currently, it is estimated that almost one out of every four children (about 15 million) live in poverty. Keep these figures in mind as we look at some things associated with poverty and how they may affect children's capacities to learn.

If the idea that a stimulating environment enriches the brain is correct, then we must accept the converse. An impoverished environment may mean an impoverished brain. Children born in poverty have both environmental and biological disadvantages that may have harmful effects from the moment of conception. These children are more likely to be carried by women who are closer to the extremes of age with respect to child bearing. Maternal age at conception which is less that 18 and more than 35 years relates to a higher incidence of premature delivery, difficult labor and delivery, low birth weight, and birth defects—all of which are known to increase the risk of neurological impairment and learning disability later on. Furthermore, there is ample evidence showing that adequate prenatal medical care and nutrition are not as available or may not be as aggressively pursued by low income women. Some studies have even shown that inadequate nutrition during women's own childhoods, long before they conceive, relates to a higher incidence of learning problems in their children many years later.

If children of poverty are fortunate and somehow escape biological risk factors, chances are that the kinds of healthy and nourishing environments known to stimulate brain development will not be as available to them. On the contrary, they are much more likely to be consistently exposed to the kinds of environmental stresses that have been suggested as having negative effects on brain development.

In place of a nice quiet home along a country lane, with Dick and Jane to play with next door, for many children, violence is their way of life. One article in the Chicago Tribune tells us that of approximately 1,000 children living in poor neighborhoods, three quarters of them had witnessed a murder, shooting, stabbing, or

---

[2]Bateman, B. "Learning disabilities: The changing landscape". *Journal of Learning Disabilities*, Vol. 25, 1992, p. 36.

[3]Baumeister, A. "New morbidity: Implications for prevention of children's diseases". *Exceptionality*, Vol. 1, 1989, p. 4.

robbery.[4] And, nearly half of these children were themselves the victims of these crimes, rape, or some other violent act. Clearly, exposure to this kind of pervasive and persistent stress will keep the adrenaline flowing. Such an environment has a negative impact on brain development, and the probability of subsequent deficits in the capacity to learn naturally increase.

Poor diet and medical care, a lower rate of immunization, and exposure to environmental poisons such as lead based paint are all more prevalent in low income areas. Level of education in the parents is likely to be lower, the incidence of one parent households is likely to be higher, and contact with educational toys and games will probably be less. There may be little if any opportunity for travel; even exposure to books and magazines may be negligible. Very importantly, the kind of constant immersion in well-structured language that is more typical in most homes will be lacking here. Along with less contact with adult models and less encouragement from parents for academic success, the overall relative scarcity and lack of variety of environmental stimulation in the critical early years are not conducive to shaping a brain that will be optimally prepared for learning later on in school. Thus, it seems clear that poverty has an adverse effect on learning potential.

There is the old adage that goes something like "the rich get richer and the poor get poorer". The saying would seem to apply with respect to learning disability; however, it would be a serious mistake to conclude that the problem is found exclusively at the poverty level. There are other risk factors operating that apply to the increase in learning disabilities. These are having an effect *irrespective* of degree of affluence. For example, fetal exposure to cocaine and other drugs has increased across the population by 300% in the past ten years. Since the mid 1980s, crack cocaine has ranked among the most commonly used addictive drugs available. In 1991, the National Force for Children's Constitutional Rights estimated that 1,000 babies who had been exposed to cocaine during their prenatal development were being born each day. Children born to addicted mothers have reached the middle grades of elementary school, and with no reason to assume any decline in drug use, they will surely continue to come.

Although the problem is relatively new, sufficient study of the effects of crack cocaine on children indicate that they are likely to have many physical and behavioral problems. Birth defects involving damage to organ systems and limbs, heightened sensitivity to stimulation resulting in increased discomfort and irritability, and permanent neurological damage have all been noted. Also, in the many instances when mothers remain addicted after the births of their babies, their continued drug use would certainly make them less efficient in caring for any baby, not to mention those who have extraordinary problems and special needs.

---

[4]*Chicago Tribune.* 4-15-93, Section 1, p. 18.

The jury is still out regarding the full effects that fetal exposure to cocaine have upon specific learning problems. In the short time that the problem has been studied, however, it does appear that many of these children have a very difficult time tolerating the high stimulus environment that characterizes most schoolrooms. They respond by either withdrawing completely or by becoming aggressive and hyperactive. In either of these cases, their subsequent ability to learn would be diminished.

Negative consequences of substance abuse from drugs other than the so called "hard" ones like cocaine have also been seen. Smoking marijuana, a harmless, "recreational" drug in the minds of many, has been shown to increase women's chances of premature delivery, which, in turn, increases their children's chances of having learning problems in school. Even women who smoke regular cigarettes during their pregnancies should know that the risk of hyperactivity, low birth weight, and mild reductions in intellectual and academic abilities will increase in their children.

Much of what has been said about the effects of cocaine during fetal development also applies to drinking alcoholic beverages. Considerable publicity has been given to the fetal alcohol syndrome. Physical problems in children including neurological impairment, abnormalities in facial appearance, particularly around the eyes, joint irregularities, and heart defects have been linked to alcohol consumption by their mothers. Research indicates that these physical problems show up in about one third of the babies of pregnant alcoholic women. And, making the situation so much worse is the fact that fetal alcohol syndrome relates to mental retardation. Some authorities now believe that it has even surpassed Down Syndrome in the number of children affected.

Of course, the range of alcohol consumption during pregnancy may extend from total abstinence to flat out alcoholism. While moderate alcohol consumption or occasional drinking by women may not cause physical defects, evidence does suggest that there are *behavioral* differences in children born to these women compared to children whose mothers do not drink at all. They have a very difficult time planning steps toward an objective, and very often they seem unable to grasp the relationship between their behavior and the likely consequences of that behavior. Hyperactivity, fine and gross motor coordination problems, short attention spans, memory deficits, and deficits in organizational and problem solving skills have all been observed. With these characteristics, it seems reasonable to conclude that if severe cases of fetal alcohol syndrome can lead to mental retardation, then milder cases would result in learning disability.

You may be thinking that little of this applies to you, your children, your acquaintances, or to the vast majority of the population at large. After all, most of us do not live in poverty, and most of us do not abuse drugs or alcohol. We go about our business, having and rearing our children, paying our bills, and living clean lives. Well, unless you have moved to a mountaintop, uncharted island somewhere, or to an isolated rural area, you should know that it has become almost impossible to stay clean.

With population growth, the movement of larger segments of the population to big cities, industrial expansion, and higher technology, the negative effects that environmental pollutants have upon all of us has increased. Toxins (a less emotionally charged word that means the same as poisons) in the environment are having their effects before and after birth. More and more, they are predisposing our children to serious health and learning disabilities.

While it is a fact that in the first few months of development, the brain of a fetus is producing cells at the fantastic rate of 15 million per hour, it is also true that this young brain has no ability to protect itself from toxic agents. Nor does it have the capacity to eliminate the effects of these substances after the fact of their damage. There is no regional center to which the fetal brain can check in for detoxification.

Prenatal exposure to cadmium, a soft white metal used in making alloys and as a protective coating for other metals, relates to movement problems in children. It is also a factor in circulatory problems that cause bleeding in the brain. Mercury is known to slow the rate of division of brain cells in the fetus and is also associated with movement problems in later childhood. Chemical compounds of which mercury is a part are hazardous, because they are found in plants and animals that we eat. Despite knowing of the dangers since 1950, we continue to hear reports of fish containing dangerous amounts of mercury due to the industrial pollution of waterways.

Lead is probably the substance which is best known for its harmful effects. Its utilization has been widespread. Many older houses were decorated with lead based paint. As this paint deteriorates, chips fall from ceilings and walls; and young children, not particularly known for their discriminatory eating habits, swallow them and hurt their brains. One of the compounds of lead, tetraethyl lead, was used as an additive to gasoline, because it made engines run smoother. However, as we all breathed lead vapors in the air coming from vehicle exhaust, our brains did not run smoother. A lead free product is the gasoline industry's contribution to maintaining the neurological health of the population. Now if we could only get the tobacco industry to demonstrate some concern for us and make a similar contribution.

Storage batteries, conduits carrying water for industrial use, electric cables, protective sheets for storage tanks, decorative glass and art objects made of pewter—lead has been used for all these purposes. Lead compounds gradually absorbed are likely to have cumulative effects, because the body eliminates them very slowly. The effects that have been documented include low birth weight, premature delivery, problems with blood vessels that reduce the number of neurons and the number of connections between them, and an overall reduction of intellectual capacity.

If you're getting the idea that living may be hazardous to your health, you're correct. At the very least, we are forced to agree with Dr. Bateman's comments in which she contends that the prevalence of learning disability is likely to continue its upward spiral. Even more ominous is the fact that there are other factors presently operating that she does not directly address in her statement. Some of these follow:

In 1960, 5% of all births were outside of marriage. Now the figure for the population at large is 30%, and some of the increase is attributable to teenage pregnancy. Currently, one million teenagers get pregnant each year, and approximately half choose to have their babies. Compounding the fact that girls in their early teens are more likely to deliver premature, low birth weight babies and that these mothers may not avail themselves of adequate prenatal care and nutrition, there is at least the likelihood that they will be less able to provide a stimulating environment for their babies during infancy and early childhood. For no other reason, the fathers are not likely to be around to help. It's probable that the early lives of these children are going to be filled with more than the typical amount of stress and less than an adequate amount of nurturing. All of these things lead to a higher incidence of pediatric disorders and learning problems late on.

Even in the fortunate instance of a child who escapes the hazards described above, there have been other changes in our country that are reasons for concern. Economic conditions have forced parents out of their homes when their children are still very young. More than half of the women who have children under six work out of the home. Furthermore, our country has the highest divorce rate in the world. If the trend continues, a majority of our children will soon be living in homes where only one parent is present.

We can agree that parents are the most important teachers a child has; they are models for intellectual, language, and social development; they shape and determine motivation and attitudes toward education; they provide the foundation for much of their children's behavior. And yet, given these important responsibilities, one reliable source indicates that, on average, teenagers now spend five minutes alone per day with their fathers and twenty minutes alone per day with their mothers.[5] On the other hand, they spend a lot of time alone with their television sets.

The extent to which television has become a source of entertainment, and, to a much lesser degree, a source of information is astonishing. Some of us remember when the first family on the block got theirs. We would cram into their living room on Tuesday nights to watch Uncle Miltie on a ten inch screen. There were actually times during the day when nothing was on, but we were so

---

[5]Bennett, William J. *The index of leading cultural indicators.* Simon & Schuster, 1994, p. 103.

enthralled with this new medium that we watched the test patterns. How things have changed.

Now, there are satellite dishes and cable networks that broadcast an astonishing array of stuff over more than 500 channels, every single second of the day and night. You may be surprised to know that there are more households in the United States with television sets than there are with indoor plumbing!

With the exception of sleeping, children spend more time watching television than doing anything else. The average American teenager spends 1.8 hours per week reading and 21 hours per week watching television. By the time adolescents reach their 18th birthdays, they have watched more that 15,000 hours of television but spent only 12,000 hours in school. And, there is good reason to believe that most of those hours in front of the tube are not filled with culturally enriching or educationally relevant experiences. In fact, by the end of grade school, the average child will have seen 8,000 murders and 100,000 other acts of violence.[6] Most of these are in living color, up close and personal.

As tempting as it might be to find a scapegoat at RCA or Sony, no one has suggested a direct cause and effect relationship between television watching and learning disability. In fact, it is difficult to find any research studies that have investigated the relationship at all. However, in the absence of hard data, common sense will do. Children who are watching television are obviously not reading, writing, using their imaginations, or being creative at all. They may not even be thinking. They are not communicating, nor are they relating to another live human in any active way. Instead, they sit passively, waiting to be entertained, all the while growing less physically fit, and, some would suggest, less intellectually fit as well.

Reading is hard, and TV is easy. There is simply no question that overcoming a learning disability requires active participation and significant effort from a student. Television provides a seductive, convenient way to escape that effort, and, in so doing, it must be considered another factor that contributes to the prevalence of learning disability.

In summary, a number of recent societal changes have been suggested as factors related to a higher prevalence of children with learning problems. More prenatal exposure to drugs, maternal age less than 17 at the time of conception, poor diet and medical care, more children living in poverty and stress-ridden environments, harmful effects of environmental pollutants, less contact with live adult models, more contact with television—all of these things are contributing to the increase.

There is more learning disability than there used to be. That is the unfortunate truth. It cannot be solely attributed to factors such as increased knowledge

---

[6]Greene, Bob. *Chicago Tribune*, 5-9-94, Tempo section, p. 1.

about learning disability or careless administration of special education programs in the schools. Much of the increase is real; there have been concrete changes in our social and cultural fabric that have placed more children in jeopardy.

When all of the factors related to the prevalence of learning disability are considered and the dust clouding the issue settles, we come back to Billy's mother. As she walked past the principal's conference room on the way out of school, she saw another set of unhappy parents. She was correct when she concluded that the learning disability business was thriving. Although she didn't say so, she would have also been correct had she concluded that the end does not seem to be anywhere in sight.

The purpose of this chapter and the last has been to help you understand learning disability. What is it? What do we know about it? How prevalent is it? Before moving on, let's review the answers to these questions:

- Children with learning disabilities have at least average intelligence.
- They are underachievers in school; that is, they have higher levels of ability than they demonstrate.
- Their pattern of learning is uneven; they are good at many things but have problems in a few areas.
- Their problems in school are not primarily due to mental retardation, sensory defects, emotional disturbance, lack of opportunity to learn, poor teaching, or language differences.
- Their learning problems are probably due to neurological impairment which affects their functioning in basic prerequisites for learning like perception, attending, memory, language development, and concept formation.
- The exact prevalence of the problem is still open to question, but most believe learning disability is common, involving perhaps 5-10% of the children in school.

Equipped with your better understanding of learning disability, it's time for you to go back to school. Much has changed since we were students. Some of us are old enough to remember ink wells, milk in little bottles instead of cartons, and the tardy bell. The closest thing to a computer was the slide rule, and the teachers were all so old. Don't be intimidated by the changes. Come back to school; there are no tests scheduled, at least not today. In the next chapter, we will examine the kinds of services and remedies that effective schools provide for children with learning disabilities and their families.

# Chapter 4

# *The Parent-School Partnership*

I'm in a dimly lit, old and musty building that I've never seen before. My skin feels moist and clammy, and I tremble as a cold shiver runs through me. There is a hollow feeling in my stomach and a stale, sour taste in my mouth. Reluctantly, I head into a classroom where I know I'm supposed to take a final examination. I don't want to be here, yet I can't leave. I see that everyone has name tags. I pick one up to pin it on, but strangely, my tag is blank. The other students are gathered in small groups, and I sense that I'm not welcome. I recognize some students I knew a long time ago in grammar school, but they act as if they don't know me. Everyone seems so calm and self-assured. I'm not at all, because I don't know anything about the subject matter. I don't recognize the instructor, I didn't read the book, I have no notes, and I didn't attend class. But for some reason, I'm in this unfamiliar room, and I have to take a test. I'm having another one of those anxiety dreams about school.

Usually I awaken from the dream before the teacher hands out the examination, but this time it continues until I actually get to look at the questions. I am amazed to discover that they aren't even printed in English. The whole class is looking at me, pointing and snickering. Three students walk by me with sneers on their faces. Incredibly, they have already finished the examination, and they wave their completed tests at me. I stand up to leave, but my legs are heavy as lead. Then everyone, including the teacher, suddenly turns toward me and begins jabbering in some totally unintelligible foreign tongue. I'm not sure, but it's probably Greek. At least it is to me. What a nightmare!

Finally, I wake up with a start and the anxiety fades. I realize it's just been a bad dream. I stretch and smile as I remember that I'll never again have to take another final examination. No indeed. Those days are gone. Now, I'm on the other side of the desk, so I give them, and others take them. I wonder how many of their dreams I'll be in?

School anxiety dreams are not uncommon. Almost everyone has them, and they continue long after we leave school. We have them, I think, because school is a place of tremendous significance in our lives. In many ways, it is our introduction to society. We enter school with excited anticipation when we are little children, still somewhat asocial and dependent upon our parents. It is a place we are expected to exit, years later, socialized and independent, ready to assume adult and parental responsibilities of our own. What happens between entering and leaving school is a long series of environmental events which overlay and interact with our unique genetic heritage to mold and shape our personalities. Its imprint is indelible, for much more than teaching us to read, write, and do numbers, school is a place where we begin to learn who we are.

When we come to school, we are grouped with other young children. We are required to adjust quickly to a new schedule, new people, and a new set of rules. And, from the first day that we venture out of the familiar and protective environment of our homes, the comparisons begin. At school, our performance is assessed. We are judged, rated, and ranked. They take the measure of us.

Wherever there is a group of children, some teachers, and a psychologist or two, there will be evaluation. Testing is one of the things that schools do. Through a rather constant series of comparisons to others our age, we learn our strengths and weaknesses, our capabilities and limitations. We come to know where we stand. This is true not just with respect to our academic aptitudes, but also our creative and artistic talents, our athletic abilities, and our leadership and other social skills.

The results of all the tests and measurements have a very significant impact upon what happens to us in school. Very early, they determine what reading and math groups we are in, who our classmates and teachers are, and if we are included on the honor roll. Later, test results may be used to decide which high school we attend, which courses we take, and whether we apply and are admitted to a college or university. The results of testing may continue to have an impact well into our adult lives. They may influence our career choices, and, at least indirectly, therefore, point us toward a particular circle of friends and associates. So, there is simply no question that at the school party, testing is an important guest that arrives early, stays late, and determines who has a good time.

For most of us, things turned out fine. The tests were passed, comparisons were more or less favorable, and positive judgments were made. We "went with the flow", not deviating significantly from the majority, making normal progress until graduation. During the process, hardly a thought was given to the adult responsibilities which loomed ahead. We didn't really listen to our parents when they said to us, "Enjoy yourself now; your days in school are the best time of your life". Now, we look back, and we know they were right. It is true that for many people, the "good old days" were when they were in school.

For other children, though, the time they are in school is not always free and easy. They are not happy there, because school is where failure is, along with the shame and humiliation that come with it. Tests are not passed, negative judgments are made, and progress isn't normal at all. For some of these children, those with learning disabilities, there is the possibility that school may be a place where they begin to suspect they are not as capable as their peers. Just like young Billy, their self-esteem diminishes, and they come to believe they are losers. There is the danger that this belief may stay with them for a very long time and have a depressing effect upon their future adjustment. **Above all, you must not let that happen to your child.**

Children who are learning disabled arrive at school with one problem. As we noted earlier, brain dysfunctions result in processing deficits which make it very difficult for them to learn their basic academics at a normal rate. This is a serious enough problem, but nevertheless, by itself, it is a singular disability. What often complicates the matter is that singular becomes plural. The primary disability in learning brings chronic frustration and failure. All too often, the result is a secondary disability, an overlay of emotional disturbance, that worsens the child's predicament in school. Naturally, the remediation of two problems rather than one is at least twice as difficult to accomplish.

As parents, your most important priority is to intervene as an advocate for your child before the learning disability becomes a dual handicap. You need to see to it that the learning disability does not grow and generalize into a larger problem, a problem with the potential to effect your child's adjustment later, outside of school. The question is: how do you do that? Specifically, what do you need to do in order to be an effective advocate for your child?

Commonly, parents of children with learning disabilities have been advised of the importance of establishing a partnership with the school. They have been counseled to work together, as a team with school personnel, toward helping their child overcome, or at least cope with the disability. This is sound advice, as far as it goes. However, it is important that you go further.

You must establish a parent-school partnership in which **you** are the majority stockholder, the chief executive officer, the president of the firm, the chairman of the board; in short, the **BOSS!** The importance of working from a position of power and "dealing from strength" cannot be overemphasized. This is not to suggest that a hostile, adversarial relationship is being recommended. Instead, the clear message to convey to the school is that decisions affecting your child will ultimately be yours, and you will therefore retain control. It is your son or daughter whose schooling and future are involved; so, quite simply, you must put yourself in a position to call the shots.

As the boss, you must be appropriately assertive and find a balance between cooperating with the school's efforts and demanding more if you are not satisfied. You need to be a knowledgeable participant who is actively and routinely involved in your child's special education. You must never hesitate to ask questions, disagree with recommendations that you feel are incorrect, or bring in your own advocates to represent you when you feel they are needed. You must know your legal rights and how they affect your family and your child in school. It is only through this type of informed and aggressive participation in the partnership that you will be able to increase the probability of your child's moving through school normally. In so doing, you will reduce the likelihood that your child's singular learning disability will grow into multiple problems that might persist long after leaving school.

In your dealings with the school, like Billy's parents, you are likely to be present at many conferences, sit with many experts you have never met, and hear a lot of language with which you may not be familiar. At these sessions, you will almost certainly be outnumbered, you will not be "on your own turf", and it would be reasonable to expect you to feel ill-at-ease. These meetings are often so intimidating to parents that they sometimes forget the fact that, of those present, they are the most expert of all. You are the ones who know your children the best; you alone have watched them grow and develop over months and years; and you alone will remain, long after the experts have left, to see what happens to your children when they are finished with school. For you, your child's learning disability does not end at three o'clock, or when the school year ends in June, or even at graduation.

As you accumulate more knowledge about learning disability and learn more about precisely what the school must provide for your child, you will find it easier to assume greater responsibility for your child's education. Then you will be in a position to take control, shed any intimidation, and use the power you have to assure that your child's special education is indeed special. You will become an effective advocate for your child. You will be calling the shots.

So let us begin. Exactly what do you need to do to form an effective partnership with your child's school? It has been suggested that knowledge is power. The first step, therefore requires that you know about laws applying to special education and learning disability.

In 1975, during President Gerald Ford's administration, the federal government enacted a law which is considered the most significant legislation relating to special education that has ever been passed. This is Public Law 94-142 (The 142nd bill passed by the 94th congress), the name of which is *The Education of All Handicapped Children Law*. Whereas this law applies to children who may be disabled in any number of ways; for example, mentally retarded, orthopedically handicapped, deaf, blind, or emotionally disturbed etc., we will examine it as it relates to children who are learning disabled.

Prior to 1975 and the passage of PL 94-142, school districts were *permitted* to establish and operate special programs for children who were learning disabled. So, if a district wanted to, a specially qualified teacher could be employed, space could be located, materials and equipment could be purchased, children could be identified and enrolled, and a special program could be offered.

With the passage of the law, however, that which had previously been permitted, became *mandatory*. The essence of PL 94-142 is that every public school district in the country *must* provide special educational services for disabled children. The law says that special education programs must be free and appropriate and that they be available for students from age 3 to 21, or graduation from high school, should that occur before age 21.

As parents, it is important for you to understand that the mandate to provide special services is upon the school district, but your child's participation is *voluntary* and may only commence after you have given your permission. You always maintain control, since your child may never be placed in a special education program without your consent. This consent should only be given after you have carefully examined all options and are convinced that special education is an alternative that offers academic and social benefits not currently available for your child in the standard educational setting.

In addition to mandating special services, Public Law 94-142 includes several other more specific provisions that are very pertinent for learning disabled children and their families. (To make certain that you read very carefully here, please be advised that there will be a quiz covering this material at the end of the chapter. Those who flunk the quiz will not be permitted to read any further; in fact, you will be required to return your book without refund. So, pay attention!)

Following are descriptions of four important provisions in Public Law 94-142. These are: 1) nondiscriminatory testing, 2) the individualized educational plan (IEP), 3) the least restrictive alternative, and 4) due process. We'll take them in order.

A basic rule in special education is that assessment must always precede placement, which is to say that no student may be placed in a special program for children with learning disabilities without being evaluated first. This initial process of evaluating a student who is being considered for placement in a special program is sometimes called a "child study", "educational diagnosis", or "psychological assessment". Whatever the term, the child who is being evaluated will be given a number of tests and will be observed in a variety of settings. A major part of the evaluation will be the responsibility of the school psychologist. The learning disabilities teacher, regular classroom teacher, social worker, school nurse, and speech and language therapist will probably be involved in the process too.

Such a child study or assessment is no small event in a student's life. Several hours are required to complete the evaluation, a child is removed from class to be examined by unfamiliar people in an unfamiliar setting, and some of the activities are likely to be difficult. At the very least, evaluation requires a departure from normal school routine and may be stressful. Public Law 94-142 recognizes the rigors and potentially important consequences of testing and requires, therefore, that it be done fairly in what is referred to as a nondiscriminatory way.

There are some basic rules built into the system, some safeguards, that school districts must follow as they attempt to practice nondiscriminatory testing. First of all, the assessment must be done quickly. No more than 60 working days may pass between the time a child is referred for testing and the time a decision is made to determine if a child is eligible for special service. Second, if a child's primary language is something other than English, testing must be done in that language. If professionals involved in the evaluation (psychologist, LD teacher, social worker, etc.) who speak the child's language are not available in the district, than an interpreter must be present for the duration of testing. It is also required that school districts use a *number* of assessment techniques rather than just one test in the determination of whether a child is learning disabled. Formal, standardized tests administered in the school psychologist's office must be supplemented by informal observations of the child in more natural settings including the classroom, gymnasium, lunchroom, and playground. Furthermore, the school is obliged to make the results of testing available to parents within 15 days of their request; however, the confidentiality of this information must be maintained for everyone else. No other individual, school, or agency may receive a child's test results unless parents sign a formal release.

The above rules are important, but they alone do not guarantee fair testing practices in a school district. Nondiscriminatory testing begins with *informed* parental consent. Testing your child may not occur without your permission. Your consent is required whether the evaluation being recommended is to be done by professionals in the school or by individuals employed by agencies outside of the school. Your consent should be given only after you understand the purpose of the evaluation, the types of tests that will be given, and how the results of testing will be used. So, let's get you informed.

Learning disability has become a test heavy field. Dozens of tests have been constructed in the past several decades, each claiming to provide important information about learning problems in children. Tests have an undeserved "mystique" about them. There is a myth that they are somehow capable of delving into the deepest depths of children's minds and revealing stuff about kids that couldn't be discovered in any other way.

The givers of tests in school, very often psychologists, share this mysterious aura and the status that goes with it. It is as if they alone, using techniques too advanced to be practiced by mere teachers or parents, are uniquely equipped to analyze children's psyches. As a result of the inflated prestige granted to tests and test givers, very often, too much credence is given to test results. Findings are accepted without question, they are considered more insightful than teacher and parent judgments, and an inordinate amount of time is given to testing that ought to be devoted to teaching. This inappropriate use of time has less chance of happening when parents come to understand the correct purpose of testing and insist that it be done properly.

With respect to the proper purpose of testing, there is some similarity between education and medicine. If you break your leg, for example, the X-Ray is a test that is given to provide information that subsequently helps the doctors fix your bone. If you can't hear well, an audiometric test is part of the evaluation prescribed that leads to improving your hearing. Similarly, if you have diabetes, a blood test is helpful in regulating your blood chemistry and controlling your illness. In all of these medical problems, testing functions as a **tool**, the purpose of which is to lead to a cure or at least a control for the condition. Thus, testing is never done for its own sake, in a vacuum, but always as a means to help solve a problem.

Although your child's problem in school is educational rather than medical, the purpose of testing should be the same; that is, **to provide information useful in fixing what is wrong.** So, as you are considering whether to give the school district permission to evaluate your child, the most important question to consider is: How will the results of testing lead to a sound, logical remedial program for my child? You want to know exactly how the information gathered during the evaluation will be used by the teacher to select different teaching methods that will help your child be a better learner. Insist upon seeing a clear connection between test results and changes in teaching method; if school personnel cannot provide you with one, the testing is likely to be a waste of time, an unnecessary interruption in your child's life, and you should withhold your consent.

Should you decide to go ahead with the evaluation, your child will be given tests that are designed to measure different things. There is no universal or standard battery of tests that is administered in all schools; however, you can count on the administration of certain types of tests. An intelligence test will be given in order to estimate that levels at which your child ought to be achieving in school. A test of academic achievement will be given to determine actual, present levels of functioning in basic school subjects. Results from these two tests will be compared to help determine if your child is doing as well in school as his or her aptitude would predict. (Remember that underachievement must be present in order to qualify for LD service.)

Additional tests that provide information about *how* your child reads, writes, and does math will be given. These tests are not so much concerned with determining grade level as they are with showing the method a child is using in the process of learning and identifying the kinds of errors that are being made. Tests like these, instruments that provide information beyond IQ and grade level, are used to diagnose a child's strengths and weaknesses in learning. They provide the kind of information that can be very useful in designing an effective remedial program.

Finally, as part of the assessment, it is very likely that tests measuring visual and auditory perceptual functioning, motor performance, and language proficiency will be given along with a test that gives information about your child's self-concept and other personality traits. These tests do not measure performance in academic subjects. Instead, their purpose is to search for correlates; that is, reasons or at least factors related to the learning problem your child is having in school.

Keep in mind that all of the findings gathered by administering these formal tests must be integrated with information from informal observations made by the classroom teacher, learning disabilities teacher, psychologist, and others on the child study team. Indeed, test results which are interpreted in isolation, with no attempt to relate them to a child's everyday functioning in the classroom, may not be useful in fixing a child's learning problem which, after all, must take place in that same classroom.

It is also true that parents are part of the assessment process. You will not escape the probing and scrutiny of the child study team. Expect to be interviewed by the school social worker and school nurse. They will want to determine if there are any family-social or medical problems that may be contributing to your child's current learning problem in school. They will prefer to speak with both parents; however, if that is impossible, interviews may proceed so long as one parent is present.

Certainly, a child study is a rigorous procedure. It is a serious intrusion into the life of a family at a time when there is likely to be worry and stress over what is happening to a child in school. So, if you agree to give the school district permission to evaluate your child, let them know, **at the beginning**, that at the end of the procedure you will be asking for a payoff. You will want to know what they have learned from their assessment that will help your child in school. You will want to know exactly how they will teach your child in a special way.

As soon as your child's evaluation is completed, ask the principal for a copy of the report. You'll want to study this document very carefully **before** going to any meeting at the school to discuss its contents. As you are reading the report, remember that the information it contains is based upon a very brief cross section of your child's life. Think of it this way. Your child has been living for a long time, let's say about eight years. The assessment done at school required perhaps four to five hours. The assumption, which is questionable at best, is that this sample of a few hours can accurately reflect your child's intellectual, academic, perceptual, linguistic, and personal aptitudes and achievements that have developed over the entire eight year span of life. No matter how carefully an evaluation is done, how skillful the professionals are, and how reliable and valid their tests purport to be, the hours involved in the psychoeducational assessment of a student who may be learning disabled are truly an infinitesimally small slice of that child's existence. Therefore, you must scrutinize the report of testing very carefully. Be prepared to challenge contents of the report with which you disagree. You may request changes or deletions of information which you feel is incorrect, misleading, or inappropriate. If you wish, you may require the school district to include, with their report, your own written explanation about any of the contents of the document.

Of course, many parents would shy away from the type of questioning and challenging attitude that is being recommended. The school personnel seem highly qualified; they have advanced degrees, impressive titles, and years of experience. All of that may be true, but it is also true that with respect to your child, none of them is as expert as you. Given the possibility that your child may soon be called "learning disabled" and removed, at least part of the time, from the standard educational program, a lot is at stake. When you consider the fact that such events may have a profound effect upon your child's present and future, in your role as advocate, you must do all that you can to get what you consider best for your child. It is only through this type of demanding parental attitude that testing becomes truly nondiscriminatory.

A second specific provision of Public Law 94-142 is the individualized educational plan (IEP). Every child who is included in a special education program must have one. The IEP is a written, detailed plan that tells exactly what the school is to provide for the child who is learning disabled. For children who have been placed in special education programs, the IEP is the most important document in their folders. It tells the levels at which students are functioning in school at the beginning of their special program; it tells where they are expected to be achieving as a result of their program; it tells who will help them get there and what teaching methods they will use; and it tells how everyone will know when they have arrived. Think of the IEP as a blueprint for your child's education, and you must think of yourself as the head architect who oversees the design and sees to it that the plans are implemented.

The IEP begins with information that tells the child's current levels of functioning in school. This information always includes levels of academic achievement but may also list levels of social and emotional development as well. Then, it lists long term, annual goals; that is, the levels at which the child is expected to be achieving one year hence. It continues with very specific, short term objectives written to describe precisely those areas of deficiency that will be attacked immediately. It tells how many minutes per week a child will be receiving special teaching, the kind of teaching that will be, and whether any supplementary services like speech and language therapy or social work are to be furnished. It describes the nature of the evaluations that will be done to measure progress. It provides a schedule for reviewing progress and developing new goals on no more than an annual basis. Finally, the IEP assures accountability by identifying the professional people who are involved in its implementation. (See Appendix I for an example of an IEP.)

Writing the IEP begins at a meeting in school. This meeting, usually called a multidisciplinary staff conference or staffing, must be held at a time that is convenient for you. If you receive notification of a staffing that is scheduled at a time that would make your attendance difficult or impossible, inform the school, in writing, that you will be unable to attend and suggest two or three other dates and times that would be convenient. Certainly, these alternatives should be as close as possible to the time originally suggested by the school.

Parents have important responsibilities regarding the IEP. Initially, you need to be sure that **all** the people who need to be at the IEP planning meeting are indeed present. The group must include the following people: you, your child's teacher, the teacher of children with learning disabilities, a person, usually the school psychologist, who is knowledgeable in evaluation and diagnostic procedures, and the school principal or a designate who is qualified to supervise programs for learning disabled children. Other people who may be invited are your child, the school social worker and nurse, and anyone else of your choosing or the school's who would be useful in providing information needed for planning.

If you arrive at the staffing and see that your child's classroom teacher is not present, do **not** allow the meeting to begin. Next to you, the teacher knows your child better than anyone. The teacher is the only person who has observed the problem over a long period of time, and the only person who knows the relative success and failure of different teaching methods. Compared with everyone else at the meeting, the teacher's knowledge of your child is unique; therefore, that person is uniquely qualified to make an important contribution at the meeting. Be adamant! Do not allow the meeting to convene unless the teacher is there.

You need to be equally stubborn regarding the presence of the teacher of learning disabled children. This teacher may soon be assuming some or all of the responsibility for teaching your child. You will have questions to ask about the special program, the curriculum, teaching methods, and ways of measuring progress. The LD teacher will need to hear a first-hand description of your child's current problems as well as methods the classroom teacher has tried up to now. For all these reasons, it is imperative that both teachers be at the meeting.

You may be told that the teachers can't be present, because there is nobody available to cover their classes. Don't buy it. Tell the person chairing the staffing to find substitutes for the teachers or to reschedule the meeting before or after school when the teachers will be available. You are the Chief Executive Officer, and these people are working for you and your family.

# The Parent-School Partnership 83

Public Law 94-142 recognizes the importance of clear communication between parents and schools. For example, in the case of a parent whose primary language is something other than English, a school district is obligated to provide an interpreter at a staffing. The intent of the law is to guarantee that all parents, irrespective of language background and proficiency, are able to comprehend the proceedings and make intelligent decisions on matters involving their children. The same reasoning applies to your ability to comprehend the proceedings. Despite the fact that your primary language may be English, if the English used at the staffing is filled with unfamiliar terminology, words that professionals may understand but parents don't, then you are entitled to and must ask for a translation.

At the conclusion of the staffing, or shortly thereafter, you will be asked to sign the IEP. Do so only if you are confident that you fully understand everything in it. If you aren't, ask for explanations of everything that puzzles you. If any of the terminology in the IEP is technical or professional jargon ("psychobabble" or "educationese") once again, insist that it be translated.

Let's take a break and try an activity for fun that exemplifies the problem in communicating that often exists between parents and professionals. In my experience as a public school teacher of children with learning disabilities, I have been present at so many multidisciplinary staff conferences that I have long since lost count. The total must be close to a thousand, however. At these meetings, I have sometimes seen a total disregard, or, at best, a rudeness when it comes to communicating with parents. School personnel, including principals, guidance counselors, psychologists, social workers, and teachers speak a language which effectively excludes parents from the conversation. For example, below, on the left, there are some statements that were made at staffings. They are real; I recorded them; they were said by educators to parents of children being considered for placement in programs for children with learning disabilities. See if you can match them to translated versions appearing on the right:

1 \_\_\_\_ Your offspring's measured intellect, as determined by his performance on a standardized, individually administered test of cognition, is in the uppermost stanine, allowing, or course, for the instrument's standard error of measurement.

A. Your child is having a hard time learning to read, because he doesn't interpret what he hears very well.

2 \_\_\_\_ Your child has a problem to which we refer medically as specific developmental dyslexia and which can be traced to underlying auditory channel deficits including sound

B. In addition to other problems, your child moves around too much.

blending, discrimination, and short-term retention of grapheme-phoneme matches.

3 \_\_\_\_ Your child's hyperkinesis is only one part of a larger syndrome that includes fine and gross motor incoordination, perseveration, catastrophic reactions, disinhibition, and neurologically based attention deficits.

C. Our best guess is that you have a very smart child.

If you don't understand much of the language in the column on the left, don't fret. Not many people do, including some of the experts. Don't let them get away with it; ask for a translation into the type of understandable English in the right hand column. (By the way, you should have answered C, A, and B, respectively.)

Even with simplified language, there is likely to be information in the IEP that will be unfamiliar to you. The names of certain tests and what they measure, procedures used in remedial teaching techniques, special equipment and teaching materials—all of these things are part of the advanced training that teachers of children with learning disabilities have. Parents, of course, have not had the benefit of that training; therefore, you must ask for precise explanations of everything. If professionals at the staffing are not able to give you satisfactory explanations, tell the chairperson that you will not sign the IEP until you have a third party look at it. Take a copy of the IEP to a parent advocacy group (See Appendix II for a list of these organizations) or to a department of special education at a nearby college or university for further explanations.

In your role as parent-advocate, it is *your* child's progress through school that is your primary concern. Whereas you care about other children with similar learning problems, quite naturally, the overall well-being of your own child will be your number one priority. The professional personnel at the school, however, have many other children about whom they must be equally concerned. There may be five or six staffings scheduled for the same week and dozens of children already enrolled in special education who must be kept track of and reevaluated. It is fair to say that given the large number of children involved, professional personnel cannot always be expected to remain on top of each child's case.

It is also true that there will be a certain amount of attrition and turnover within the staff. Teachers retire, psychologists transfer to other districts, social workers go into private practice; for whatever the reason, it is likely that some of the professionals who knew you and your child at the beginning of the proceedings will not be around for the duration. To guarantee that your child does not get lost in the shuffle, it is imperative that you keep accurate, up-to-date records of everything that happens in your child's case. At home, keep a file folder containing all correspondence and documents relating to your child in school. Invitations to staff conferences, reports of testing, your child's report cards, and the original IEP and updated versions should be readily available. Careful record keeping is something that good bosses do.

Next, we come to a third specific provision of Public Law 94-142. The words "least restrictive alternative" appear in the law. This is a term that applies to the practice of integrating special education programs, as much as possible, into the standard educational program. "Mainstreaming", a word that means essentially the same as least restrictive alternative, has been used more commonly when educators and lay people talk about teaching disabled children, in regular classes, with their nondisabled peers. A small slice of history is in order.

A look backward at early attempts to provide programs for disabled people reveals that segregation was common. For example, it was not unusual to find facilities for the mentally retarded and emotionally disturbed located in out of the way rural areas, set apart from the rest of the population. It was as if these conditions were communicable diseases requiring quarantine in order to isolate their germs and protect the rest of us. Usually these facilities provided very little in the form of education or training. Instead, they offered basic custodial care, and many didn't even do a good job at that.

As time passed and a more enlightened attitude toward disabling conditions developed, provisions for special education were made within the public schools. It was felt that including disabled children with their nondisabled peers would allow for better understanding and tolerance among both groups. Language in PL 94-142 is very strong in support of mainstreaming. It says that to the greatest extent possible, school districts shall educate disabled children along with all other children.

For a minute, think back to the options that the child study team had in Billy's case. After determining that he was eligible to receive special education services, they had to choose between a part-time program in a resource room or a full time program in a special classroom. Although it wasn't considered in Billy's case, a third option which is available in some school districts is placement in an entirely separate, special school where all the children are learning disabled.

The idea is that as distance and separation from the regular or standard educational program increase, the school setting for the disabled child becomes more restrictive. So, a resource room arrangement, in which the child with learning disabilities is removed from the regular class for only a portion of the day, is considered less restrictive than placement in a special class. And, a special class arrangement, in which the child with a disability at least attends a school where nondisabled children are present, is considered less restrictive than placement in a special school.

Back to the present and your own family, your ultimate goal is the return of your child to the standard educational program. From the day that you give the school district permission to place your child in special education, you must constantly remind all of the participants that permanent placement is not an option, that you are demanding special services that result in movement back toward less restrictive settings, and that ultimately you expect normal progress through school for your child.

As a good general rule, the further children are initially placed from the regular class setting, the longer it will take for them to get back. Be very conservative, therefore, when it comes time to give your consent for placement. Insist that your child's classroom teacher consult with the learning disabilities teacher and apply some special teaching techniques in the regular class **before** you allow your child to be removed, even for a part of the day. Ask to see written documentation and records that show the results of those techniques. Do not accept mere verbal accounts and descriptions of what was tried.

If you become convinced that regular, part-time contact with a learning disabilities teacher outside of the regular classroom is required, get to know the resource room program first. Find out specifically how much time your child will be in the resource room each day. It may not be more than half of the time your child is in school, and more typically, it should be about 40 to 60 minutes every day. Find out what will be missed in the regular class when your child leaves and what provisions will be made to make up the work. Get to know the LD teacher, visit the resource room, determine how many other children will be taught with your child, ask the teacher to explain and demonstrate what is unique about the teaching methods used in the resource room, find out how you will be apprised of your child's progress and exactly what criteria have to be met to assure you child's exit from special education.

Full time special classes and separate schools for learning disabled children are considered quite restrictive settings and should only be considered appropriate in the most serious cases. Although quite a controversial issue in special education today, the majority viewpoint of authorities in the field now seems to be leaning toward reserving full-time placement alternatives for children with learning disabilities whose problems are compounded by multiple handicaps or for those who have not responded to educational treatments in less restrictive arrangements. And, even in these relatively few cases, placement is never to be considered permanent; the goal is always to move the child back to the standard educational program as quickly as possible.

Finally, we come to a fourth specific provision of Public Law 94-142. This is the portion of the legislation dealing with due process. Along the way to participation in special education, there are many mutual decisions that you and representatives of the school district will have to make. Questions having to do with testing, the content of the IEP, and the most appropriate placement for your child will need to be answered. Usually, the district makes recommendations to answer these questions, and the parents indicate their agreement, or lack thereof, by either granting or withholding their consent. Experience has shown that in a small percentage of the cases, there will be disagreement. The law provides a system to resolve disagreements between parents and school districts in an objective and impartial way.

Let's say that you have given the school district permission to test your child, and they have concluded, as a result, that full time placement in a special class for children with learning disabilities is required. You, however, do not agree with the test findings or the recommendations and will not give your consent for such a placement. If a mutually satisfactory compromise cannot be worked out, a third party will be called in to hear the case, weigh evidence, and render a decision. These third parties—former teachers, professors, lawyers, or just interested citizens—have received special training that entitles them to function as impartial, due process hearing officers.

The request for a due process hearing may come from either party to the disagreement; that is, the parent or the school district. Such a request must be in writing to the Superintendent of Schools, and upon receipt, the child's position in school is frozen. Therefore, no change in placement can occur until the dispute is settled.

At the outset, you and the school district will have to agree upon a hearing officer to be chosen from a list of five provided by the State Board of Education. If none of the people on the list is familiar to you, this would be another good time to rely upon a local parent advocacy group to help with the selection. The person chosen will be responsible for scheduling the hearing at a time that is mutually convenient for you and the school. You are entitled to bring people to represent you and your child. Some parents will bring an attorney, a psychologist they have contracted who has done additional testing, another parent who can provide support as a knowledgeable advocate, or all three.

Although the meeting is not held in a courtroom and the hearing officer is not a judge, an impartial due process hearing does bear a certain similarity to a judicial proceeding. Witnesses are called, questioned, and cross examined. Testimony is recorded, objections may be made by either side, and ultimately, the presiding officer must decide on the outcome. The hearing officer's decision must be sent to you, by certified mail, no longer than 10 days after the hearing.

If either party to the dispute is not satisfied with the results of the hearing, an appeal may be filed with the State Superintendent of Public Instruction. And, if such a state level appeal does not result in satisfactory resolution of the case, parties are always free to pursue the matter in court. The hope is, of course, that a mutually acceptable plan can be worked out long before such legal intervention is required, and most of the time it is. The due process procedures included in Public Law 94-142 were not written into the legislation with frequent use in mind, but rather as a set of legal safeguards to be used sparingly, in those very few cases where conflict resolution, by people acting in good faith, could not be achieved. You should consider these procedures only after all other attempts at mediation with the school district have failed.

Of course, parental responsibility for their children in special education programs does not end with the initial placement. You will need to stay involved in monitoring your child's progress. We sometimes forget that public schools are indeed public places, and, of necessity, they must maintain an open door policy. Therefore, as a parent you are welcome to visit and observe. Most schools set aside two days during the school year for formal parent conferences and visitation. Certainly, you should be present on those days, and, in addition, it would be a good idea to visit more often, on a monthly basis if possible. You might want to send a note to the teacher in advance, but there is nothing wrong with simply dropping in unannounced, once in a while. Of course, you will want to stop at the school office and pick up a visitor's pass before entering your child's classroom.

These visits should not be casual, "let's sit back and see what's going on" observations. On the contrary, they must be businesslike, with an exact purpose. You will want to make sure that the work provided in the special education program is aimed directly toward satisfying the objectives written in your child's IEP. If you don't see the connection between an activity in the special program and an objective on the IEP, do not hesitate to ask the teacher for an explanation at the end of the lesson.

Again, I have had parents tell me that they hesitate to participate in the kind of regular and active observation recommended above. They do not wish to be considered meddlesome; they are afraid they will be viewed as troublemaking, "oh no, here they come again", people. The fact is, of course, for your child's benefit, you need to be as meddlesome as you see fit until you are absolutely satisfied that the school gets it right. You have lent them what is most precious to you, after they detected "flaws" considered serious enough to warrant removal from the standard educational program and placement in special education; you are therefore entitled to keep coming as often as you like to make sure the school is fixing the flaws to your satisfaction.

At the end of the school year there will be another formal meeting to discuss your child's case. This meeting, called an annual review, is a legal requirement. The principal or a designate, your child's teachers, and you are to be present. The purpose of the meeting is to review the amount of progress that has been made toward objectives and to make plans for the following year.

You will want to be prepared for this year end review. Go over the annual goals and the short term objectives in the IEP before you go to the meeting. Be prepared to ask for specific evidence that details the exact amount of growth your child has made during the year. This evidence should consist of classroom work samples and anecdotal records that the teacher has kept as well as results of formal testing done during the year.

Never lose sight of your ultimate goal. You are looking forward to the day when special education will no longer be needed and your child can move through school normally in the standard program. Therefore, one recommendation you want to hear at the annual review would be for a **reduced** amount of time in special education.

Think of it this way. A year ago you made a decision to separate your child from the regular school program, at least part of the time. You did so because you felt that exposure to a team of experts in education and child development would result in the remediation of the learning disability and whatever academic deficiencies were present. Now, after a year, with respect to your child's progress, there are only three possibilities. Either your child has made progress, there has been no change, or there has been additional regression compared to other children. If the first alternative has happily occurred, then intervention from special education is working and a reduction in such a program would be logical. If, on the other hand, there has been no progress or even more regression, then special education hasn't worked and a reduction in time spent would be equally logical.

Sometimes schools and teachers develop a possessive attitude toward children who have been placed in special education programs. If there has been progress, they will want to keep a child in special education arguing that even more gains are likely to occur; and if there has not been progress, they will want more time to make it happen. Be very wary of these kinds of arguments. While they have a certain amount of logic on the surface, and may therefore seem attractive to you, long-term, continuous participation in special education often develops its own inertia. One year quickly merges into the next, and children and their parents become so firmly settled and comfortable that the goal of return to the standard education program fades and may ultimately be forgotten.

As a way of protecting against permanent, full-time placement, all children who have participated in special education programs must be fully reevaluated a minimum of once every three years. This is the same kind of rigorous, multidisciplinary assessment that is done when a child is initially referred. Should your child still be in special education after this three year period, the results of the reevaluation will give you the opportunity to determine precisely how much growth has occurred. In any case, **three years is enough.** For children with learning disabilities, three years in a self-contained, special program is ample time and opportunity for the school to remedy the problem. If, in fact, the problem still exists, your child is likely to do just as well coping with it in the regular educational program, and you should terminate full-time placement in special education. Any further contact should be restricted to part-time help in a resource room and consultation between your child's regular class teacher and his former teachers in the special program.

In this chapter, you have learned about important provisions of Public Law 94-142, The Education of All Handicapped Children Law. This law has not been stagnant since it was enacted in 1975; rather, it has been expanded and amended as time has gone by. In 1990, under President Bush, the Individuals with Disabilities Education Act (IDEA) was passed. This law reinforces the mandate of PL 94-142 upon school districts to provide special education services and adds some new provisions to the earlier law. For example, it requires that the term "handicapped children" be replaced by "children with disabilities". It has expanded school districts' sphere of responsibility to include service to children who are autistic or who have suffered from traumatic brain damage. Finally, it makes it necessary for school districts to give additional attention to older disabled children, those at the high school level, by requiring that a plan for their transition from school to the world of employment be included in their IEPs.

During the last two decades, mandatory legislation has forced the public schools to expand their role in the education of disabled children. It is true that the system for providing special education to disabled children is still evolving and is certainly less than perfect. It is also true that we have seen very significant improvement from the days before such legislation when school districts were essentially free to provide as much or as little special attention as they pleased. Of course, passing laws in no way guarantees that those laws will be correctly implemented. But they do, at the very least, provide the framework for a good system. It is up to you, the parents, acting aggressively, with knowledge and persistence, to insure that the system works to the maximum possible advantage for your children.

In the next chapter, we'll begin to take a look at some of the treatment programs for learning disability that are available outside of your child's school. You will want to become an intelligent consumer as you explore such things as nutritional and drug therapy, visual training, and after school tutoring programs.

Wait a minute here! Did you really think I had forgotten? While it is true that in a quiet room, you can actually hear my arteries hardening, and the old professor's memory is not what is used to be, the promise of a quiz has not slipped my mind. It's time to see what you have learned. Follow the directions appearing below as you take this quiz. An answer key is provided which will help you score your exam and determine if you qualify to go on to the next chapter. Good luck, and please keep your eyes on your own paper!

Directions: The following quiz consists of 10 multiple choice questions that assess your understanding of learning disability and related material. For each question, choose **one** alternative that you think is most correct and print your answer on the line next to the number of the question. You may **not** look back in your book to find or verify answers, and there is a 20 minute time limit which will be rigidly enforced.

1. \_\_\_\_\_ Learning disability may be caused by neurological factors which slow the development of basic psychological processes. The term "basic psychological processes" refers to:

    A. Brain chemicals which control our ability to pay attention
    B. Overall intelligence as measured by standardized IQ tests
    C. Attending, memory, perception and other prerequisites for learning academic subjects
    D. Processes that psychologists use when they send patients their monthly bills

2. \_\_\_\_\_ In recent years, learning disability has become the largest branch of special education. This rapid growth would probably **not** be attributed to:

    I. A reluctance on the part of school districts to call children mentally retarded
    J. Grants given to districts to start programs for children with learning disabilities
    K. The influence of poverty, drug abuse, and environmental toxins
    L. A high cholesterol diet and more men wearing tight jockey shorts

3. \_\_\_\_\_ Which of the following statements about learning disability is correct?

    E. Children with learning disabilities have average or above average intelligence
    F. Learning disabilities are due primarily to laziness and poor motivation
    G. Learning disabilities are caused by visual and hearing impairments
    H. Learning disabilities are caused by poor teaching and lack of opportunity to learn

4. \_\_\_\_\_ The essence of PL 94-142, The Education of All Handicapped Children Law, is:

    V. Public school districts must provide special education for all disabled children between 3 and 21 years of age.
    W. All disabled children between 3 and 21 years old must go to school
    X. All disabled public school districts have between 3 and 21 years to come into compliance with the law
    Z. Every person between 3 and 21 years old must have a disabled friend

## 92    Coping with Learning Disabilities

5. \_\_\_\_\_    The letters IEP stand for:

   C. Intense energetic professor
   D. Innovative educational program
   E. Individualized educational plan
   F. Insane European playwright

6. \_\_\_\_\_    Which of the following would **not** be included in an IEP?

   O. A child's current levels of academic achievement
   P. Short-term educational objectives
   Q. Special services a child would need like speech therapy or physical therapy
   R. The name and phone number of an intense energetic professor

7. \_\_\_\_\_    Which of the following would **not** be needed to satisfy the nondiscriminatory testing requirement of PL 94-142?

   Q. Testing a child in his or her native language
   R. Providing an interpreter if there are no testing personnel who speak the child's native language
   S. Using a number of tests for assessment rather than a single one
   T. Using separate but equal tests when assessing children from minority groups

8. \_\_\_\_\_    A multidisciplinary staff conference is a meeting where:

   E. School personnel and parents gather to review results of testing and determine if a child should be placed in special education
   F. Principals and assistant principals meet to discuss ways of disciplining teachers who have been vocal critics of their schools
   G. Psychologists and social workers gather to show video tapes on methods of corporal punishment that leave no marks
   H. Bureaucrats at the school district central office meet to discuss creative budgeting in order to attend educational conferences on Oahu

9. \_\_\_\_\_    In Public Law 94-142, the term "least restrictive alternative" refers to:

   Q. Relaxing school rules so kids feel free to express their creativity
   R. Putting a misbehaving child in a time out room in place of caning
   S. Teaching children with disabilities in settings where nondisabled children are present
   T. Placing children with disabilities in alternative schools

10. \_\_\_\_\_ Which of the following would **not** be provided for under the due process section of Public Law 94-142?

    Q. Allowing a parent who disagrees with test results to have a child evaluated by professionals who practice outside of the school district

    R. Convening an impartial hearing to resolve differences between parents and the school

    S. Providing an appeal procedure when parties to a due process hearing do not agree with the initial decision

    T. Allowing a process server to serve papers on parents telling them when they are due in court

Well, how did you do? Use the following answer key to score yourself. Allow one point for each correct answer.

| Question | Answer |
|---|---|
| 1. | C |
| 2. | L |
| 3. | E |
| 4. | V |
| 5. | E |
| 6. | R |
| 7. | T |
| 8. | E |
| 9. | S |
| 10. | T |

Readers who scored at least 9 points (some imperfection is interesting) may proceed to the next chapter. Sorry, all others must turn in their books and await the second edition which will come in larger type and have pictures.

# Chapter 5

# *Outside of School: Diet, Vision, and Learning Centers*

I've been a teacher in classrooms where the students were as young as six years old in first grade and as old as sixty-five in graduate school. Among many other things, I've learned that every class has a different personality. Some groups are businesslike, even a little tense, as they attend to their lessons in a quiet and determined quest for knowledge. Others are much more relaxed, almost carefree, confident that sufficient knowledge will come to them in good time. Some are noisy and boisterous, learning just as much as any other class, but needing to be more rambunctious in the process. They have a will of their own and can be stubborn and difficult to manage.

Despite the diversity in character between classes, there is one constant that will be present in every class irrespective of the age or ability level of the students. Cheating. You count on it. It happens often enough that new uses of words have developed to talk about it. For example, terms such as "crib sheet" and "pony" refer to notes that students surreptitiously sneak into classes to help them improve their exam performance. Furthermore, teachers' arsenals of commands include many dictates that are meant to convey their disdain and somehow slow the younger generation's moral decay. Examples include: "Keep your eyes on your own paper", "Honor the honor code", "Cheating may result in suspension from the university", "Do your own work", "No copying", and one that grudgingly accepts the inevitable, "If you must cheat, at least pick someone smarter than you".

It is a fact that cheating has been the subject of many controlled, scientific studies by educational psychologists. Using sophisticated experimental designs, advanced inferential statistics, and, as we have become more technologically advanced, hidden spy cameras, data are gathered and analyzed in order to either accept or reject hypotheses that have been formulated with enough precision to attract support from various governmental or private agencies that have granted big sums of money to verify that students cheat—a fact that most seasoned teachers would verify for nothing.

I will save you the time and effort that would be required to go to the library and read all those studies. The one overriding finding is: "Yup, students cheat". They do it often and with an amazingly diverse collection of devious techniques. Not just rubbernecking to eyeball a neighbor's exam paper. That's commonplace enough to be considered gauche. Truly imaginative cheaters do things like pay a gifted and equally unscrupulous friend to take an exam for them, carefully search trash bins outside of faculty offices for rough drafts of exams just before final week, or hook up wireless transmitters with tiny, very sensitive microphones and receivers in order to communicate with a trusted ally hiding in a stall in the rest room with a copy of the textbook. Now, if we could only channel all that creative effort toward more socially acceptable ends.

This is not to imply that all students cheat all of the time in all classrooms. It's more like a few students cheating most of the time and almost all students cheating some of the time. Really, it's not much different than what happens as their parents consider taking deductions for charitable contributions, travel expenses, and business lunches on their 1040A. Hmmm.

I tell you all of this, because I must say, in all candor, that I was not pleased with the test taking behavior of some of you at the end of the last chapter. I needn't mention names (you know who you are); suffice it to say that a few of you have been less than honorable. To the woman in Wilmette, did you really think I wouldn't see your furtive glances under those mirrored sunglasses? To the gentleman (hah) in Geneva, might I suggest some Lava soap to remove all that indelible blue ink from your hairy forearms. And finally, to the couple in Keokuk, I certainly admire your eyesight, but the old fingers on the cheek to represent letters of the alphabet trick didn't fool me for a minute.

To the rest of you, congratulations on your test results. I was pleased, as you should be, at your retention of important information. I promise you that there will be no more major examinations, although I do reserve the right to pop a quickie quiz on you at any time. Now, let us return to the business at hand.

To this point, we have looked at aspects of learning disability that apply to you and your child during the school day. That leaves us with 18 hours to consider. As parents, you know that learning disability is more than a six hour inconvenience. Problems continue before and after school, on weekends, and over vacations.

As Billy's mom noted, the number and variety of treatments for learning disability and related characteristics like attention deficits and hyperactivity can be overwhelming. In a sense, parents of disabled children are a captive audience; they may be "easy marks", because they are willing to try any approach that is advertised as a way to cure learning problems, or at least lessen their effects, in children. Often, selecting a treatment regimen is not proceeded by a careful and objective study of research findings or even by talking to authorities who may be less emotionally involved. This parental susceptibility to embrace unproven approaches of questionable value is exemplified in the following account of another family and a child with a disability. While the disability is certainly more serious than those exhibited by the large majority of children with learning disabilities, this mother's writing will still help us explore some of the factors that influence parents when choosing treatments for their children.

## John, Our Son

John was born the middle child in a family of five sons. He joined his brothers in a happy, healthy, and very noisy household. My husband and I were delighted with our "team", even though we replaced more broken windows, the result of endless games in the back yard, than any other family in the neighborhood. Our boys were all we could have hoped for—ambitious, some more than others, academic, when the mood prevailed, competitive, and full of affection and brotherly respect for each other. None of the neighborhood bullies picked on one brother, because they knew they would have to contend with the rest of the clan.

Our entire life pattern changed one May, some years ago. At that time, John was eleven years old, had almost completed the sixth grade, and ranked as a superior student, both academically and socially. He was president of his class, an altar boy, and very active in clubs and sports. Even at this early age, John had decided he wanted to be an orthopedic surgeon and had already written to Northwestern University to ask about their medical school. On May 7th, he complained of a headache. I took his temperature, which was normal, and decided he might be coming down with the flu, from which one of his brothers had just recovered. His unexpected and welcome vacation from school was thoroughly enjoyed with special treats and favorite shows on TV.

The headache persisted and the doctor prescribed an antibiotic. Each day the head pain became more severe and prolonged. The doctor changed the medication and told us he was concerned about the possibility of meningitis. Just a week after the symptoms began, John had a frightful convulsion and had to be rushed to the hospital. The attending neurosurgeon speculated that he suffered from either a brain tumor or abscess, and that both were inoperable. When lab tests were completed, John's illness was diagnosed as encephalitis—a name that was entirely unfamiliar to us, but would gain dreadful meaning over the next ten years.

John lapsed into a coma and slept for three months. Fortunately, both my husband and I had several devoted brothers and sisters who cared for the other boys, so John was never without either parent being with him during these critical weeks. In spite of the fact that he was completely paralyzed, blind and deaf, he became known as the little boy who refused to die. It was quite a surprise to all the medical personnel, who had labeled the case as hopeless, when John finally began to move—first, just a nerve in the leg, than an eyelid, next his toe or finger. Of course, he had suffered brain damage as a result of his long sleep, but no one could determine how much or how lasting. A noted neurologist, brought in as a consultant, told us that John's intelligence was unimpaired; his opinion was that the damage was chiefly in the communication center of the brain.

We brought John home from the hospital in September. Unable to walk, he was carried by his dad and brothers. Days of endless practice passed in teaching him to stand and showing him how to put one foot in front of the other. I held him upright to assure his balance, and his dad pushed one foot forward and then the next. When John was able to walk unaided, the same procedure was followed in teaching him to climb the stairs. Fortunately, both sight and hearing were restored, although he was unable to communicate verbally. John, our son, had totally lost his ability to speak.

As his physical strength returned, he became more active and agile. This was the most trying period of all. John changed from a quiet little recluse to a hyperactive little bundle of nerves. His father and brothers spent hours running with him, playing ball, and finally reteaching him to ride the new bicycle he had received for his eleventh birthday, the previous September. The mechanical skills returned quite readily. John's brothers and his dad and I accompanied him to the neighborhood high school pool, where special classes in swimming were held for handicapped children. By the end of the semester, John had remembered most of the movements necessary to swim.

During the next two years, John progressed slowly. He learned to smile again—just a half smile and crooked—but to his family the most beautiful smile in the world. We constantly searched for new means or methods to help John. We came to believe that the problems of the handicapped had still not been adequately addressed in our community and that there were precious few authorities to whom we could turn for constructive advice.

Then, in a local newspaper, I read of a new treatment being developed in Philadelphia to help brain damaged children. The facility was called the Institute for the Development of Human Potential, and it was directed by two men named Glenn Doman and Carl Delacato. We spoke with John's pediatrician who felt the Institute might be worth trying, so we applied for admission. A short time later, we were notified that John's name had been added to a long waiting list of applicants.

Because of the long time before he would be accepted in Philadelphia, we enrolled John in a similar program being conducted in Chicago at the Loretto Research Institute. One of my most vivid memories of the program was the long delays. When your child is hyperactive and has to wait for hours at a time sitting on a folding chair in a dimly lit corridor amid similarly afflicted children, it becomes a situation that parents come to dread.

John was examined by a physician who recorded his case history from the time he was an infant, and after numerous consultations, our son was accepted as a patient. The directors of the Loretto Institute were devoted and kind. They outlined John's daily program (a Herculean task for the entire family) and drilled us in the therapy.

We kept John at Loretto for nearly a year, until we were notified that he could come to Philadelphia. It was a difficult decision to make. We pondered whether we should stay with the Chicago branch of the Institute, where John seemed to have made some progress—he had learned to feed himself for the first time in three years—or go to Philadelphia, the "mother house" of the program. Because we were afraid of passing by an opportunity that might never again be available, we flew to Philadelphia with John and one of our older boys to help manage.

It was an exhausting and expensive trip. For three days, John, his dad and I were subjected to long hours of examinations, lectures, and drills. When John was officially accepted as a patient, a new series of exercises and procedures were outlined. This program was definitely a family project. We talked it over with our other boys, Bob 17, Jim 15, Bill 11, and Tim 6. We discussed the pros and cons and listened to each boy's thoughts and beliefs. Because they were to play such an important role in John's program, we felt we had to consider their time and energy. Our boys voted unanimously for the plan, because as one of them said, "John would do it for us". I was never prouder of my team of men.

It was an exhausting program. The initial step was patterning. This is a technique that requires five persons to move a patient's body through a prescribed exercise four times a day, seven days a week. We had to get down on the floor, one person assigned to each of John's limbs, and another person to his head, and creep across the room. John was fortunate to have a father and three big brothers devoted to his recovery. Together, we were the first crew of workers for a patterning session each morning before breakfast. At the end of each exercise, the crew was beat, although the session lasted only seven minutes. John was a big boy and resisted the motions forced upon him.

At ten o'clock, while the rest of the family was at work or school, John and I went to the fire engine house in Evergreen Park, where the wonderful firemen gave him his second patterning of the day. In the afternoon, the physical therapists at Little Company of Mary Hospital patterned him for the third time. In the evening, just before dinner, the early morning crew performed again.

Patterning was just one phase of the Doman-Delacato program. John's dad was directed to build a crawl box, twenty feet long. Its purpose was to keep John on his stomach and make him crawl a prescribed distance. Because the structure had a top and sides, he had to wiggle forward on his stomach to reach the end.

Another aspect of the program was creeping. The Institute wanted John kept on the floor all day, except for meal time and toilet privileges. The theory was that by taking John back to an earlier stage of development it would be possible to "reorganize" his damaged brain and bring him back to normalcy. We were told that we had made a mistake by reteaching John to walk when he originally came home from the hospital.

John resisted this creeping technique very vigorously. He could now run like a gazelle and saw no reason why he should stay on the floor. As we look back at the treatment now, we can see its many fallacies, but at the time we were ready and anxious to accept any theory that might be beneficial to our son. What kind of parents would we have been had we not tried this?

In the short time left in each day, John was required to participate in other aspects of the therapy. To stimulate his tactile sense, we placed objects inside a bag or box so he couldn't see them. John had to identify them using only his sense of touch. To stimulate his language development, he listened to a tape recorder which constantly repeated certain words and phrases. We stimulated his visual sense by having him follow the movements of a flashlight or pencil with his eyes.

You would think that by the end of the day, we all would have dropped off into deep sleep, not to be aroused until the following morning. That would have been nice, but John's treatment did not end at bedtime. Another part of the therapy required that he sleep in the correct position. It was called the cross pattern sleeping posture. John had to be on his stomach with one arm extended and the opposite leg drawn upward. So, throughout the night, at two hour intervals, either my husband or I had to go into John's room to check his position and move him if necessary.

With all that had to be done to meet the plan set forth by the Institute, we always felt that we had never quite finished the job; we were never able to accomplish all that the Institute advocated. We couldn't help but wonder how other families managed, families that did not have brothers willing to help and access to the other kinds of assistance that we did.

John stayed with the program for two years, at which time his father and I finally began to disagree with some of the prescribed methods. We felt that our son had actually regressed from having to stay on the floor all day. His appetite waned, he became stoop shouldered, and he seemed to lose all interest in his surroundings. We believed the Institute was eager for results and was getting desperate in prescribing methods to attain them.

We are not sorry we went to Philadelphia, because we have always wanted to do anything possible to aid our son. We came to believe, however, that at best, John's participation in this program helped to develop his leg and arm muscles, but did little to eradicate the damage to his brain. Because Mr. Doman assured us and other parents that some day our children would take their natural place among their peers, we feel that the Institute's claims for success were unfounded, or, at the least, very exaggerated.

For several years after terminating our contact with the Institute, John had a tutor who helped him rediscover the alphabet and numbers. He has become a gentle, loving, sweet boy. His hyperactivity has diminished somewhat, and he is a welcome and valued participant in the social activities of our family.

As I look back, it hasn't been an easy ten years, but I feel our family has accomplished a great deal. As John's parents, we always tried to teach our boys that just because he is different, there is no reason to be ashamed or apologetic. Our Tim, at the ripe old age of seven, proved the point when he introduced his family to a new friend. When the little visitor asked why John couldn't speak, Tim replied, "John has been sick for a long time, but he is getting better every day". I was so proud of my little Irishman.

Our other boys have always been encouraged to entertain their friends in our home. We want them to keep their activities as normal as possible. John loves to ride in the car and whenever anyone mentions going anyplace, our favorite passenger is found waiting at the door, with coat and hat. We plan our vacations so all can enjoy themselves; our favorite was a trip down the Mississippi on a houseboat. The boys took turns steering the "Queen Mary", swabbing the decks, and exploring the islands. Once again, we are fortunate that John has so many brothers to share their experiences and interests with him.

We have added a new, but most prominent, member to the family in the last few years. My husband thought that a dog would be a good companion for John, so a Dalmatian named Chuck became our sixth son. He is John's dog, but everyone in the family enjoys him. It is remarkable that an animal has the instinct to realize when one boy needs more affection and attention than the others.

In spite of the fact that John requires much more time and energy than all the other boys together, we try to share our interests and enthusiasm equally. We want all the boys to have a happy home, to have enjoyable experiences and wonderful memories. We have tried to guard against devoting all our thoughts to our disabled son and neglecting the others. During their vacations from school, one of the older boys has always volunteered to care for his brother, so my husband and I can spend some time away together. As our children grow up and leave home—the eldest is married, the next is just home from the Peace Corps, and another is in college in Wisconsin—we are blessed to always have another brother to step in and help with John's care.

It is probably because of John's disability that I became interested in special education. My previous teaching experience had been with normal children. Because of our constant search for help for our son over the last ten years, I became aware of the pressing need for teachers in this field. If I can just help one disabled child and his or her family find the way to share a more normal life, I'll feel justified in returning to the classroom. It hasn't always been easy to pick up the techniques of note taking, term papers, and exams after being away from the classroom for so many years. My family thinks it's "real cool" that I'm a student again.

What lies ahead for John? We will never give up hoping that someday the broken wires in his brain will be rerouted and our son will be able to recall the knowledge and experiences he learned the first eleven years of his life. His speech and language are still very poor. He talks with his eyes and can make his wants known in a manner recognized by family members. There still isn't anything his dad and I wouldn't do to aid in his recovery. Of course, we all have our "blue" days when we reminisce about things that might have been, but for the most part, we try to live one day at a time and focus on the good parts.

If I could offer any advice to parents of disabled children, I'd tell them to make the most of each day, to love their children and enjoy them for themselves. Exhibit your devotion and love of the other siblings and teach them love, understanding, patience, (you'll need a great deal of that) and consideration for each other by demonstrating these characteristics yourself.

---

Here, just as in Billy's case, there is much that can be learned from this family's experience. What is so vividly apparent throughout the story is their unusual ability to come together in the face of a tragedy to care for their son and brother. A young, vulnerable, and cherished member of the clan has been wounded, and the elders are moved by a powerful need to hasten the healing process. This is a most profound expression of love. In the end, it seems obvious that the unselfish efforts expended by the individual members of this family had merged to make them a stronger unit than they otherwise might have been.

The fact that mother, after all the years of exhausting effort within her own family, went on to pursue an advanced degree in special education so that she might help others is, to me, truly remarkable and inspirational. Having this woman in my class at the university provided me with a lesson in determination, fortitude, and elegance that I shall never forget. She is beautiful, in the truest sense of the word. This is amazing grace.

Mother's writing is important for other reasons as well. She gives us insight into some of the dynamics that operate in parents as they attempt to find help for their children. Consider the following excerpts from her story:

1. "We constantly search for new means or methods to help John."

2. "Because we were afraid of passing by an opportunity that might never again be available, we flew to Philadelphia . . ."
3. "As we look back at the treatment now, we can see many of its fallacies, but at the time we were ready and anxious to accept any treatment that might be beneficial to our son. What kinds of parents would we have been had we not tried this?"
4. "We are not sorry we went to Philadelphia, because we have always wanted to do anything possible to aid our son".

Their highest expression of parental love includes a willingness to try **any treatment** that **might** be beneficial. We understand this willingness, for when a child is hurting, it is difficult to be coolly dispassionate and take the time to evaluate various treatments objectively. There is a need to get active, to try something, anything that offers even the slightest hope for improvement. So, as we consider this family's loss and think about the fear and disappointment they faced in seeing John's unusually high potential vanish at age 11, it becomes easier to understand why they would be willing to invest the time, tremendous effort, and money in an approach which, in the opinion of most authorities in medicine, psychology, and special education does absolutely nothing to reorganize impaired neurology or, in simpler terms, to fix damaged brains.

This is not to suggest that advocates of the Doman-Delacato therapy aren't sincerely concerned about disabled children or adults. There is no doubt that they are, but what is troublesome is the lack of acceptably controlled and objective research that would lend support to their considerable claims.

The "constant search for new means or methods to help John" that mother writes about is not unique to this family. Searching for a cure is one stage that many families pass through as they struggle to adjust to disability in a child. It is quite common for parents to pursue every possible approach, however experimental and however unfounded, for indeed, "What kinds of parents would we be" if we didn't do all we possibly could for our children?

An assertive approach in your dealings with the school, an approach in which parents are in full control, has been recommended. In fact, the same kind of active and aggressive demands for excellent special services inside school should be practiced by parents when seeking additional therapy for their children outside of school. But, a quick choice of any program that **might** be helpful, as understandable as it is, must be discouraged and delayed.

There is a good deal of wisdom to the old adage: "Look before you leap". It is important that at least some objective evaluation of the many and varied approaches for treating learning disability precede the participation of children in such approaches. The goal is to help families make wiser, more well-informed choices when selecting treatments for their children; treatments which, in the end, will not be considered fallacious and wasteful of time and effort but will be viewed as having been valuable courses of action toward remediation of the problem.

This chapter and the next will familiarize you with some of the therapeutic approaches available and will give you information that ought to help you decide whether any of them would be appropriate for your child. We will examine dietary treatments, visual training, Irlin lenses, after school learning centers, and drug therapy as possible types of intervention.

As part of an informal study conducted at an elementary school in Chicago, I asked a group of almost 50 students in seventh and eighth grade to tell me their favorite foods for dinner. Pizza turned out to be their first choice, by far. Some of the students told me they would eat it seven days a week if they could, and a few even went so far as to tell me their favorite toppings and whether they preferred the crust thick or thin. Students, who seemed otherwise untalented in oral communication skills, waxed eloquent as they described the correct proportions, contrasting flavors, and complementary textures of cheese and tomato paste. Some actually salivated during their descriptions.

Also on the preferred list, but distance runners up to the Italian delight, were steak, ribs, Big Macs, Double Whoppers with cheese, Kentucky Fried Chicken, spaghetti and meat balls, fajitas, gyros, tacos, and one oddball vote for tuna noodle casserole. (This last choice met with some groans and came from a student nobody liked.) Health foods were conspicuous by their absence. There wasn't a single vote for a fresh garden salad, steamed vegetables with tofu, or a broiled chicken breast with the skin removed.

My informal study does not qualify as controlled scientific research that deserves to be praised for its excellent experimental design. Nevertheless, one is tempted to conclude that the diet currently preferred by our nation's youth is a delight for both cardiologists and the owners of a multitude of pizza parlors across the country.

The effect of diet upon the growth and development of children is something that concerns almost everyone who works with them in any capacity. Some authorities have even maintained that diet has an important relationship to learning disability and hyperactivity in children. Perhaps the most noted of these authorities is Dr. Ben Feingold, a pediatrician from California. Dr. Feingold's theories led to the development of the Kaiser-Permanente diet, one of a number of controversial treatments for learning disability. Again, a little history is in order.

In the late 1960s, as a result of careful observation of patients in his own pediatric practice, Dr. Feingold theorized that many children were learning disabled and hyperactive because of an unusual sensitivity to a substance called "acetylsalicylic acid" which is present in aspirin. Forms of this substance, salicylate radicals they're called, are found in some natural foods, primarily certain fresh fruits and vegetables, as well as in all foods that contain artificial coloring and flavoring. The theory is that these substances are able to enter brain cells, have a toxic effect upon the central nervous system, lead to observable responses such as hyperactivity, and therefore interfere with normal learning.

Time factors apparently played an important role as Dr. Feingold refined his theory. He points out that artificial additives, particularly flavorings, were not used in our country, to any significant degree, until after World War II. He furthermore contends that the dramatic increase in hyperactivity and learning disability began at the same time or shortly thereafter. So, the implication is clear. There is indeed no free lunch. The time saved by families who turned to quickly prepared convenience foods that contained substantial amounts of synthetic additives would be paid back by caring for a generation of children who were hyperactive and learning disabled, because they ate them.

The best result of a theory occurs when an effective treatment is derived from it which ultimately leads to benefits for children. And so, from his theory, Dr. Feingold derived his special diet, the purpose of which is to reduce the ingestion of salicylates, thereby eliminating the sensitivity to them. The consequence would be a cure, or at least management, for the hyperactivity, along with a subsequent lessening in the learning disability.

Dr. Feingold was anything but conservative in describing the potential utility and benefit of his dietary treatment. He believed that more than five million children in our country were hyperactive and learning disabled and that half of these were likely to have a fully beneficial response to the diet. He also felt that an additional twenty-five percent would have a partial benefit, at least to the extent that drugs would not be necessary to manage their behavior. Clearly, the good doctor was not bashful; these were no small claims.

This dietary treatment was highly publicized in both the professional and popular press. Dr. Feingold appeared on television talk shows, gave press conferences, wrote a book and magazine articles, and appeared at governmental hearings all the way up to the federal level. Perhaps the clearest evidence of the very positive and widespread public reaction to this treatment is the fact that at one time not many years ago there was a National Feingold Association in the United States with more than 100 local chapters and a total membership in excess of 20,000 families. That's a lot of people believing in the idea: "You are what you eat".

In the Feingold diet, along with careful avoidance of aspirin, two groups of foods must be eliminated. First, *every* fruit and vegetable from the following list must be omitted: apples, cherries, nectarines, apricots, oranges, peaches, plums, prunes, grapes, raisins, blackberries, raspberries, strawberries, boysenberries, almonds, currants, tomatoes, cucumbers, and pickles. By-products of these foods such as fruit jellies and vinegars are also on the list of no-nos. The orchards of forbidden fruit would seem to cover vast acreage.

Second, *all* foods with artificial colorings or flavorings must be omitted. If you were to carefully read labels on your next trip to the supermarket, you would see that a full roster of such products would require its own thick book, so the following is only a representative sampling: 1) Luncheon meats including salami, bologna, ham, bacon, sausages, meat loaf, and hot dogs, 2) Breakfast cereals and instant breakfast foods, 3) Bakery goods, for example, cakes, cookies, sweet rolls, doughnuts, and pies, 4) Candies, both hard and soft, 5) Poultry, including barbecued chicken, all self-basting turkeys, and prepared stuffing, 6) Desserts, including ice cream, sherbet, jello, puddings, and flavored yogurts, 7) Fish products, particularly frozen fish filets and fish sticks that are dyed and flavored, 8) Beverages, including all diet and soft drinks, iced tea, powdered lemonade, cider and chocolate milk, 9) Miscellaneous and sundry foods and medicines including butter, mustard, soy sauce, catsup, chili sauce, colored cheeses, Bufferin, Excedrin, Alka Seltzer, Empirin, Anacin, all toothpastes and powders, mouthwashes, antacid tablets, cough drops and syrups, throat lozenges, vitamins, and many prescription medications.

To help parents implement the diet, Dr. Feingold provided a list of instructions. For example, one requirement is that a daily diet diary (try saying that three times, fast) be kept. Parents are required to record everything that the child eats along with noting any behavioral or academic changes exhibited by the child. He contends that the greatest probability for a successful outcome occurs when the entire family adheres to the diet. (No more of those plump, red, succulent hot dogs for you either folks.)

Dr. Feingold furthermore suggests that prohibited foods be removed from the home entirely so as to eliminate temptation and dietary "cheating". Recognizing the importance of sweets like baked goods, candies and ice cream to most children, if not their parents, he points out that it is possible to avoid the artificial additives in these foods by preparing them, from scratch, at home. He is really quite adamant in insisting that dietary compliance be perfectly maintained. He says that anything less than 100 percent adherence, even one forbidden sip or bite, can result in an unfavorable reaction that may last for as long as three days or more.

As you can see, the Feingold, Kaiser-Permanente diet is a demanding intervention program. Its requirements are tough for the entire family. Careful grocery shopping and food preparation are vital and demand a corresponding increase in time and effort. Similarly, keeping an accurate record of everything that is eaten as well as noting all changes in behavior are difficult, time consuming tasks.

From a practical viewpoint, one must wonder if it is really possible to implement this treatment at all, especially given today's economic situation that requires both parents to work in so many families. It is also true that the number of households in which only one parent is present has grown dramatically in the past decade. In situations where both parents must work or where there is only one parent available, the amount of time and energy to devote to extensive and detailed food preparation and recording data in a diet diary is limited. It's difficult, also, to understand how a parent would be able to control what a child eats outside of the home, on all those walks to and from school, to the park, or to a movie, with friends who have an insatiable desire for junk food, which happens, of course, to be laced with artificial additives.

On the other hand, nobody ever said that fixing learning disability was going to be easy. Difficult problems usually require difficult solutions; therefore, many parents would be more than willing to invest the time and effort if, in fact, it could be shown that the approach in question yielded positive results. So, the question becomes: Just what are the results? What does the research say?

Dr. Feingold first developed his theory and subsequent diet therapy as a result of clinical experience with a sample of five children in his own pediatric practice. Most people who do research, including Dr. Feingold, would contend that this group of children is too small to constitute a study from which reliable conclusions can be drawn. A larger sample of children is needed.

There is also the possibility that these five children represent what would be referred to as a "biased sample" in research studies. One question is: can a person who has developed a theory and a treatment, especially a person who sincerely cares about children and wants to help them, be truly objective in evaluating the effectiveness of his own treatment upon his own patients? At best, I think the answer is "maybe", and it must be very difficult.

It is also likely that the parents would be another source of bias. For example, it is not unusual for parents of children with learning disabilities to travel from one specialist to another, sampling one treatment after another, and being disappointed one time after another. It may be that they finally arrived at Dr. Feingold's office, only after they had tried a string of other approaches that hadn't worked. A degree of desperation, developed as a result of repeated frustration, can easily lead to a parental mind set that is less than objective when it comes time to evaluate the results of the latest treatment. They want something finally to work, so it does.

The publicity that touted Dr. Feingold's treatment can also be viewed as a possible source of bias. When an approach is widely advertised in the popular press, and when it is presented as an healthier alternative to more invasive approaches like drug therapy that have side effects, it is easy to see why this became an attractive choice. The attraction, added to the fact that so much time and effort are required of parents, might lead them to overstate any observed benefits. "Why, of course it worked; look at how much effort we put into it", and "Didn't you read the article in the Sunday Supplement?" would not be surprising statements.

So, to reduce the possibility of bias and investigate the effectiveness of this approach more acceptably, we must look at the results of research studies conducted by those with no vested interest in the outcome, who utilized a larger sample of children selected to participate on a random basis, and whose improvement was evaluated by observers other than, or at least in addition to, their parents.

Such research studies do exist. They present inconsistent results which, at best, provide very weak support for the Feingold diet as a treatment for learning disability, hyperactivity, and related characteristics. Often, for the same group of children, parents noted some positive changes in behavior resulting from the diet, teachers noted less change, and objective measures in the form of neurological and psychological tests and laboratory observations showed no changes in learning or behavior at all.

In a few studies that reported positive results for children on the Feingold diet, there was no deterioration in behavior or learning after the same children went back to eating candy bars and cookies and drank soda pop, all of which contain the forbidden additives. This would suggest that any initial, positive changes in behavior might not have been due to the Feingold diet at all. Instead, changes might have been related to the novelty of the diet, modifications in overall nutritional status in the children that would have occurred on any different diet, or simply to a placebo effect; that is, the children perceived they were being attended to in a new and interesting way.

In one review of 23 research studies of the Feingold diet, it is reported that the behavior of children improved to a degree that was only slightly better than chance. Their ability to pay attention longer and their overall learning ability remained essentially unchanged.[7] While research on the behavior of children seldom *proves* anything, these kinds of findings do, at least, cast serious doubt upon the effectiveness of the Feingold diet.

Given the inconsistent and negative findings that are reported in the research, it seems fair to conclude that the basic tenets of the theory—that certain foods have toxic effects upon children's brains, that these effects lead to learning and behavioral problems, and that these effects can be eliminated through dietary controls—cannot be supported in any general way. There may be a few children who suffer from the unusual kind of sensitivity that Dr. Feingold suggests and who may even benefit from dietary intervention, but their number is certainly extremely small; much smaller that the millions he talks about.

---

[7]Kavale, K. et al. "Hyperactivity and diet." *Journal of Learning Disabilities*, Vol. 16, 1983, pp. 324-330.

So, what does it all come down to for you? As a parent, you aren't primarily concerned about all those other kids who participated in research studies. You're concerned about your own child who may be one of the few children who would benefit from a special diet. Of course, the choice will ultimately be yours. If you choose this treatment, at least go in with your eyes open. Be prepared for a routine that will be very difficult to implement and a treatment for which research findings do not report any widespread benefit. It would also be a good idea to read the following conclusions written by the National Advisory Committee on Hyperkinesis and Food Additives in a report to the Nutrition Foundation:

1. No controlled studies have shown that hyperkinesis (a synonym for hyperactivity) is related to the ingestion of food additives.

2. The claim that hyperactive children improve significantly on a diet that is free of salicylates and food additives has not been confirmed.

3. The nutritional qualities of the Feingold diet have not been evaluated, and it may not meet the long-term nutrient needs of children.

4. The diet should not be used without competent medical supervision.[8]

Speaking of keeping your eyes open, let us turn next to the field of optometry. Learning disability has been an attractive problem into which many professions have dipped their fingers. In the rush and clamor to help children, it seems that almost everyone wants a piece of the action. Optometry has not been an exception. We'll take a look at what it has to offer.

Most people think that when they read, their visual sense plays a primary role. After all, in reading we use our eyes to scan lines of print as we try to comprehend an author's meaning. It seems logical, therefore, that learning disabilities, in the form of reading problems, might be the result of defective vision. Before we explore this proposed relationship between defective visual functioning and learning disability any further, it would be a good idea to review what is involved in normal vision.

Take a minute and reread the preceding paragraph. (Go ahead; it's OK, I don't mind waiting . . . ) Now that you've finished, let's assume that your vision is normal in every way. Given that happy fact, consider some things about your eyes that were involved as your read those 84 words.

You should be very pleased to learn that at least one part of your body is perfectly formed. You have wonderful eyeballs! Not too long and not too short; just perfect. To see the words clearly (vision specialists call this "normal visual

---

[8]National Advisory Committee on Hyperkinesis and Food Additives, New York, The Nutrition Foundation, Inc. 1980.

acuity"), it is necessary for the light waves carrying the images of those words to fall at precisely the right place on your retina, the light-sensitive part of the eye at the back of the eyeball that transmits information to the optic nerve and then to the brain.

You may not have known it, but if you saw the words in the above paragraph with normal visual acuity, your eyes were refracting light waves properly. Deviations from normal acuity are called refractive errors. Without getting too complicated, these errors happen because of abnormal shape of the eyeball. As a result, the light waves carrying the images of the objects being seen (in this instance, words in print) are not refracted properly and do not reach the right place on the retina. The result is blurred vision.

Refractive errors are quite common and are usually easy to correct with prescription lenses. Examples of refractive errors are myopia, which is nearsightedness, hyperopia, or farsightedness, astigmatism and presbyopia. In astigmatism, blurred vision results because the cornea, the surface of the eye, is uneven. It can occur by itself or in combination with myopia or hyperopia. Presbyopia is seldom found in children; rather, it waits to plague those of us beyond the age of 40. What happens is that, with age, muscles in the eye lose their ability to change the shape of the lens as we look at objects at different distances. Usually, the ability to see things up close is affected the most, so to read comfortably, either bifocals or longer arms are required.

Cataracts are also classified as a refractive error. Here, the soft, clear lens of the eye becomes hard and cloudy. Vision is affected to varying degrees depending upon the location, size, and density of the cataract. When cataracts are surgically removed in children, whatever refractive error remains can be corrected with glasses or contact lenses.

There is more to seeing normally than the proper refraction of light waves. When you read the words in the paragraph, you also had to be able to keep your eyes in focus long enough to see individual words and to move your eyes smoothly across the page from left to right. So, we can conclude that in addition to some other obvious assets, you've got a fine set of eye muscles.

In a few people, including some with normally shaped eyeballs, there are muscle disorders in the eyes that make it difficult for them to keep things in focus, even for very short periods of time. Examples of muscle disorders include: nystagmus, a condition in which there are involuntary jerky or quick rolling movements of the eyes, and strabismus, when the muscles controlling eye movements are out of balance. In this latter condition, often called cross-eye or walleye, there may be double vision and a loss of depth perception, along with the primary problem in focusing. Sometimes, if strabismus goes untreated and double vision remains, amblyopia develops. What apparently happens is that the brain, bothered by two similar but not identical images of the same object, shuts down the input from one of the eyes. That eye weakens over time and may actually lose its ability to see. The term "lazy eye" is sometimes used as a substitute for amblyopia.

So, in summary, a person whose vision is functioning normally during reading has eyeballs of the correct shape and muscles controlling eye movements that are working as they should. As a result, there is clarity of vision that can be maintained long enough and the process of reading, this uniquely human and miraculous ability to gain meaning from the printed word, begins. It is important to underscore the idea that reading only **begins** with the eyes; the process ends in the brain, a fact to which we shall return when discussing the effectiveness of visual training as a remedial reading technique.

Now, back to optometry and the relationship between visual problems and learning disability. Optometry is a profession that is primarily concerned with prevention and correction of visual disorders. Practitioners, holders of the Doctor of Optometry Degree, examine, diagnose, and treat children and adults in order to increase and maintain their visual efficiency and eye health. Results of the optometric examination may lead to the prescription of a variety of treatments including eye glasses, contact lenses, and visual training. It is this latter treatment, visual training, that is most pertinent to parents of children with learning disabilities. It is also correct to say that it is the most controversial treatment of those offered by optometrists. We'll examine it in some detail.

Visual training is a term that has some synonyms. It is also called visual therapy, eye exercises, orthoptics, and eye training. Whatever the term, this treatment seems firmly entrenched in the practice of optometry. The American Optometric Association endorses visual training as an important part of the profession, and the technique is taught in all colleges where prospective optometrists are prepared to practice their profession.

Visual training consists of a number of non-surgical treatments to correct the kinds of muscle disorders described above. The patient participates in a sequence of exercises which are designed to remedy problems with eye movements and focusing disorders including nystagmus, strabismus, and amblyopia. A very wide range of specific treatments is available. One may be as simple as patching an eye to force the other amblyopic or lazy eye to work harder and contribute more to vision. A second may involve moving a small beam of light across the field of vision to enhance the ability to follow or track a visual stimulus smoothly. Another may be complex and involve the use of sophisticated computer programs to keep track of eye movements and provide feedback to the patient to reduce the nystagmoid, jerky movements. Of course, the kind of exercises that are prescribed are determined by the doctor and will relate to the nature of the visual problem that is present.

Visual training is an aspect of optometry that has been the subject of some rigorous debate. In the early and middle 1970s, a lively, often heated exchange occurred between optometrists and ophthalmologists (medical doctors who specialize in diagnosing and treating visual problems) regarding the usefulness of visual training to correct visual problems in general and as techniques for correcting reading problems in particular.

At one extreme position on the debate were optometrists making rather extravagant claims about visual training as a cure for dyslexia. At the other extreme were ophthalmologists who saw little use for visual training as a treatment for muscle disorders, let alone as a cure for dyslexia. As is the case with most controversies, the truth is probably somewhere in the middle.

Now, almost 20 years later, with the benefit of 20/20 hindsight, we can see that the controversy centered on two questions. First, does optometric visual training help to fix cases of muscle disorder like cross eye or lazy eye? And second, will the same visual training techniques be useful in the remediation of severe reading problems?

In one review of research reported in 1988,[9] more than 200 studies were cited in support of visual training as a way to facilitate visual problems including poor focusing, lazy eye, eyes turning in and out, and involuntary jerky movements of the eye. It is interesting, though, that in only *one* study out of this very large collection of research was there any report of visual training having any positive effect on reading disability. And, in that one study, the effect was very weak.

How can we best interpret this research, and what are the implications for you, as parents? Consider the following examples: Let's say there is a child who inherited some genes from his father, and , as a result, he has a refractive error resulting in blurred vision, particularly up close, at reading distance. Unfortunately, this young boy also has a neurological impairment, a brain dysfunction, which is severely impeding his progress toward learning to read. He is dyslexic. Wouldn't you agree that prescription lenses, although perfect for fixing the blurred vision, would do absolutely nothing for his neurological problem and his dyslexia? With his new eyeglasses, what we would have would be a dyslexic boy with good eyesight.

Now, consider another dyslexic child whose visual acuity at reading distance is normal. She, however, has a muscle disorder, let's say cross eye, that interferes with her ability to maintain focus on words in print. I think we could also agree that vision training exercises would be an effective treatment for the strabismus but would leave this girl just as dyslexic as she was before. We would have a reading disabled girl with stronger eye muscles.

---

[9]Cohen, A. "The efficacy of optometric vision therapy". *Journal of American Optometric Assoc.* Vol. 59, 1988, pp. 95-105.

The point is that the source of reading and learning disabilities is within the central organ, the brain. Therefore, remedial procedures like visual training which ameliorate problems in the peripheral organ, the eyes, will not be beneficial. This is not to diminish the importance of visual training; merely a plea to keep its utility in proper perspective.

The eyes are involved in reading. Of that, there is no doubt. Optometric examinations that detect problems in visual functioning should be followed by appropriate treatment, corrective lenses and/or visual training. However, you must know that, at best, optometric visual training will maximize your child's *potential* for learning to read, but the actual remediation of the reading problem will remain the responsibility of teachers. It seems correct to say that visual training is useful for improving eye problems that create discomfort during reading, and should be considered very valuable for increasing the effectiveness of visual functioning in general, but, beyond that, there is no relationship between the eyes and reading.

There are two more things to consider about the relationship between visual training and the improvement of reading disability. First, the most basic assumption of optometrists who have prescribed visual training has been that the problem with vision comes first and the reading disability second. If your eyes aren't working correctly, the effect is a reading problem. Isn't it possible, though, that the cause and effect relationship of visual functioning and reading proficiency might actually be in the reverse order from what vision trainers propose? It might be that a child's problem with reading comes first and leads to the onset of a visual problem. This idea is supported by the fact that there are some children whose visual problems are apparent only when they are reading; they are less of a problem or vanish altogether when looking at a series of pictures of doing other visual tasks that do not require a translation of letters into sounds. If this reverse order of cause and effect is indeed the case, then the implication for treatment becomes obvious. The best approach for the child would be to work directly on the reading problem or to work on the reading and visual problems simultaneously.

Finally, recent study of dyslexia suggests that severe reading disability is more closely related to auditory and language factors than to visual processing. Perhaps the most dramatic example of this is the fact that blind children, a group of students whose disability leaves their hearing and linguistic functioning untouched, are able, with Braille, to learn to comprehend the printed word; that is, to read. On the other hand, deaf children, with perfect visual acuity and no eye muscle disorders, but whose auditory and language development are interrupted, are often severely delayed in learning to read.

So, once again, what does it all come down to for you, the parents? If you choose to enroll your reading disabled student in a program of visual training, do so with a realistic expectation of the probable benefits. Understand that when the treatment is over, your child is very likely to be able to use vision more efficiently and comfortably. This is a significant outcome, the importance of which should not be minimized. However, the reading disability will remain and will need to be attacked by professionals in special education or remedial reading who have been trained in the use of special teaching techniques.

Before leaving the area of visual perception and turning to other treatments that have been proposed for learning disability, we should look at a more recent and equally controversial cause and remedial procedure for dyslexia that has hit the learning disability scene. This is the scotopic sensitivity syndrome and the use of colored lenses for reading.

The word "scotopic" is not part of our everyday vocabulary; we can agree that it does not come up very often in casual conversation. In fact, it's doubtful that even one percent of the population has ever heard it, never mind know what it means. Being part of the larger majority; that is, the other ninety-nine percent, I simply assumed when I first heard reference to scotopic sensitivity that a person suffering from such a syndrome could manage the problem effectively and thus continue leading a reasonably normal life by never eating scotops. This I silently pledged to do, because being plagued by allergic reactions to oysters, shrimp, lobster, and assorted other foodstuff, not to mention cat dander, the very last thing I needed was to be done in by a couple of quick bites of undercooked scotop during a hurried lunch between classes. I languished in such ignorance until, on television, I saw a portion of Sixty Minutes that explained the theory underlying the scotopic sensitivity syndrome and the treatment derived from it. Among other things, I learned from Morley Safer that the word "scotopic" refers to ones's ability to adapt to darkness. Perhaps a little background will shed some light or at least help us adapt.

In 1983, Helen Irlin[10], a psychologist, proposed the idea that some dyslexic children, maybe as many as 50%, suffer from a disorder in visual perception which she claims occurs in people whose retinas are unusually sensitive to light waves of particular frequencies. Although the frequencies involved vary in different people, everybody with this syndrome has a difficult time reading because of print distortions that are made worse by the contrast of black print on a white page. There it is; scotopic sensitivity, a problem adapting to black print on white paper.

Irlin also believes that this is a unique type of visual problem that is totally different from the refractive or muscle disorders we have already described. In fact, it is her contention that the scotopic sensitivity syndrome cannot be diagnosed during a standard optometric examination and that the condition cannot be treated successfully with traditional visual training.

---

[10]Irlin, Helen. "Successful treatment of learning disability". Report to the American Psychological Association, August, 1983.

Irlin lists the following characteristics of the scotopic sensitivity syndrome:

1. Distortion of print including the shapes of letters, reduced amount of space between words, words that run together or are missing entirely, and words spinning backward across a page.
2. Movement of print in ways that makes the words appear to be shimmering, vibrating, or wavering to the reader.
3. Swirling of an entire page of print in a whirlpool effect.
4. Seeing "rivers" of white or colored lines running through or between the print.
5. A very narrow span of vision as if the reader were looking down a thin tube. The field of vision is so restricted that the reader may only be able to see two or three letters in a word at a time.
6. Blurred or double vision that only occurs when looking at a page of print.
7. Seeing shadows or circles of light around individual letters and words.
8. Problems in depth perception, frequent loss of place during reading, skipping lines, hesitations, and rereading lines unintentionally.

In cases of scotopic sensitivity syndrome, all of the above problems would not be present in any one person; however, even two or three of them would create symptoms that would be serious impediments to reading. In fact, the contention is that these problems make reading, even for short periods of time, an extremely fatiguing task that requires tremendous effort and concentration.

Helen Irlin reports that children and adults who attempt to read under these conditions show signs of visual strain including red, itchy, and watery eyes. Often, they will open their eyes very wide as they read and frequently blink and squint. With all these symptoms plus commonly occurring headaches, it would not be surprising if those who suffer from this syndrome do everything they can to avoid reading altogether.

Irlin's treatment for the scotopic sensitivity syndrome requires the reader to wear tinted lenses during reading, the purpose of which is to filter out those specific light frequencies causing the sensitivity. Since the troublesome frequencies vary from one person to the next, the color of the lenses will also vary and need to be precisely determined and selected from a total of 150 different hues. Once the exactly correct color is determined, wearing glasses tinted to that hue results in improved visual perception during reading and the elimination of headaches, eye strain, double vision, distortions of print, and the other bothersome symptoms listed above. It follows that individuals will then be able to read more comfortably for longer periods of time and reading achievement will improve.

The validity of the theory that forms the basis for the scotopic sensitivity syndrome and the effectiveness of the colored lens treatment for the management of dyslexia are not black and white issues. (I know, I know, it's a bad pun, but I couldn't help myself.) On the contrary, many people have reacted with skepticism and criticism. For example, this therapy is being used more in Australia than it is here. It is reported that in some schools down under, **all** children wear their colored lenses or place colored plastic overlays over material when they are reading. But, it is interesting that in the same country, in 1987, the Australian College of Ophthalmologists went on record expressing their opposition and belief that there was no basis for accepting the Irlin approach as a useful method for the treatment of reading disabilities. A similar difference of opinion exists in the United States, so, once again, therefore, it is necessary to turn to the results of research in order to try to be objective in judging the effectiveness and potential utility of this therapy.

It is not an exaggeration to say that the relatively few research studies designed to examine this approach in a carefully controlled and objective way have yielded conflicting results. Actually, the words "confusing mess" come to mind after reading the research. So, let's review one of the important tenets of Irlin's theory and then propose a study of our own.

The theory that forms the basis for treatment tells us that the frequency of light waves that cause the sensitivity varies from one person to the next. This is why the lenses come in 150 different colors and why it is necessary for each person to undergo a careful diagnosis in order to determine the exact lens color that will work the best. Given this basic premise of the theory—that the same color lenses that work the best for some children would not work well for others—let's get on with our research.

We'll find 100 children, all of whom have equal degrees of reading disability and all of whom are judged to have the scotopic sensitivity syndrome. To make our research better, these 100 children are equally intelligent, the same age, come from the same socio-economic background, have had schooling of equal quality, and are equally motivated to wear the lenses and participate in our research. In the real world, it would probably be impossible to control the research this well; perfectly designed studies only exist in textbooks. Nevertheless, what we're attempting to do is include children who are the same in all important ways so we can better evaluate the one variable we are studying, the effectiveness of the Irlin lenses as a means for improving reading achievement.

The first part of our experiment requires that we do careful testing to identify the optimal lenses, the most appropriate hue, the ones that ought to work the best for each child. We'll call these the "good lenses". This we determine, and at the same time, we are able to identify a lens color for each child that would be less than optimal; that is, the lenses with hues that would, theoretically, not be effective in filtering out the offensive frequencies for each child in question. We'll call these the "bad" lenses. Then, on a random basis, half the children in our research would be assigned good lenses and the other half would get bad ones. As a way of reducing subjectivity, bias, and the effects of prior expectations, the children, their parents, their teachers, and we who are conducting the research will not know which children have the good lenses and which don't.

We'll let six months go by during which time the children in both groups will receive an equal quantity and quality of reading instruction. At the end of this period, we will retest the reading of all the children, which, you recall, was equally poor for both groups at the beginning of our study.

If the theory and treatment for the scotopic sensitivity syndrome are correct, then certainly the children in our research who wore lenses optimal for them; that is, the good ones, should be performing at a significantly higher level in reading than the children who wore the bad ones. I think Helen Irlin would like that result. But, in reality, there is at least one research study, similar to ours, which indicated that the color of the lens didn't matter.[11] Both groups made gains in reading comprehension with their lenses, and, in fact, there was a slight difference in favor of the children who wore the less than optimal lenses, the bad ones. These findings would suggest that Irlin's theory and the treatment derived from it are questionable, and that the gain in reading achievement could more logically be attributed to a placebo effect. The children in both groups perceived that they were being treated in a new and interesting way, and it was this perception, not the lenses at all, that had a positive effect on their motivation and subsequently higher achievement in reading.

There is other research that casts some doubt on this approach to the remediation of dyslexia. Remember, it is Irlin's contention that the scotopic sensitivity syndrome is a unique problem of visual perception. She contends that is different from the kinds of visual problems (muscle disorders like cross eye, for example) detected during an optometric examination that respond to visual training. Let's do another experiment to test that contention.

We'll find another 100 children similar to the previous bunch. Again, they are equally delayed in reading, are judged to have the scotopic sensitivity syndrome, and are equally bright. In fact, just like the subjects in our previous research study, these children are the same with respect to all things except one. The difference between them is that half will wear the colored lenses and half will participate in traditional visual training exercises with an optometrist. At the end

---

[11]Robinson, G. and Conway, R. "The effects of Irlin colored lenses on students' specific reading skills . . ." *Journal of Learning Disabilities*, Vol. 23, 1990. pp. 589-596.

of six months, we will retest the reading achievement in both groups. If Irlin's contention is correct; that is, if the scotopic sensitivity syndrome is a specific problem in visual perception different from all of the rest, then the children who wore the tinted lenses should be achieving at a significantly higher level in reading then the children who had visual training.

In a study designed in a way similar to ours,[12] the authors reported that both groups appeared to have fewer annoying visual symptoms like watery eyes and headaches and were therefore much more comfortable during reading. However, neither group had made any measurable progress in learning to read. The findings of this research suggest:

1. The scotopic sensitivity syndrome may *not* be substantially different from the kinds of vision problems that optometrists work with all the time. In fact, it may not be a distinct problem in visual perception at all.

2. For some children, wearing tinted lenses results in more comfort during reading.

3. Wearing colored lenses is no more effective for the remediation of dyslexia than any other form of visual training.

So, at the present time, with the limited amount of acceptable research on the technique, about the only thing that can be said with certainty is that the jury is still out on the scotopic sensitivity syndrome. Until more controlled studies are done, parents would be wise to approach this treatment with caution. And, while it might be correct to say that colored lenses are as effective as visual training exercises in helping some children reduce eye strain, increase their visual comfort during reading, and, in general, improve the overall functioning of their vision, it is also correct to say that visual training exercises are more likely to lead to a cure for these problems, while colored lenses create nothing more than a dependency. For just as soon as the lenses are removed, the problems come back. It's kind of like looking at the world through rose colored glasses. When you take off your specs, there's the same old stark reality.

Up to now, we have considered therapies that involve dietary modification and visual functioning in the remediation of learning disabilities. It is obvious that these treatments are very different in their approaches. What you eat is emphasized in one and what you see is emphasized in the others. Despite these clear differences, all of the therapies discussed thus far do have something in common. They attempt to remedy academic learning disabilities in roundabout, indirect ways. They are concerned with nutritional and visual perceptual factors that may be "relatives" of aca-

---

[12]Blaskey, P. et al. "The effectiveness of Irlin filters for improving reading performance". *Journal of Learning Disabilities*, Vol. 23, 1990, pp. 604-611.

demic achievement, but are probably no closer than second or third cousins. More specifically, they propose non-educational solutions for educational problems.

Authorities may continue to disagree about the relative effectiveness of the Feingold, Irlin, and visual training approaches to help children who are learning disabled. There can be no argument, however, that children who are learning disabled are first recognized because of problems in academic achievement. Their teachers do not refer them to special education because of salicylates in their diets, lazy eyes, or unusual sensitivity to light waves of a certain frequency. No indeed, children who are learning disabled come to the attention of their schools because they aren't learning to read, spell, write, speak, or do math at a satisfactory level. Then, at least in the opinions of some critics, instead of getting immediate help for their specific academic deficiencies, these children are taken on a trip over a very circuitous route. Fruits and vegetables are removed from their tables, or colored glasses are placed over their eyes. Or, in more extreme cases like John's, they are not allowed to stand up but must inch forward, on their bellies, through a box.

With the best of intentions, we have hoped that these indirect approaches will somehow lead to improved learning in school. But sadly, in too many cases, hopes and good intentions have not been enough. Often, at journey's end, the children come home, still deficient in their reading or other academic subjects.

When the same critics are asked what they have to offer, they urge a more straightforward attack on academic problems. They will say that as of now, given the current state of the art, the best way to help children with reading disabilities is to teach them to read. Immediately. Working *directly* on children's academic deficiencies is likely to be more beneficial that treating peripheral factors like diet and visual perception. It's kind of like not bothering to invite the distant relatives to the wedding, because they're not likely to bring nice presents anyway.

Suggesting such a "frontal attack" is not meant to diminish the possible importance of nutrition, visual perception, or other factors which may relate to academic achievement, nor is it meant to minimize the important contributions that other professions make to the learning ability and overall welfare of children. Such forthrightness simply reminds us that we are at an early stage in our understanding of learning disabilities. The most basic questions about definition and prevalence haven't even been answered yet. This is a time when research findings about remedial methods are ambiguous and equivocal. We haven't studied enough and done enough homework to develop a firm rationale for our remedial practices. Parents are confused, because the experts are too, and until such time as the confusion abates, it would be better for more children who are learning disabled if *educational* solutions to their problems were given primary emphasis. The children need to participate in remedial activities designed to improve academic deficiencies directly. Right now, it does indeed appear as if the best way to teach children to read is to teach them to read.

So, you will want to make sure that your children have a healthy, nutritious diet. Also, you will want to see to it that any visual problems are corrected. But when you're done with those things, you will want to get on with the business of dealing with the reason your child came to the attention of the school in the first place—learning problems in one or more academic subjects.

Many parents with concerns about their children's academic achievement have turned to private learning centers that offer programs in the late afternoon and evening. Sylvan Learning Center is the largest of these after-school programs. More than 500 Sylvan centers are currently operating in the United States and Canada. These are franchised businesses that owners buy from a central corporation. At the present time, they offer a wide range of supplementary education programs to thousands of students; and, since their inception, more than one million children and adolescents have participated.

Let's see precisely what Sylvan Learning Centers have to offer and determine whether any of their services are appropriate for children with learning disabilities. Our objective remains the same: to help you decide if an approach that is advertised as a way to help children do better in school is something that you might want to pursue for your child.

Dr. T. H. Bell, United States Secretary of Education from 1981 to 1984, during President Reagan's administration, is Chairman of the Sylvan Education Advisory Council. Dr. Bell has said:

> Sylvan Learning Centers use curriculum materials and teaching techniques that are among the most effective I have observed. The education directors are carefully trained. The education that is provided utilizes the very best of education theory and practice. The diagnostic materials are excellent. Education is carefully planned to provide both remediation of deficiencies and enrichment. The results have been phenomenal. The increases in grade equivalents in reading and math are outstanding. Study skills and habits have been improved tremendously. . . . Lives have been changed. There are countless students who have been downcast and discouraged when they have begun Sylvan programs. These students are becoming happy, enthusiastic learners. Many who have been afraid to open a book have become avid readers. Personalities have blossomed. Often the shy, mumbling child has become the extrovert. . . . I believe that Sylvan offers to parents and students an excellent opportunity for our youth to gain full benefit from the regular education system and prepare themselves for full and productive lives.[13]

Dr. Bell has certainly been generous with his acclaim of the Sylvan Learning Centers approach. In his quote, he alludes to many aspects of sound education practice: up-to-date curriculum materials and sound teaching techniques, well-trained teachers, thorough diagnostic procedures, and an emphasis on remediation of academic deficiencies. He addresses important, positive side effects on children's personalities, attitudes toward school and learning, and overall preparation for success in life. This is no faint praise; on the contrary it's somewhere between lavish and effusive. His reference to such excellence required a closer investigation.

Over the course of a few weeks, I visited several of the Sylvan centers in the metropolitan Chicago area. I spoke with present and past educational directors of these centers and some of the teachers. These people were extremely cordial and helpful. They were happy to share time with me, and I never felt rushed. I was given full tours of their centers, and I was able to examine the surroundings, the teaching materials and equipment, and the materials used for diagnostic testing. All my questions were answered in a direct manner, and it was my impression that the professional people employed by Sylvan were quite competent, happy to be working there, and sincere in their belief that the Sylvan approach was an excellent way to help children.

I was also able to have brief, casual conversations with four parents and their children who were participating in these programs. Although four families is too small a sample from which to generalize about the reactions of thousands, still, I can say that these parents were pleased with the centers, and the children were happy to go. (One 11 year old boy did frown and tell me he'd rather be playing ball, but that's how 11 year old boys tend to be.) The parents told me they had seen the progress their children had made and would not hesitate to recommend Sylvan Centers to other families.

My visits helped me learn a good deal about the Sylvan Learning Centers. Much of what I saw and heard was very impressive. For example, a wide variety of programs is offered for children and adolescents of different ages and varying needs. For young children, or older children who are behind in school, there is a beginning reading program that emphasized phonics and comprehension. There is an academic reading program for students between second and twelfth grades. This is designed to develop higher level, critical thinking skills that are important in reading all subjects. For children in elementary school, there is a math program that teaches and reviews basic arithmetic operations, problem solving, and math applications. For older children who need further help in math or who wish to expand their existing math skills, there are Algebra courses available. A writing program develops sentence and paragraph writing skills, reviews the basics of

---

[13] Sylvan Learning Center, Advertising Brochure, Front insert, 1991.

punctuation and grammar, and encourages creative written expression. For preteens and adolescents further along in school there are courses designed to develop study skills, help students with time management and organization, and teach strategies useful in taking tests. For students getting ready to apply for colleges, Sylvan offers SAT and ACT reviews.

These courses are supported by a full complement of materials and equipment. The textbooks, workbooks, math manipulatives, computer software and hardware were recent and no less complete and appealing than those I have seen in excellent public and private schools and clinics. Teaching materials were neatly displayed and arranged in ways that were conducive to easy utility. The centers were attractively furnished, away from traffic and other noises, and well-lit. The work areas were sufficiently spaced to allow different groups of children to participate in simultaneous lessons without undue distraction. All in all, I felt the atmosphere was warm, yet businesslike. These were places, it seemed to me, where children could be helped to learn better.

There were other things about Sylvan that impressed me. The center directors and the teachers must hold state teaching certificates. Of course, holding a license to teach does not automatically mean that a person will be a good teacher. However, it does mean, at least, that the teacher has graduated from a college or university that offers an accredited course of study in teacher preparation. Certified teachers have taken courses in educational psychology, child and adolescent development, methods of teaching the various academic subjects, measurement and evaluation of student progress, and characteristics of the exceptional child. They have satisfactorily completed a supervised practicum or student teaching. This provides them with classroom teaching experience in elementary and secondary schools, under the watchful eye of an experienced teacher. All other things equal, selecting a professional who is certified to teach children would be the preferred choice over one who is not.

Children who come to Sylvan get one on one instruction from these certified teachers in groups which are never larger than three. This instruction comes after an educational diagnosis, the purpose of which is to identify a student's academically relevant strengths and weaknesses. Individualized goals are written into a program plan for each child, and instruction is geared toward utilizing a child's academic strengths while working to remedy his or her weaknesses.

Sylvan recognizes the importance of regular communication with parents and schools. After every 12 hours of instruction, parents will be invited in for a conference with the center director or assistant director. Progress is reviewed and plans for the future are discussed. After 36 hours of instruction, but only with the consent of the parents, a conference will be held at a child's school. The objectives are to keep the teachers at the school apprised of progress and to assure that there is consistency between teaching methods applied at school and in the center.

A formal reevaluation of academic achievement is also done after 36 hours of instruction. Tests are administered to quantify the degrees of progress children have made, determine if continued contact with the center is necessary, and, if so, pinpoint areas in which children need further assistance. The results of the retests are also used to determine whether parents can take advantage of one other option offered at Sylvan Learning Centers. This is the Sylvan guarantee which promises that children who are enrolled in basic reading or math programs will improve at least one full grade in reading comprehension, vocabulary, math computation, or math applications after the first 36 hours of instruction. If the results of these standardized and nationally normed achievement tests do not indicate one year of progress, Sylvan will provide 12 more hours of instruction at no further cost to the family.

Humorous stories or jokes can be classified into different categories. There are ethnic jokes, dirty jokes, one liner jokes, knock-knock jokes, and good news-bad news jokes. As an example of the last category, a gentleman is talking with his physician on the phone. The doctor says, "I've got good news and bad news for you. The good news is that you've only got 24 hours to live". In an obviously shocked state, the patient replies, "If that's the good news, what could the bad news possibly be?" The doctor answers, "I forgot to call you yesterday".

My investigation of Sylvan Learning Centers, like the gentleman's physical examination, did not provide news that was all good. While I believe there is much that is very good, indeed excellent, about the services they have to offer, my visits did result in some areas of concern. Some bad news, if you will.

Sylvan centers are not exclusively or even primarily concerned with the problems of children who are learning disabled. They do not claim to be; the center directors I spoke with were quite open in admitting that children with learning disabilities might need special educational services that were different from what they had. Each center is, after all, operated as a business venture, and like any other business, they need to sell their product to the largest possible group of consumers in order to maximize their profits. Therefore, the market they seek cannot be restricted solely to those with learning disabilities but must include **all** children and youth who need or want supplementary educational services for any reason.

There are many aspects of program operation at Sylvan which indeed indicate that children with learning disabilities are not their primary concern. First, the diagnostic testing that is done before a student begins the sequence of prescribed lessons does not include the administration of any tests that are typically part of an LD evaluation. After meeting with a student and the parents, reviewing records, and talking with school personnel, if the need for special education testing seem indicated, the parents will be referred elsewhere.

Second, special education certificates that are required of teachers who have been specially trained to teach children with learning disabilities are not a prerequisite for employment at Sylvan. While it is true that their teachers must hold general state teaching certificates, at the present time, the course of study that leads to such certification requires only one introductory survey course in special education. As someone who has taught that survey course more times than I can count, I know that it covers all areas of childhood exceptionality—mental retardation, deafness, blindness, emotional disturbance, etc.—and coverage of learning disability is necessarily limited to a cursory lecture of about three hours. Someone with a general teaching certificate, therefore, will not have been exposed to special diagnostic techniques or teaching methods used in teaching children with learning disabilities. Again, I must emphasize that having a special certificate does not always make one a more effective teacher than a person who doesn't have one, but, on balance, there is something to say for the advisability of relying on specialists for special problems.

Third, Sylvan does not limit its services to children who are behind in school. A large percentage of their clientele, as many as half at the centers I visited, do not have academic problems at all. These children don't come to the centers for the remediation of learning disabilities; instead, their parents bring them for enrichment activities. At a time when higher education is being pursued by almost everyone, competition for entrance to colleges and universities has naturally increased. So, concerned parents, hoping to give their children a leg up on the competition, enroll their students at Sylvan. This is fine, but it is also a further example of the broader market, beyond children who are learning disabled, that the centers hope to attract.

Fourth, there is the question of fees. Currently, the charges for lessons at Sylvan Learning Centers range from $33.00 to $37.00 per hour. The diagnostic evaluation at the beginning is an additional $160.00 to $185.00. If the amount charged for diagnosis is spread over the duration of the lessons, it is fair to say that parents would be looking at fees of about $40.00 per hour. Assuming that a student comes to a center 3 times a week for a total of 48 lessons that are spread over 16 weeks, the bill would come to $480.00 per month, and the total would be $1,920.00. Generally, none of this money would be reimbursed by health insurance policies.

Businesses exist to make profits. To use an overworked phrase, "That's the bottom line". Professional people are entitled to charge fees for their services. That's one of the things that makes them professionals. And, relative to current charges for medical, legal, and psychological services, the fees at the Sylvan Learning Centers are not out of line. It's just that many people would not be able to afford an extra $500.00 per month, even if they could be guaranteed that their children's learning problems would be remedied.

When Willie Sutton, the notorious bank robber, told authorities he robbed banks because "that's where the money was", he got it exactly right. Although larcenous, Willie was no fool. And, neither is Sylvan, for they too have gone where the money is. Of 13 centers serving the Chicago metropolitan area, most operate in affluent suburbs, and not one is located within the city limits. Apart from any question of the effectiveness of their methods for the remediation of learning disabilities, it seems clear that children with learning disabilities from poor families could not possibly benefit to the same extent as children with learning disabilities from rich ones. That is also, I'm afraid, the bottom line.

Finally, to me, giving parents a guarantee of one years growth in a child's academic achievement is a very questionable practice. Guarantees are for simple things like new cars, toasters, and washing machines. Learning and academic achievement in children result from very complex neurological factors that are made even more complicated by environmental influences such as the differing degrees of motivation that children exhibit and the differing qualities of teaching they receive at home and at school. I think Sylvan is mistaken and would be well-advised to rethink their policy of offering a guarantee. While it may be attractive as a marketing technique, at the same time, it opens the door for criticism and suspicion.

I'd like to know, for example, if the same achievement test that is administered to a child at the beginning of instruction is the one that is given 36 weeks later to verify if a year's growth in academics has occurred. If such is the case, it is possible that some of a child's academic growth would not be attributable to the Sylvan lessons at all but simply due to practicing the same test twice. I'd also like to know if the same people who are responsible for teaching a child, and therefore have a vested interest in satisfying the stipulations of the guarantee, are the ones who do the testing. It would be better if an outside person, with no stake in the outcome, were brought in to measure the precise degree of academic growth.

These questions should not be taken as a condemnation of the Sylvan Learning Centers. They do help a lot of children and their families. I just wish they would be satisfied with that assistance; it is a very significant accomplishment that is tainted and diminished by offering a guarantee. You may remember that Billy's mother closed her narrative by reminding parents that there are no guarantees when it comes to learning disability in a child. She was correct.

So, after all the good and bad news is aired, the initial question remains: Would parents of children with learning disabilities be wise to enroll their students at a Sylvan Learning Center? I'm certain there would be some benefits for the children. They will have skillful, caring teachers in a small group situation. Whatever academic skills have already developed will be practiced. Consistent and healthy doses of positive reinforcement for effort will help increase confidence and self-esteem. Study habits and organization skills are likely to improve.

I'm also certain that there would be benefits for parents. Anxiety levels in parents usually diminish as they take concrete steps to help their children. Tension between parents and children resulting from nightly tutoring sessions at home or battles over unfinished homework assignments would be reduced. Having an advocate at Sylvan who is available to discuss problems and willing to cooperate and share information with teachers in school can be comforting and helpful to parents.

These are important benefits to children and parents, and they must be carefully considered in the decision to enroll your child. What you must also consider is the probability that despite these benefits, at the end of the course, your child's learning disabilities are just as likely to be present as they were before. Learning disabilities are stubborn and very persistent. They resist remediation even in the face of special teaching techniques that are applied by specially trained teachers. It may be wishful thinking to assume that the Sylvan Learning Centers, without those techniques of teachers, would be able to remedy the problem.

As always, there are no easy decisions, and no one who can make them for you. We have looked at the pros and cons, the advantages and disadvantages, the good news and the bad regarding dietary and visual perceptual therapies for the remediation of learning disabilities. We have also looked at out of school learning centers to see what they have to offer. Now that you are better informed, the hope is that you will be in a better position to make what ultimately must be your own decision.

In the next chapter, we shall move inward through the skull and investigate a therapy that has a more direct effect on the central organ, the brain, the most advanced and wondrous computer there is. Drug therapy will be discussed alone, separate from any other treatment, because it is the most controversial therapy of all.

# Chapter 6

# *Outside of School: Medication*

There is a film called "Hyperactivity" produced by the CIBA pharmaceutical company. Its purpose is to explain the problem to parents and prospective teachers. The film shows interviews with physicians and hyperactive children who are asked to comment on the problem and give what they think may be the causes. One of the doctors says, with obvious assurance, "Hyperkinetic impulse disorder is due to disinhibition of the diencephalon as opposed to cortical control". An 11 year old hyperactive boy says, through obvious tears, "It's just the way I am; I feel weird when I have to sit still."

Maybe they're both right, but, for me, the boy's explanation is surely more meaningful. He tells us that he has no control over the matter, and he would change if he were able. It is easy to see his sadness and sense his frustration. There are many others like him. In the film it says "theirs' is a life without harmony". They suffer throughout their early lives, unable to manage their impulses and actions, blamed for disruptive behavior, often shunned by their classmates, and sometimes punished by their teachers. We need to try to understand this problem, at least to the extent of recognizing that it isn't their fault.

As you know, the current belief of most people studying learning disability is that neurological dysfunction is the source of the problem. Although not a unanimous opinion, it is widely held that certain aspects of this neurological dysfunction, specifically biochemical irregularities in the brain, operate to increase the activity levels of children. They become hyperactive. The hyperactivity reduces a child's attention span (Attention Deficit Hyperactivity Disorder, shortened to ADHD, is now the preferred term), and the resulting inability to process information for long enough periods contributes to the learning disability.

The relationship between hyperactivity and learning disability is not a simple one. They are not always coincidental; that is, both problems are not necessarily present at the same time in the same child. Furthermore, hyperactivity is a characteristic that is not found exclusively in children with learning disabilities. If you were to read about other disabilities like mental retardation, autism, and emotional disturbance, you would discover that hyperactivity is considered a characteristic that is commonly associated with those problems as well. In fact, some authorities contend that hyperactivity is a problem that goes along with almost every pediatric disorder.

The following statistics will help clarify the relationship between learning disability and hyperactivity: 1) Currently, the estimate is that somewhere around three to five percent of all children are hyperactive, 2) Among this three to five percent of hyperactive children, the best guess is that about one third are learning disabled, and 3) Among the population of children who are learning disabled, but have no other disability, about twenty percent are hyperactive.

So, while it is correct to say that there is not a perfect overlap between learning disability and hyperactivity; still, there are many children in whom both problems exist concurrently. Without help, the behavior of these children will make child rearing somewhat less than a perfect joy for mothers and fathers. These are parents who are likely to learn the true meaning of exhaustion and who come to value peace and quiet as if they were rare and precious gems. The same behavior also increases the amount of frustration and anger in teachers. There will be difficult days in the classroom as the best planned lessons are ruined by children with high energy levels who are impulsive and difficult to manage.

To help children manage their own behavior, lessen the parental frustration, and quiet the teachers' classrooms, a large number of young people are being medicated. Several recent surveys report that one to two percent of all elementary school children are given drugs to reduce their hyperactivity.[14] This is a percentage that translates into hundreds of thousands of children.

It is this use of stimulant drugs as a treatment to manage hyperactivity, attention deficits, and learning disability that we shall discuss next. As you would expect, it is quite a controversial therapy. Before examining both sides of the issue, it would be a good idea to describe the behavior of hyperactive children in more detail. In the classroom and at home, what are they like? We need to take a closer look at hyperactivity and the dilemmas it creates for teachers, for parents, and, of course, for the children.

When teachers are asked to prioritize aspects of their jobs they consider important, maintaining order and discipline is usually close to the top of the list. Disruptive children who are difficult to manage are a primary source of job dis-

---

[14]Gadow, K.D. *Children on medication: Vol.1, Hyperactivity, learning disabilities, and mental retardation.* San Diego, College-Hill 1986.

satisfaction. Two or three hyperactive children in a classroom have helped more than a few teachers set land speed records for exiting school buildings on Friday afternoons at three. Whooooosh! And, the same teachers do not have quite the same spring to their steps when they return to school the following Monday morning at eight. In fact, you have probably encountered speedier escargot. The teachers will never admit it, but some are hoping in their heart of hearts that the little flesh and blood dynamos broke down over the weekend. Not a dread disease or anything; maybe something like a recurrent bad cold with a fever or an upset stomach that lasts until June.

The typical classroom is a place with a lot of rules. Depending upon the teacher's personality, need to maintain control, years on the job, and amount of remaining sanity, these rules are more or less strictly enforced to govern behavior. Examples are "sit still", "pay attention", "no talking", "stay in a straight line", "wait your turn", and "shhhhhhhhh". These are common and have been around for a long time; almost certainly you heard them during your own years in elementary school.

After we graduated, other rules made their way into the classrooms of today's youth. Included are "no make-up", "no short shorts", "no pony tails", and "no earrings", which, amazingly, are now being applied equally to students of both sexes. Most recently, we have had to add "no guns or knives" to the list of school rules. The enforcement of this one is assured by security guards manning metal detectors at the entrances. In one generation, teachers have had to switch from "put away your tops, yoyos, and trading cards" to "put away your weapons".

Concerns about learning and learning disability are placed on the back burner when children and their teachers no longer consider their classrooms and school corridors to be secure havens and are worried about finding a safe route home after school. It is true that at many schools, young people feel as if their personal wellbeing is at risk, and "runnin' for your life" has been added to the list of three R's.

For hyperactive children, the classroom may be an even riskier place than it is for other children. The rules require that they conform in ways that are impossible for them, and the threat of punishment is high. They simply cannot sustain attention and sit still for acceptable periods of time. It's not just the quantity of their movement that may be greater than normal; the quality of movement is unusual also. Even if the total amount of movement is not significantly different from other children, they may get in trouble because their choices are bad. They get up and move around at inappropriate times, without legitimate purpose and without a goal in mind. Their teachers describe them as restless, impulsive, disobedient, unable to concentrate, jittery, or, more to the point, a pain in the butt.

Parents, too, use a series of adjectives that would not be considered complimentary. Moody, unsatisfying, irascible, immature, fidgety, and driven are but a few. Asked for more detail, parents will likely say their children can't sit still, they move their legs, tap their fingers, flit from one activity to the next without finishing anything, don't play or get along well with other children, or behave in a frenzied way as if they have a motor running that cannot be turned off. It has been said that hyperactivity is a dual tragedy, for in the close environment of a hyperactive child, there will always be a set of parents. These are parents who get very little respite from the rigors of child rearing, which, in the best of circumstances are difficult, and when complicated by hyperactivity, may approach overwhelming.

Although some of the research on hyperactivity suggests that it may be specific to certain situations; that is, more likely to occur in the classroom than at recess or after school, many parents will swear that there really is no time when it isn't a problem. Some parents even say that it is a 24 hour problem. After a day of frenetic activity, their children do not fall asleep easily, and even when they do, they are more restless and move around more than other children.

With all of the above problem behaviors, it is easy to see how hyperactivity can have such a negative effect upon a child's adjustment to school and family life out of school. Therefore, it should be no surprise to learn that medication, the purpose of which is to help eliminate or reduce those behaviors, is taken by so many children each morning, with or without their orange juice, as they get ready to leave for school. Nor should it be surprising to learn that many people are very seriously opposed to the practice of having small children, three or four years old and even younger, take powerful chemicals into their bodies every day. Let's look at both sides of the issue in as fair and calm a way as possible.

Those people who advocate using stimulant drugs to control hyperactivity enter the debate with a strong, pragmatic argument. They work. Follow-up studies have consistently shown that about 70 to 80 percent of hyperactive children who take medication improve to varying degrees. Often, this improvement will be evident immediately and is so obvious that teachers can hardly contain their joy. One day there is an unmanageable child, a wild, unconstrained energy source leaving fingerprints on the walls, and soon after appropriate medication and dosage are applied, the same child is able to control his or her impulses and is no longer a problem in class. Teachers walk back into school with renewed enthusiasm and a faster pace. What is it that is happening to create such a quick and obvious change? What is going on in the brain of a hyperactive child before and after the medication is taken?

It is tempting to assume that somehow the brains of hyperactive children are overaroused. Logically, it makes sense that since the overt, observable behavior is so exorbitant, the inner workings of the brain must also be excessive. The brain can be a sneaky devil though, and sometimes just the opposite from what would appear logical turns out to be the case.

Recently, some agreement has been reached among scientists who study the central nervous system. They are saying that the brain of a hyperactive child is actually in a state of underarousal. The explanation goes like this: In the routine course of daily events, there are many times when it is necessary for children **not** to do things. They must be able to inhibit a tendency to respond. They are not supposed to listen to the clock ticking at the same time as teacher is talking, they are not supposed to watch television while they are pouring their milk, and they are not to study the cracks on their desks instead of their weekly spelling words. We are beginning to understand the mechanism that enables children to attend to things which are important and relevant in their surroundings and not be distracted and responsive to less important things.

In the brain, messages are carried from one nerve cell to another with the help of certain chemicals. The chemicals that send messages between neurons are called neurotransmitters. There are dozens of neurotransmitters that have already been identified, and the feeling is that there are probably many more that will eventually be discovered. They all have names like "norepinephrine" that are impossible to pronounce and only the last kid standing in the spelling bee can spell, but it's more important to understand what they do than to be able to say or spell them.

When things are working normally and the brain is in a proper state of arousal, certain of these chemicals **stop** the transmission of unnecessary messages. Thus, as a result of appropriate chemistry, we are able to be behave appropriately. We come to school and are able to sit still, inhibit any tendency to be impulsive, and selectively attend to the learning tasks at hand without being bothered by everything else.

Hyperactive children, however, are apparently using too little of the chemicals that are needed to stop brain messages. It may be because the cells that have the chemical are damaged or the connections between the cells aren't sufficiently sensitive to the chemical, In either case, the chemicals involved in inhibiting transmission of messages are in a state of underarousal, and the child responds to everything in a haphazard, seemingly purposeless way.

The effect of stimulant drugs like Ritalin, Dexadrine, or Cylert is to bring the chemicals responsible for inhibiting neurotransmissions back to a higher state of arousal. The drugs activate the chemicals, and the result is that children are better able to filter out the irrelevant stimuli that were previously so distracting.

Of course, most parents and teachers of hyperactive, learning disabled children are not particularly interested in the biochemical explanation of drug therapy. If getting through the day at school and the rest of the time at home can be made so much easier with appropriate medicine, many people will not ponder a whole lot about connections between neurons, the inhibitory effects of chemicals, and the arousal level of neurotransmitters. It's more like "Hey, if it works, let's get on with it; don't confuse us with the facts, just point out the closest pharmacy". Such a hurried approach is understandable, given the hardships and huge inconveniences that hyperactivity brings with it.

It has been stated that approximately two thirds to three quarters of the children for whom stimulant medication has been prescribed show an immediate and obvious benefit. Specifically, these children are able to pay attention longer, they work more accurately and faster in class, and their fine and gross motor coordination improves. Teachers and parents report less fidgeting, less crying and fewer temper tantrums, less distractibility, less impulsivity, and, in general, less frustration at school and reticence to attend. And, as their ability to pay attention improves, so do their memories. Then, it is only a small step to the assumption that the drugs make children more effective learners.

The opinions of parents and teachers are supported by objective reports of research that have described the effects of stimulant medication on a variety of psychological and physical abilities. Attention span, impulsivity, reaction time, motor performance, productivity in the classroom, the ability to plan and concentrate—all these important areas of functioning have been investigated in controlled research studies, and findings indicate a very high improvement rate attributed to the use of stimulant medication.

With all the benefits that have been attributed to drug therapy, at this point you may be thinking seriously of partaking yourself. As middle age progresses and we get our unsolicited AARP membership cards in the mail, there are few of us who haven't already begun to notice some problems in sustaining concentration, slowing of reaction time, and memory loss, not to mention depressed function and vigor in other, really important areas. You should know, therefore, that the positive effects listed above are not restricted to hyperactive children with learning disabilities. Nonhyperactive children and adults like you will pay attention and concentrate for longer periods of time with the same drugs. (Sorry, for the other problems, you might want to try eating a lot of oysters or ground ginseng root.)

So, where is the controversy? If a couple of pills a day can create positive changes in behavior such that so many children will improve in so many ways, why is there a debate at all? Who would hesitate to help children become more effective learners, both in and out of school, when treatment is so readily available? Indeed, some medical practitioners have forcefully advised not to hesitate, that to hesitate is to lose. For example, consider the following remarks: "To those who have seen the results of such treatment . . . the present limited use of drug therapy is as upsetting as it is unbelievable . . . stimulant drug therapy . . . is the treatment of choice . . . withholding it represents an injury to the patient and his family".[15] Here is one medical doctor who concluded that depriving children of drugs, and utilizing other treatments, psychotherapy for example, constituted nothing short of medical malpractice.

Representative of an opposing viewpoint, here is another statement: "I have never prescribed stimulants for these patients, and I never will... Stimulants merely mask the symptoms without curing the disease... the hyperactive child's problem can almost always be identified and treated if the physician is willing to take the time and trouble..."[16]

The totally contrasting positions reflected in the above opinions capture the flavor of the debate. Here are two members of the medical profession who, in the early and middle 1970s, were obviously at polar extremes regarding the use of stimulant medication for hyperactive children. One said he would never prescribe them, and the other contended that it would be malpractice not to. It's hard to imagine a wider divergence of opinion.

While the extreme positions represented in the above quotes may have softened a little in the subsequent two decades, the controversy continues to this day. Much of the debate comes from a concern about the question of side effects, both physical and psychological. You need to know about these side effects.

You may remember that Billy's parents were very anxious about side effects at one of their meetings with the pediatrician. The doctor explained that the two most common side effects were insomnia and appetite loss. He went on to say that in a smaller percentage of cases, children taking stimulant drugs begin to have head aches and stomach aches. Finally, he mentioned that in a very few instances, severe depression, interference with growth, and cardiac irregularity have been suspected.

The list given to Billy's parents was certainly correct; however, it was not complete. The doctor could have also mentioned anxiety, psychotic-like behavior including hallucinations, changes in liver function, inactivity, drowsiness, dizziness, nausea, lethargy, nightmares, euphoria, dry mouth, pallor, black circles under the eyes, fearfulness, talkativeness, dazed appearance, tremor, and nervous tics. With regard to the latter, there is some concern that children with a predisposition for Tourette's Syndrome, a tic disorder accompanied to varying degrees by repetitive behaviors including throat clearing, snorting, sudden screams, cough-

---

[15]Wender, P. Minimal brain dysfunction in children. p. 130

[16]Walker, S., III. "Drugging the American child: We're too cavalier about hyperactivity." *Psychology Today.* Vol.8, 1974, p. 43.

ing, eye blinking, and the utterance of obscene words, increase their risk of this condition when taking stimulants.

Whereas this alarming list of consequences to stimulant medication appears frequently in discussions of drug therapy, it must be stressed that these side effects occur in a very small percentage of cases. Almost always, children whose appetites wane and sleep patterns become worse will revert to their previous levels after three to four weeks on the medication or with some change in dosage. Sometimes, though, a "rebound effect" is noticed. For example, as the effect of the drug wears off later in the day, a child may become even more restless than earlier. Another dose in the afternoon or closer to bedtime may be required to relax a child enough to permit sleep. This has become less of a problem as newer forms of medication are used that are "time released"; that is, their effect is spread over a longer period of time.

Regarding the reported suppression of growth in height and weight, most of the follow-up studies indicate that if their has been some inhibition, it is very slight, and any losses will be made up during a growth spurt which occurs when children are removed from the medication. Consequently, many physicians will recommend that there be periods of time, "drug holidays" they're called, often during vacations from school, when children do not take their pills. Others maintain that any growth inhibition will be made up anyway and that children must take their medication throughout the year, since there is as much to be learned outside of school as there is within the classroom .

Another of the consistent concerns about stimulant drug therapy for childhood hyperactivity has been the possible relationship it may have to drug abuse later on during adolescence and adulthood. The opinion of most authorities in this area is that despite the logic and legitimacy of the concern, no connection between stimulants and increased levels of drug abuse has ever been found. It is true that children do not report any pleasurable reaction or "high" while on the medication. On the contrary, they place it in the same negative category as any other medicine and are quite happy when they don't have to take it any longer.

It is interesting, though, that the opinions of authorities are not always shared by parents. Read what one mother had to say about her boy who was diagnosed as hyperactive and placed on Ritalin by a child psychiatrist. Incredibly, to me, the diagnosis was made and the treatment began when this child was 11 months old!! This child stayed on the medication throughout his early childhood.

Here is at least one maternal opinion that runs contrary to the statements of those who have downplayed any relationship between drug therapy as a treatment for hyperactivity and drug abuse. In fact, this mother came to believe that stimulant drug therapy and drug abuse were one in the same. Furthermore, it is legitimate to question the judgment of those who would prescribe these drugs to children as young as this one. While the use of stimulant medication for preschool children, particularly those who haven't even reached their first birthdays, is unusual, one has to wonder how it could be justified at all.

> The drug seemed to calm him down but he suffered severe side effects . . . one was suicidal tendencies . . . he also had a loss of appetite and insomnia and he mutilated his hands and fingers. The drug made him so nervous that he kept picking on his nails and cuticles. His skin was torn to his knuckles. . . . When he was five he used to ask me for the pills in the morning, he got into such a habit. He'd say, "I feel so awful when I take them, I wish I never had to take them. I will do anything to not have to take these pills anymore.
>
> When I stopped giving them, my son went through periods of depression, anxiety, and sleeplessness. Then he would sleep all day. He wouldn't get up and get dressed. He would stay in his pajamas all day and not even wash himself. He was extremely unhappy and had pains in his stomach. Some doctors say there are no withdrawal symptoms from Ritalin. . . . If what my son went through is not withdrawal, I don't know what it is. It reminds me of heroin withdrawal on a milder level.[17]

It is difficult to do the kind of research that would provide a definitive answer to the question of whether there is any increased probability of later drug abuse in populations of children who have taken stimulant medication in their earlier years. In some of the studies that have been done, there have not been adequate control groups. In other studies, sometimes the drugs were given to children who were already aggressive, were associating with socially maladjusted peers, and had taken to engaging in delinquent behaviors prior to being medicated. Since aggressive behaviors and juvenile delinquency by themselves relate to higher than normal levels of substance abuse, it's hard to know the degree to which these children would have abused drugs, even had they not been given stimulant medication.

So, as long as we must wait for the type of controlled research that would determine, with more certainty, whether there is any increased probability of later drug abuse in populations of children who have taken stimulant medication when

---

[17]Hughes, R., and Brewin, R. *The tranquilizing of America.* p. 113.

younger, it would seem prudent to at least accept the possibility that such a relationship exists and reserve it as an area of concern. And, if such a concern indeed exists, it ought to be reflected in continuous monitoring and meticulous follow-up of all children who take the drugs. Unfortunately, there is some reason to believe that such careful follow-up has not always been the case.

It is known that in some instances, months have passed between the time a child first takes the medication and the next visit to the doctor. Parents have been allowed to manipulate dosage based solely upon their own observation of behavioral changes without making subsequent visits to the doctor. Sloppy supervision in some families has allowed children to become responsible for taking their own medication. Instances of children saving their pills and subsequently selling them to nonhyperactive friends have occurred. Whereas Dexadrine is classified as a central nervous system stimulant, an amphetamine, and its generic designation is "dextroamphetamine", on the street, it has a much simpler name. Speed. Clearly, it has a market that extends beyond hyperactive children.

Thus, in some cases, it seems that the fervor of those who advocate the management of children's behavior with drugs has not always been present to the same degree when it comes to keeping tabs on the consequences. And, there are other concerns.

Think back to Billy's father. I think he was a smart guy. He was concerned about the possibility of side effects beyond those involving physical development; that is, those consequences of drug therapy that might have had a negative influence upon his son's psychological well-being, motivation to succeed in school, and self-esteem. Dad recognized the potential of the pill to destroy or at least weaken Billy's assumption of responsibility for his own successes and failures. Children on medication for long periods of time may come to assume that it is their pills rather than their own efforts that are responsible for changes in their behavior.

Many child psychologists and other authorities in child development have expressed the same kinds of concerns as Billy's father. They speak of the concept of "learned helplessness". It's an important idea that may be affecting the school performance and motivation in general of many children who are learning disabled. We need to examine this notion of learned helplessness in some more detail.

Failure and the frustration that goes with it are common in the school days of children with learning disabilities. Their perceptual handicaps are not so severe as to impair their ability to perceive differences between their own poor performance in school and the more satisfactory accomplishments of their nondisabled classmates around them. So, on a regular basis, they see themselves as unsuccessful in their academic and social pursuits. Despite initial attempts to succeed, their failure persists, and children with learning disabilities come to believe that there is no relationship between effort and success. Since their efforts do not pay off, why bother? They develop an unwillingness to try to learn new things, and even if they can be convinced to do so, they approach novel situations very passively and with an expectation of failure. No longer seeing any use in trying is what is meant by learned helplessness.

The relative percentages of success and failure in school are very important in determining the factors that a child will identify as reasons for that success or failure. For example, let us assume that you were a successful student in school. You consistently achieved above grade level and your name always appeared on the honor roll. While you might not have perceived that the percentage of your success in school was 100; nevertheless, your efforts were more often fruitful than not, and failure was relatively rare. Therefore, it is probable that you concluded very early that the success you encountered was due to you own abilities and efforts. For you, it was always worth trying, because the outcome was almost always a good one. On those few occasions when you were not successful, it was natural to assume that the reasons were outside of you. Maybe bad luck or a bad teacher.

Now, let us assume that you had some learning disabilities and were not so successful in school. You didn't make the honor roll even once and success was relatively rare. You probably learned very early that it was not worth trying, because the outcome was hardly ever good. You came to believe that it was a factor within you, specifically your own lack of ability, that caused you to fail, so you stopped putting forth any effort. In those few instances when you were successful, you attributed it to luck, a teacher being nice to you, or some other factor outside of you that you couldn't control.

So, what we see is a difference in factors that are thought to be responsible for success and failure. The able learner attributes success to his or her own abilities and efforts and failure to external factors. The disabled learner, the child who has learned to be helpless, attributes failure to his or her own lack of ability and success to external factors. Certainly, the first approach is healthier and goes hand in hand with positive self-esteem.

We begin to understand the feelings of Billy's dad. He was concerned that his son's reliance upon medication might teach him that factors other than his own efforts in school would be responsible for any future success. Despite the possibility of positive changes in behavior like improved attention and less impulsivity, Billy would be learning that his own efforts didn't count; he would be learning to be helpless.

Billy's dad has a point. He is not alone in his concern. It has been stated very eloquently by others: " . . . the easy way out may be the hard way back. For if the current trend continues, our nation will be peopled with millions of young citizens who have learned at a very early age to approach the tasks of learning and living with a fundamental and insidious question: namely, 'Where's my pill'?[18]

Thus, it is possible that for all the short term benefits that accrue from stimulant drug therapy, over the long haul we may be teaching children to shift responsibility for their accomplishments in life from their egos to their medicine. By masking the present symptoms, we may be helping children handle their short term debt. However, there is the possibility that since the basic problem remains, in the long run they still wind up having to pay the piper. Maybe with interest.

There is also the question of how drug therapy prescribed for children may affect the motivation of adults. Teachers, for example.

With the exception of summer vacations when I was much younger, I have never been anything but a teacher. I have taught in affluent suburbs where the drop out rate was less than 2% and over 95% of the high school graduates went on to college. And, I have worked in inner city schools where the drop out rate in high school exceeded 50% and only 10% of the rest pursued higher education. I have known students in elementary schools whose abilities have ranged from severe mental retardation to the highest levels of intellectual giftedness. I have seen "educational innovations" such as team teaching, open classrooms, behavior modification, and new math come and go. With all of the years and varied experiences, I have come to one certain realization about teaching school: It is one heck of a difficult job.

Usually, critics of the teaching profession, those people who buttress their arguments by alluding to our six hour days and long summer vacations, have not been teachers themselves. They may not have first hand knowledge of how difficult it is to be responsible for 35 to 40 children or adolescents especially when that responsibility goes beyond instruction in basic academics to include concerns about teen age pregnancy, drive by shootings, gang recruitment, child abuse, parental disinterest and other social problems that have had a recent impact on school achievement. To those critics, I say, "Come on into the classroom and see how exhausting teaching can be". When they refuse my offer, as they invariably have, I do not hesitate to remind them that without us they might have never even become literate enough to communicate their criticism.

Given the possibility that I am correct in my belief that teachers have a difficult job, and understanding that we are certainly no different than members of any other profession, we will try to find ways to make our work day easier. We may get to school early, before any other teacher, to sneakily hoard more than our fair share of the new shipment of writing paper. We may be extremely kind to the school custodian in order to get new light bulbs right when we need them. We may curry favor with the principal to increase the probability that the three really bad children in 5th grade will be assigned to the *other* sixth grade teacher next

---

[18]Myers, P. and Hammill, D. *Learning disabilities.* p. 427.

September. These things are OK. I suspect that similar motivation occurs in every profession as people attempt to increase their comfort level on the job. But sometimes, we cross the line. When teachers encourage parents to put their children on drugs to control their hyperactivity, this is not OK. We have done this last thing, and it must stop.

In our role as teachers, we are trained to observe the behavior of children, and it is our responsibility to inform parents when we see behavior disorders in their children. However, it is not our place to diagnose neurologically based conditions, nor should it ever be our role to coerce or even suggest the prescription of pharmacological or medical treatments. Regrettably, there is ample evidence that this has happened. As an example, one report tells of an elementary school teacher who had three hyperactive boys in her class at the beginning of the year.[19] The teacher said, "I'll have those three on medication by Thanksgiving or they won't be in this class". In November, after teacher had accomplished her mission and was asked how she had managed it, she replied, "It took a bit of pressure".

In my own experience as a teacher of children with learning disabilities in Chicago, I have seen many similar incidents. Often, the first suggestion some of my teacher friends would make to parents of difficult children was to get a prescription for Ritalin from a physician. And sometimes the teachers would continue pressuring parents throughout the school year, even to the extent of mentioning the names of particular physicians, until the parents finally relented. This may not qualify as abuse, but it is certainly misuse, both of drugs and the appropriate role of teachers.

If you have been reading carefully and paying attention to this point, it should be clear to you that the controversy surrounding drug therapy is complicated and has many facets. There are advantages and disadvantage, pros and cons, advocacy and criticism, even from members of the same profession. One hopes, of course, that parents will make their own decision about this form of treatment *after* a careful examination of both sides of the issue.

In the final analysis, it would be good if the tempting attractiveness of the obvious short term benefits of drug therapy would be given less weight than a consideration of the probability of academic and social changes in the long run. To me, the most important question that parents of learning disabled, hyperactive children should be asking about drug therapy is:

> ▸ What evidence is there that this medication safely contributes to *long term improvements in academic achievement and social adjustment?*

Will my child learn better in school and get along better with peers?

---

[19]Ross, D. and Ross, S. *Hyperactivity.* p. 198.

There is sufficient evidence supporting the contention that the majority of children who take stimulant medication show *short term* benefits in important areas. As noted throughout this chapter, they are less hyperactive, less impulsive, and better able to pay attention for longer periods of time. However, it has been stated that the most important gains that could be attributed to drug therapy would be *long term* improvement in academic learning and social adjustment.

Unfortunately, the evidence concerning whether short term gains translate into improved academic and social functioning over the long term is not clear at all. I have not been able to locate a single study with findings that indicated improved relationships with other children or better emotional adjustment in those children who have been medicated for a number of years compared to children who never were.

Appropriately aroused neurotransmitters do not automatically erase a history of emotional disturbance and negative encounters with other kids. By themselves, pills will be very limited in their ability to promote friendships. About the best that can be said is that medication may increase a child's *potential* for improved socialization with peers, because the incidence of really obnoxious behaviors decreases. Whether that potential is realized, however, will depend upon the same set of factors that determine positive social relations for all of us: self-concept, motivation, extroversion, sharing, and other personality traits that people find attractive when selecting friends.

With respect to long term benefits in academic achievement, the results are more mixed. There are at least as many research studies that report no academic benefits as a result of drug therapy as there are that do. As time has passed and more insight has accumulated, it has become increasingly apparent that the relationship between drug therapy and academic achievement is more complicated than previously thought. It is probably naive to assume that it is as simple as "you take your pills and you do better in school".

Some people who have reservations regarding drug therapy have proposed the notion of "state dependent learning". They suggest that what children learn while in a medicated state will not necessarily be demonstrated when the drugs are not present in their systems. The unmedicated state represents an environment that is totally different from the drugged state during which the learning initially occurred; therefore, it is doubtful that the material previously learned will be retained or applied.

If these contentions prove correct; that is, if state dependent learning is a real phenomenon, there would be some very serious implications. It would imply that hyperactive children might "unlearn" or regress when they are no longer on medication. Such an eventuality would increase the tendency to rely upon medication for longer periods of time. The end result would be "you do better in school as long as you take your pills, you do better in school as long as you take your pills, you do better in school as long as you take your pills, and on and on and on".

Further complicating the relationship between medication and long term benefits in academic achievement is the fact that changes in different types of behaviors appear to be related to different dosage levels of the medicine. Reducing hyperactivity and impulsiveness (socially relevant behaviors) seems to require higher dosages than are required to improve concentration and memory (academically relevant behaviors). There may not be one level of dosage that is equally effective in optimizing both social behavior and academic achievement. So, in an attempt to eliminate disruptive classroom behavior, dosage may be so high as to actually impede academic progress. In place of an overactive child with learning disabilities, there is an underactive, but equally learning disabled child. This problem in finding the best dosage is exemplified in the following passage:

> Children who . . . have been on active drug treatment appeared . . . distinctly more bland or "flat" emotionally, lacking both the age-typical variety and frequency of emotional expression. They responded less, exhibited little or no initiative or spontaneity, offered little indication of either interest or aversion, showed virtually no curiosity, surprise, or pleasure, and seemed devoid of humor. The reactions of the children strongly suggest a reduction in commitment of the sort that would seem to be critical for learning. There would then appear to be not only a reduction of the disapproved behaviors that interfere with learning, but also of the desirable behaviors that facilitate it. The net effect on learning would presumably be nil.[20]

Some parents have also reported the kinds of effects described above. They have used terms like "zombie", "robot", "sleepwalker", and "chemical straitjacket" when describing the effects of medication on their children. Most of the time these words are used during the first days after medication begins, at the time when the swift and dramatic changes in behavior are so obvious. It has been suggested that children are so overwhelmed at their "new selves", that they appear to be in a dazed, trance-like state.

On occasion, some parents have even expressed a yearning for the "good old days" when their child was hyperactive. Their "new" child is too quiet, too con-

---

[20] Rie, H. E., Rie, E., Stewart, S., & Ambuel, J.P. "Effects of Ritalin on underachieving children: A replication". *American Journal of Orthopsychiatry*, Vol. 46, 1976b, p. 320.

trolled, too different from the old one, who, despite the problems, was the one they had come to know and love. Usually, with some downward modification in dose, children regain some spontaneity and emotionality, and the parents' concerns about drugs controlling their children decrease.

Once again, it is necessary to stop and ask some questions. What does all of the information on drug therapy mean to you? How can you interpret it in a way that will help you decide whether to pursue it for your child? I think it may help if you consider the following summary:

1. There is plenty of evidence supporting the immediate effects of stimulant medication on the reduction of hyperactivity, impulsivity, and attention deficits.
2. Decrease in appetite and insomnia are common side effects; more serious consequences like suppression of growth, depression, and cardiac problems are really quite rare.
3. There does not appear to be solid evidence of a link between stimulant medication in childhood and later drug abuse, although better research needs to be done.
4. There is the possibility that children may come to depend upon their medicine instead of their own efforts to modify their behavior.
5. Drugs may lead to motivational changes in adults. Teachers, for example, may view medication as a quicker, easier solution to problems than behavioral treatments.
6. At best, long term, beneficial effects of drug therapy upon social adjustment and academic achievement are questionable.

Given the above summary, I advise parents to think long and hard before choosing drug therapy for their children, If, after a careful consideration of both sides of the issue, you are willing to give it a try, understand that medication, by itself, will never be enough to completely remedy the kinds of behavioral problems for which it is prescribed. The severity of the problems which led you to pursue drug therapy in the first place is so great that medication, if it is to be used at all, must only be provided as an adjunct to other treatments including a sound program of special education in school.

Finally, if you do choose drug therapy for your child, it is an absolute necessity that you insist upon complete medical assistance and follow up. A thorough and comprehensive medical examination must precede the prescription of medication. A schedule of subsequent visits for monitoring progress or problems must be provided for you. Just as you are the Boss in school, so too must you be in your dealings with any professional person whose treatment will have an effect on your child outside of school.

# Chapter 7

# *Into Adolescence*

Billy's mother thought about the future. You may remember that she began to fantasize about her son's adult achievements even before he was born. Her adjustment to his learning disability was made difficult when she realized that her grand dreams for him might not come to pass. John's mother, too, wondered what would happen to him. She hoped that somehow the broken wires in his brain would mend, that he would regain his former level of competence and go on to make a satisfactory adjustment as he got older. These boys are unique, as all children are; but there is nothing unique about parents who worry. None of us escapes.

The anxiety and uncertainty about the future that all parents feel may be even greater in those whose children have learning disabilities. It's harder to foresee what might happen as they get older when learning and development through their early childhood years are unusual. Of course, attempting to predict the future accurately is very hazardous business in any case. Parents can never know precisely what is in store for their children. Given that reality, there is still some information that has accumulated from follow-up studies of children with learning disabilities that is useful in at least giving us some clues about what is likely to occur as they mature.

What can you expect? What will happen as your student gets older, moves on to high school, perhaps goes to college, and finally reaches adulthood? The objective here is to tell you as much as we have learned about learning disabilities in adolescents and young adults so that you and your student can make the kind of intelligent plans and decisions now that will benefit everyone down the road.

Begin by imagining an elementary school with a student population of about 600 children. Think about spending a few days there and carefully observing the surroundings and the people. If you were to watch the children in their classrooms and the gymnasium, have lunch with them in the cafeteria, go to recess and attend assemblies with them, walk the halls and listen to their conversations, you could not help but notice the tremendous diversity that was represented. In so many ways, you would see the striking differences that children exhibit. You would be struck by how much they vary in aptitude and talent, in hopes and aspirations, in motivation and emotion, in personality and appearance.

Then, let's say you could find those same 600 people 30 years later. Their diversity, clear and present so early in their lives, would be even more obvious as adults. A few will have achieved to the highest levels academically and vocationally while others will have dropped out of high school and assumed positions on the unemployment rolls. A handful will be wealthy philanthropists, and some will be on welfare. A few will be psychiatrists, and a few will be mentally ill. Some will be selling insurance and some will be selling cocaine. Talented ones will have successfully pursued careers in the arts or athletics, and larcenous ones will be in jail. A few will be teachers (also talented, we hope), others will be in public service, and some will be dead. The fact is that this group, like any other, would exemplify the full range of adult achievement and adjustment.

An infinite variety of genetic factors interacts with countless environmental influences to make every child unique. This is true whether the child in question happens to be learning disabled or not. When students are labeled with terms like "LD", there is the danger of assuming that they somehow relinquish their individuality and become the same. We know better. Beyond sharing the label and some problems in school, children with learning disabilities are just as variable; that is, they are no more or less alike than any other group of children.

Follow-up studies of students who had been classified as LD in school indeed show that they too are very diverse with respect to their adult adjustments and achievements. We can say with absolute certainty that learning disability in school does not guarantee a life of failure or minimal accomplishment. On the contrary, there is plenty of evidence of adults with learning disabilities who have managed to become extremely successful.

However, the same follow-up studies do suggest that satisfactory adult adjustment is more difficult for those who are learning disabled. A larger percentage drop out of high school, do not go on to higher education, have a very difficult time finding suitable employment and satisfying social pursuits, and, in general, have a harder time adjusting to the independent living requirements associated with adulthood. And, there is reason to believe that for many people, including the learning disabled, the transition to adult living is becoming even more difficult because of some recent changes in our society that are having serious effects on the nature of childhood and adolescence.

For a large group of young people, things are profoundly different now. In the relatively brief span of a few decades, some of the rules which used to apply have become obsolete. An example of one kind of change, here is an incident that happened not long ago at a public elementary school in Chicago.

A thin, young girl was alone on the stage in the school auditorium. She stood tall and erect, hands clasped in front of her, with long, black hair hanging straight to the middle of her back. All of us who were present were really impressed with her poise as she waited for silence in the audience. She was in front of a group of 400 of her schoolmates, 15 teachers, and about 50 parents. The girl was almost 14 years old, and she was an honor student in seventh grade. She was participating in her school's annual oratory contest. Students were taking turns making speeches, reciting poetry, or giving dramatic readings of literary pieces they had chosen, memorized, and carefully rehearsed. With a strong voice, appropriate pace and inflection, and natural gestures, this young girl presented the plaintive plea for life of a fetus about to be aborted. Her oral interpretation so impressed the judges that she was awarded the first place ribbon and a small trophy.

The young girl's success qualified her to participate in the district-wide oratory contest. She would leave her own school and go to a central location to compete against other students who had won contests at their schools. However, this trip would require consent from her parents. At least one of them would have to sign a form giving permission for their daughter to travel away from the school grounds. The girl took the form home and brought it back the next morning. Her mother had signed it for her. When the girl returned the form to her teacher, she said, very quietly, "I can understand why the school thought I should get permission from my mother, but I felt a little silly, because I have a 6 month old baby of my own at home."

This is one of the things that has happened. Children are having children.

Any discussion of adolescence today is complicated by the fact that many of the traditional aspects of the passage from childhood no longer apply. The essence of childhood has changed in the last generation. Increasingly, young people don't have a childhood. This is true for many children, certainly not all, not even a majority, but a growing number. And, the trend seems to be continuing.

Another way to appreciate the differences between childhood today and what it was just a generation ago is to look at the kinds of concerns parents had 30 years ago compared to those at the present time. Recently, while cleaning out some old files, I came across a collection of anecdotes I had saved from counseling sessions with parents of children with learning disabilities. These sessions took place in the mid 1960s; the parents and I were discussing the kinds of incidents that had made their parenting a real adventure, if not a test.

One mother told me about her 11 year old son who, in retaliation for what he thought was an unfair grounding, removed all the canned fruits and vegetables from their pantry. Carefully, he proceeded to steam off the labels and glue them back on to other cans with different ingredients. For a few weeks to follow, family members were never quite sure what they would be having to accompany their main course at dinner.

Junior's impish (and I must admit, creative) act of revenge required his sustained concentration for the better part of an afternoon, and mother, who told me her son's teachers had been complaining about his short attention span since first grade, couldn't help but wonder what had happened to it. Strangely, he had been riveted to his "canned goods caper" for three hours at home, and yet at school, he would be distracted from his reading and math lessons after three minutes. Incidentally, this no-nonsense mother was equally creative in devising a punishment that fit the crime perfectly. Sonny boy was required to polish off a double helping of "vegetable surprise" every night as a side dish.

Another mother told me about her 12 year old son who had been banned from a neighbor's backyard pool for bad behavior. His generally obnoxious and rowdy demeanor had included making sounds to simulate escaping bowel gas by slapping his arm down over a hand cupping his arm pit. He alternated between demonstrating this talent, repeatedly pulling on the bra strap of the neighbor's 14 year old daughter, and imitating a whale by spitting pool water on their expensive and terrified Siamese cat.

Everyone agreed, except the boy, that his banishment from the pool had been well-deserved. Mother intercepted him late the next night headed out the back door carrying a pail filled with super strength, liquid laundry detergent. It was immediately clear to everyone involved that the boy was not planning to help the neighbor lady with a couple of loads of dirty wash. We were left to speculate about how much Tide would have been required to fill a moderately sized, suburban back yard with bubbles.

A third tired mother related a problem her son and his friends had with a family across the street. The boys would ride their bikes over the neighbor's newly seeded front lawn as they pedaled around the neighborhood. After a few polite requests to ride elsewhere had no effect, the man of the house berated them several times, made some pointed comments regarding the boys' maternal heritage, and finally threatened to call the police.

The boys, apparently budding macho men who would not be pushed around, thought it would be cute to insert a garden hose through the mail slot adjacent to the front door of the neighbors' home while they were away the following afternoon. Luckily, mom saw the boys out of the kitchen window before they could turn on the water and determine, in their own nasty and vandalous way, whether priceless antiques float.

The truth is, of course, that episodes like these happened in all families, whether the perpetrators were learning disabled or not. They were considered part of the every day "challenge" of parenthood that made us look forward to the time when our little challenges would grow up. Then, they would have their own children and get everything that was coming to them. As somewhat detached grandparents, we planned to sit back in silent glee and marvel at the wisdom and remarkable perception of whomever it was that first said, "What goes around comes around".

Well, sadly, I think, what came around hasn't always been what we expected. As I read the anecdotes I had saved for all those years, they seemed like humorous, almost quaint remnants of a bygone era. They created a mood of pleasant nostalgia, kind of a longing for the simpler days of yore. But now, for some families, they are about as representative and relevant as episodes of Ozzie and Harriet, Leave it to Beaver, and the Brady Bunch are to present family life. Many of the current generation of parents would be thrilled to trade the problems facing them and their children today with those their parents had to deal with. They might even be willing to help steam off some of the labels.

A generation ago Bob Dylan sang, "The Times They are A Changin'". We listened and nodded in agreement. How insightful, we thought. Except we really had no idea what was coming. None of us, including the songwriter, could have predicted the magnitude of the changes we were in for.

Close your eyes and think back a few decades. It doesn't matter if you were a campus radical, blue collar worker scrimping and saving for a down payment, long haired hippie on a commune, or a conservative, first year law student. Whatever your background and however different your aspirations, chances are you had some things in common with your age mates. One of the things most of us shared was that we grew up during a time when the vulnerability of children was recognized. Childhood was a protected time. It was a time without heavy responsibility, a time to play, to go to school, to make friends and get to know yourself. It was a time when we could venture forth and take some risks, but still find comfort in the knowledge that if we stumbled or fell, the security of a stable family would be a safety net to catch us.

We enjoyed the present. During that period of our lives, we experienced what has been referred to as the "lyrical joy" of childhood. We reflected on the future only on those few occasions when some visiting uncle would pinch our cheek and ask, "So what do you want to be when you grow up?" Worry was something adults did. Clearly, the times have "A Changed", for now, one generation later, an increasing number of our children must worry too.

They worry about beginning to experiment with drugs when they are eight and nine years old. They worry about returning from school to a home where one of their parents doesn't live and the other doesn't get home from work until four hours later. They worry about having to assume adult responsibilities like child care and preparing meals for their younger brothers and sisters. They worry about being sexually active when they are eleven and twelve years old. They worry about whether thirteen year olds are supposed to get up in the middle of the night to feed their babies or let their own mothers do it.

They worry about shooting, because they see the carnage every day. They see people shooting at each other, people who get angry and frustrated over important matters like traffic jams on the expressway. They see maniacal snipers shooting down at random targets from high rise, vertical slums. They see gangsters drive by and shoot their friends who made the monumentally stupid mistake of wearing the wrong color clothes one day or pointing the brim of their baseball caps in the wrong direction. They worry about where they can get a gun to do some shooting of their own. They worry about condoms and pills and abortions and AIDS. They worry about dying in a city where one person is murdered every 10 hours. And, as perhaps the most striking evidence of their worry, increasingly, they are dying at their own hands. Each year, a half million young people attempt suicide.

The point is that for many of our children, the joy of childhood is not so lyrical anymore. In fact, for a lot of them, there is no joy at all. What has happened in one generation, across large segments of our society, is that the time traditionally reserved for childhood has shortened, and, in some instances, vanished altogether. We must recognize the effects of these changes on our children, and we need to understand what the changes have come to mean for adolescents, all of them, including those who happen to be learning disabled.

It must be reiterated that the kinds of societal changes affecting childhood described thus far do not yet impact the majority of young people. But, for the growing minority who are being affected, it would do us well to understand that the more traditional and common problems encountered as most children make the transition to their teenage years can no longer be viewed as priorities. It's difficult to convince young people of the necessity to do well in high school and how present academic achievement will relate to future career choices and ultimate fulfillment of the American dream when for so many, childhood has become nothing more than a desperate struggle for survival. I think it was put best by one very bright, very direct, and very learning disabled teenager who said, "Dyslexia don't mean nothin' if you're dead." His grammar may have been a little off, but he sure had a point.

Given the depressing reality that recent changes have created for a minority of our children, let's examine the more traditional challenges associated with the transition from childhood to adolescence that still apply in the majority of cases. These challenges may pale in comparison; nevertheless, they remain difficult hurdles.

Of course, children with learning disabilities get older. Each birthday is separated by the same 365 days that every other child must wait, although you may sometimes wonder why the days seem a little longer at your house. But rest assured, with patience, you will see them grow up. However, you may not see them move out! Regarding this increasing reluctance to vacate the family abode, the following words were a headline over an article in a recent edition of the Chicago Sun-Times: "Young Adults Slower to Leave Nest".[21] The article tells readers something they probably already knew, particularly if the readers are parents with big grocery bills and small closets. You can't get the kids to move out, and when they finally do, there is a really good chance they'll be back.

The article points out that for the first time in six decades, the age at which young adults are leaving home has increased. According to information gathered during the 1990 census, 21% of all 25 year olds had not yet flown the coop, as it were. That figure is up from 15% just ten years earlier. It's more than the fear of homesickness that keeps them whistling their altered version of "There's No Place Like Home" (as long as it's my parents'). Many would like to leave, but a tight job market, sluggish increases in wages, and the high cost of living, particularly housing, have made it impossible for them to strike out on their own.

If making the move to independent, adult living is now more difficult for everyone, there is reason to believe that it is even harder for young adults with learning disabilities. Some follow-up studies of learning disabled young adults between 20 and 27 years of age indicate that slightly more than half are still living at home with their parents.[22] What ever happened to justice and fair play?

It will be apparent, as you read on about adolescent stages of growth, that those who are learning disabled sometimes get a double whammy. The same difficult problems in adjusting that transitions from one segment of the life cycle to another create for all of us are compounded and magnified by the continuing influence of their lingering childhood disabilities. The fact is that learning disabilities can be stubborn and long lasting. They too grow up, but just like the kids, they may be slow to move out.

Suggesting that learning disabilities may be permanent is not meant to be unduly pessimistic or alarming. It's just a realistic recognition of the fact that in most cases, learning disabilities are not transient things. They do not come and go; they are not something that children grow out of. The consensus of those in

---

[21] Schmidt, Randolph, E. *Chicago Sun-Times*, 4-8-94, p.30.

[22] Cobb, R.M., and Crump, W.D. *Post school adjustment of young adults identified as learning disabled while enrolled in public schools.* (Final report) Washington D.C. ERIC document 253209.

the field, people who have watched children with learning disabilities develop into young adults, is that learning disabilities first identified during childhood, or residuals of them at least, will persist into adolescence and adulthood. Such persistence is likely to have a continued effect on social adjustment and academic achievement; however, as children with learning disabilities get older, another concern becomes paramount. For just like everyone else, they must eventually confront the transition from school to the world of work and adult responsibility.

Many of the findings of research studies on learning disabilities in older students are not promising. Often, there appears to be little reason for optimism. This information will be presented as it is, without any attempt to soften or "pretty" it up. As you read on, you may find yourself yearning for a pair of Helen Irlin's rose colored glasses. It may help to resist the temptation if you remember that research is done on groups of people; its findings tell us only what is *generally* true for the group as a whole. Obviously, though, your child is an individual, and there is always the possibility that he or she may be an exception to the general rule. Especially if everyone works at it.

We'll begin our discussion with graduation from elementary school. Those who were happy and excited eighth grade graduates in June move on to high school as nervous ninth graders in September. The fish perceive their relative size diminishing as they enter the larger pond. So much is altered with the onset of adolescence. Students change, and so do their schools. We'll take a look at the students first—all students, including the learning disabled, who are entering their teens.

Adolescence has been depicted as a time of stress and disorganization. A psychological and physical "storm" makes the earlier years seem like a period of relative tranquility. Often, there is the mistaken assumption that the turbulence and turmoil associated with the transition to adolescence apply in almost every case. Actually, the large majority of children handle the passage smoothly, with a minimum of difficulty. However, to do so requires that young people make a number of important adjustments and resolve some difficult conflicts.

First, adolescence is a time to test wings. It is when we begin to reach toward the level of independent functioning expected of adults. Remaining emotionally dependent upon one's parents is "baby stuff"; the idea now is to act grown up. But, for many adolescents, there is a conflict between their wanting to cut some ties with their parents and not being confident or secure enough to do so. Thus, their rock is a need to demonstrate their independence and their hard place is a desire for the continued safety and security of dependence upon their parents.

There is the story of a policeman and a young boy that exemplifies how wobbly and tentative the first steps toward achieving independence can be. The policeman gets curious and concerned when he notices the youngster walking around and around the block. Finally, the officer stops the boy and says, "What are you doing?" The boy politely replies, "I'm running away from home, officer". Of course, the policeman is puzzled. "If you're running away", he asks the boy, "why do you keep walking around the same block?" "Because", the boy says, "My mother doesn't let me cross the street". Like many jokes, it contains a grain of truth. And, if you're the boy, it's not so funny.

Second, there are issues of body image. Puberty doesn't mess around, and it is not always kind. Changes in facial appearance can be dramatic as features mature and baby fat fades away. Pug noses elongate; so do feet, and the word "gawky" comes up in the conversation with increasing regularity. Rapid growth spurts affect the shape of the entire body. Some parents believe that between midnight and six A.M, after the TV and stereo have been shut down, you can actually hear them growing. Since teenagers are often extremely self-conscious about their looks and particularly concerned about how others see them, accepting their new physical appearance can be very difficult. One bad zit may require a three day break from school.

Third, there is emerging sexuality. C'mon, you remember, dontcha? New looks and new shapes are accompanied by new urges. Traditionally, the elders have passed the necessary knowledge down to the young ones. The transfer is exemplified in the following anecdote: A concerned and conscientious father approaches his pubescent teenage son and says, "Son, you've gotten older, and it's time we had a talk about sex". The youngster smiles knowingly and replies, "Sure dad, what do you need to know"?

Until recently, the anecdote could be interpreted as a wry and mildly humorous commentary on each successive generation growing up a little faster than the preceding one. Now, however, things are different. Things aren't humorous at all, because in many respects today's youth had *better* know more than their elders. This generation of adolescents must deal with sexually related matters that weren't even issues for their parents. Things we never even dreamed of. Attitudes of sexual permissiveness have flourished. So has teenage prostitution. Kissing games like spin the bottle and post office have been replaced by oral sex. Schools distribute and give lessons on the use of condoms and birth control pills. On average, teenagers become sexually active when they are 15 and have had four different partners by the time of high school graduation. At the same time, there have been dramatic increases in one parent households, percentages of unwed mothers, AIDS, and other sexually transmitted diseases. The fact is that even if dads or moms are still around, to provide adequate coverage as they speak of sex with their offspring, they will need to know a whole lot more than gramps or granny ever did.

As issues relating to sexuality have changed, it seems a safe assumption that more young people may not be equipped with sufficient knowledge and understanding to adjust easily to their adolescent "awakening". As a consequence, they may be confused. They will worry a lot and devote much time and energy to this new and mysterious facet of their development.

Fourth, and related to their needs to become less dependent upon parents, there is the area of peer relationships. Adolescence is a time to fit in. It is important to wear the right clothes, look the right way, say the right things, drive the right cars, and belong to the right groups. It is not a time to stand out. Physical, psychological, and behavioral differences are magnified in high school. The approach of the "normals" toward those who are unfortunate enough to be classified as "weirdos", "dweebs", "nerds", "geeks", or "dorks" may be described as similar to sharks in a feeding frenzy.

As adolescents strive to sever their emotional dependence upon parents, peer pressures and peer values become increasingly potent influences upon behavior. And, to the extent that these pressures and values do not agree with those being emphasized at home, the probability of conflict and confrontation with the family increases. "You can either wear a ring in your nostril or cut your girlfriend's initials into you hair, but you can't do both!" "Oh yeah, watch me!"

Finally, adolescence is a period when it is necessary to begin thinking about preparing for a career and entering the work force. Childhood fantasies about pitching in the major leagues, being the next Michael Jordan, or even practicing more important vocations like policeman or nurse are reevaluated. Students begin to give more serious consideration to selecting vocational goals that can be realistically attained and are in accord with their maturing interests and abilities. Those with the aptitude and desire to go to college will be faced with more competition and increasingly difficult admission requirements, not to mention increasingly difficult tuition payments.

Each of the above aspects of typical adolescent development, by itself, has the potential to be stressful. Taken together, their combined effects can make adjustment so hard that some people look back at their teen years as a time of pain and frustration. What compounds the problem is the fact that it's not just the kids who change. So do their schools. The changes happening to adolescents take place in schools that are nothing like the ones they just left and had grown accustomed to. Consider the following differences between elementary school and high school:

First, there is a difference in the approach to teaching. In any classroom, there are three major variables that interact as the process of learning moves forward. There is the student, there is the teacher, and there is the subject matter to be learned. As a student moves from grade school to high school, very often, the relationships between these three variables suddenly shift. In grade school, teachers teach children; but in high school, teachers teach their subjects. As a result, high school teachers are less likely to be sympathetic to individual differences between students and may not be so willing to accommodate those with problems.

Second, as students enter high school, they will have more teachers. The close attachments to their teachers that children have in grade school can happen because students have only one or two teachers all day long, for the entire year. High school is different, because students have seven or eight teachers, each of whom may be responsible for five or six different classes and approximately 150 students. The greater quantity of teachers who must teach a greater quantity of students makes close, personal relationships harder to come by. Even guidance counselors have such large case loads in many high schools that they find it impossible to either guide or counsel students on a regular basis.

Third, assumptions about academic abilities and student motivation are different in high school. Students are expected to function as independent learners with less need for constant intervention and assistance from their teachers. They must have sufficiently developed reading skills to explore various subject areas on their own. Higher level thinking skills involving analysis, organization, synthesis, and evaluation are required, and students are expected to apply these skills on their own as they read longer assignments, comprehend them, and retain the material. It is also assumed that achievement levels in mathematics and written expression will have progressed to the point that high school students will be able to apply these tools independently as they gather and express information.

The point has been made that for those young people still fortunate enough to have enjoyed the protected period of time called childhood, their transition to adolescence will be a period of rapid change. They will be required to adapt to modifications within themselves and their schools. The fact that the majority of children weather the storm and complete the passage with a minimum of difficulty is testimony to the flexibility and resilience of youth.

Sometimes, however, there will be a special, smaller subset of adolescents, those with learning disabilities, who have a more difficult time with the transition to high school or may not make it at all. For these young people, there is a higher probability of their becoming statistics when school districts quantify their annual drop out rates. Therefore, we need to examine the characteristics of adolescents with learning disabilities, characteristics that have effects above and beyond those that affect all other teenagers. These are problems that placed them at increased risk as they enter and attend high school.

First, the academic delays that initially bring young children to the attention of their teachers in grade school will continue in evidence when they arrive at high school. More often than not, early remedial attempts will not have proven to be fully effective. It is not uncommon for teenagers with learning disabilities to score four years below grade level on standardized tests of academic achievement. So, at a time when their nondisabled peers are applying their academic skills at a high level; for example, gathering information from a variety of sources, critically evaluating material they have read, and analyzing and synthesizing bits of information into logical sequences and meaningful wholes, teenagers who are learning disabled may still be struggling with their vowel sounds.

It is indeed a struggle for them to complete term projects on their own when their basic sight vocabulary is still limited, when their rate of reading is still painfully slow, and when they can't remember the content of a reading passage even if they are able to plow through it. Quite simply, the type of independent academic functioning that is expected in high school may be impossible when, on a good day, the learning disabled adolescent's level of functioning in academic subjects remains bogged down, no higher than a fourth or fifth grade level.

Second, as students with learning disabilities enter high school, they are likely to bring residual deficiencies in activity level, attention span, listening, concentrating, motor proficiency, language development, and organizational skills with them. Even these prerequisites for academic achievement continue as problem areas. Their effects are described below.

Contrary to an earlier, popular belief that hyperactivity and attention deficits diminished with the onset of puberty, more recent evidence suggests that they don't go away. There may be changes in how they show up; nonetheless, they continue to be present. For example, even in cases where hyperactivity is no longer accompanied by overt, obvious signs of excessive movement, it remains to have an effect upon thinking. The adolescent body may no longer be hyperactive, but the mind continues to be. One high school boy compared what was going on inside his head to the rapidly changing images on a television screen when the buttons on the remote control device are pushed. It's just that someone else with very fast fingers had control of the device.

If anything, attention deficits become a more serious impediment to learning when students get to high school. Often, teachers in high school classes stand in front and talk. They impart wisdom to their students who are expected to sit passively and listen. Given 40 or 50 minute periods in high school and this lecture approach demanding sustained attention for the entire time, it should not be surprising when these students don't do well on their exams.

Problems involving the coordination of fine motor skills have an effect upon the legibility, spacing, and overall neatness of the longer and more frequent written assignments required in high school. Even if typing or word processing skills can be used to circumvent these problems, they will remain to affect note taking endeavors in class. Clumsiness in gross motor skills may limit achievement on the athletic field or dance floor, places where other high school students, those without learning disabilities, can gain a measure of status among their peers and esteem for themselves.

Lingering language deficits in adolescents with learning disabilities have serious ramifications in high school. Reading comprehension and written expression in class require a sufficiently large vocabulary, appropriate utilization of grammatical forms, and the ability to interpret and construct compound and complex sentences. Talking with friends outside of class demands a rapid give and take of oral language skills. Students must be able to shift from standard English required in the classroom to whatever "lingo" their friends are using on the street. It is very probable that delays in these communication skills will have a negative impact upon both academic achievement and peer relationships.

The busy routine and higher expectations for independent study in high school require adequate organizational skills. Demands are placed on students to develop routines to manage their time and systematize their efforts. It's called "getting your act together". When the act requires attending six or seven classes a day, remembering which textbooks and notebooks to bring, keeping track of the multiple in-class and homework assignments, deciding which of these assignments to do first, finding time to look for a part-time job after school, and wondering if classmates go out on dates with those who need remedial instruction from special teachers, it's easy to see how a student who is learning disabled, and therefore likely to be deficient in organizational skills, could be overwhelmed in high school.

A third concern upon entrance to high school is that there will be continuing problems in social adjustment. During the late 1960s and '70s, when children with learning disabilities were first being recognized in the public schools, special education programs tended to emphasize remediation of their academic deficiencies to the exclusion of all other problems. Beginning in the 1980s, and to the present time, there has been growing awareness and concern about other problems that children with learning disabilities have. We know, at this point, that academic problems do not exist in a vacuum but have "spillover" effects upon social and emotional development. Children who are learning disabled come to school as whole children and to focus attention upon only one part, the academic, is to provide them with an educational program that will be only partially beneficial, at best.

The importance of attending to socialization skills is underscored when adults with learning disabilities are asked to tell what aspects of their lives are most difficult for them. Most often, they will mention problems in social adjustment rather than academic deficiencies. Their delays in reading, math, or written expression have less influence upon their ability to adapt as adults than their deficits in interacting with other people. It seems clear that in the long run, a social skills deficit is a greater barrier to successful adult adjustment than anything else. So, it is important to examine the kinds of problems with social skills that students with learning disabilities may bring with them to high school.

One of the disturbing things that many parents notice about their children and adolescents with learning disabilities is their lack of friends. It is not unusual for them to be socially rejected and isolated. The relationships between people that develop into friendships are complex and sometimes delicate. To be satisfactory, these relationships require mutual understanding, tact, tolerance, and a good deal of give and take between the participants. Friendship is indeed a two way street, and lasting friends must be able to walk in both directions.

When children have difficulty in their interactions with others, it is natural, at least initially, for parents to assume that the others are responsible. It is tempting to blame other kids or even some teachers for their lack of understanding and tolerance of disability. In most instances, however, a careful and more objective analysis of social adjustment problems and failed friendships for children with learning disabilities will reveal that they themselves are the ones who are behaving in socially inappropriate ways. Let's see why this is so often the case.

Perception has been defined as the ability to interpret things that we see and hear. It is an ability that is so important in learning that the term "perceptual handicap" has been used synonymously with "learning disability". We have come to understand that in addition to being important in learning to read and write, perception is important in social learning as well. The term "socially imperceptive" has been used to describe the behavior of adolescents with learning disabilities as they struggle with their social interactions.

They are deficient in social skills, because they aren't "tuned in" to the feelings of others. They don't seem able to pick up or interpret subtle cues from facial expression or body language that we use when it is necessary to choose the most appropriate response to people close to us. It seems harder for them to judge the moods of people around them; they may not perceive when classmates are happy or sad, approving or disapproving, seeking company or preferring to be alone. They have been described as lacking tact and sensitivity.

A series of studies conducted over a five year period at the Chicago Institute for the Study of Learning Disabilities tells us more about the social lives of learning disabled students in school.[23] The findings of this research indicate that children with learning disabilities are not well-accepted by their classmates. Just the opposite tends to be the case. When they are grouped or paired with other children in classroom situations requiring cooperation, they resist going along with majority decisions. Their classmates and teachers describe them as nonproductive, needing more interactions with the teacher, and hostile. They blurt out inappropriate remarks or are mean and competitive in group conversation.

---

[23]Bryan, T. In Collin, C. (Ed.) *Keys to success.* Monograph of the Michigan ACLD conference. 1983.

While it is true that the kinds of problems in social adjustment described above will not always accompany learning disability, and, in fact, some adolescents with learning disabilities will have real strengths in the social sphere, more often than not, learning problems and social skills deficits go hand in hand. These deficits are so obvious that parents, teachers, other children, and even perfect strangers are able to detect them after just a few minutes of observing the interactions between students who are learning disabled and those who aren't.

With this truly distressing combination of academic delays, lasting problems in activity level, attending, motor skills, language and organizational skills, all of which are often compounded by social maladjustment, it follows that emotional disturbance is a fourth problem that many teenagers who are learning disabled have in high school.

One of a number of activities that child or adolescent psychologists will use to help verify signs of emotional disturbance is called "Incomplete Sentences". It is a way of encouraging young people to bring their feelings to the surface and talk about them. It might be interesting for you to try some yourself. When you have finished, you can compare your completed sentences to those of an adolescent with learning disabilities who participated in the same activity. All you need to do is read the beginnings of the following five sentences and complete them any way you like:

1. When I'm alone I think about _____
2. I wish I weren't _____
3. The thing that is hardest for me is _____
4. In my spare time I like to _____
5. I wish other people would _____

While this may not be the most sophisticated or valid way of detecting signs of emotional disturbance, the content of the completed sentences is at least suggestive of problems that warrant further attention. One student in a high school learning disability program wrote in the following: 1) what heaven must be like, 2) such a goddamn loser, 3) just getting up in the morning, 4) read books about death and dying, 5) go away and leave me alone.

No degrees in psychology, psychiatry, or special education are needed to diagnose the depression in this student. Any reasonable person in charge of his education would give priority to his emotional problems over his academic disabilities. The bad feelings about himself, the fact that he is so sad and resigned to his fate, his alarming preoccupation with death—all these things are so obvious that one would be justified in being concerned about his safety.

Signs of depression and deflated self-worth are not uncommon in adolescents who are learning disabled. They may not be as apparent as they are in the above case, but the signs are there. Students with learning disabilities must go to school where they are reminded of their deficiencies every day and where they come to believe they cannot compete. They perceive limited respect from their peers and teachers. They view themselves as failures, or, at best, relatively inept compared to their classmates.

The feelings of helplessness that began during their younger years grow during adolescence, and many students give up any semblance of trying and leave school entirely. We find out, from numerous surveys, that from 30 to 50% of students who are learning disabled leave high school before graduation. Compared to the general population of high school students, this is a significantly higher drop out rate. And of serious concern, another rate that is significantly higher has to do with the incidence of juvenile delinquency.

When two things go up at the same time, it is tempting to assume that one causes the other. For example, as more people move into a particular area, pollution increases. One sensible conclusion is that population density causes pollution. Similarly, as cigarette smoking increases, so does the incidence of lung cancer, so we logically assume that one causes the other. (Not bound by this logic, of course, are chief executive officers in the tobacco industry.) Closer to our area of interest, we have examined the rapid and large increase in learning disability in the last several decades. During the same time, there has been a huge increase in criminality across the entire population. Is it possible that a cause and effect relationship exists between the two? To answer the question, we need to consider some statistics describing the general crime rate first:

Since 1960, the population of our country has increased by 40 percent. During the same period of time, however, the number of violent crimes has increased by more that 500 percent. The rate of violent crime in the United States is higher than in any other industrialized country. Since 1990, twice as many Americans have been murdered than were killed in the Viet Nam war.

In many urban areas, it has become almost impossible for law enforcement to keep up with the problem. The police are clearly outnumbered. For example, in the 1950s there were 3.2 police officers for every violent felony committed. Now, just the opposite is the case; there are 3.2 violent crimes committed for every police officer. The fact that Americans own more than 200 million guns does not help.

With respect to this increase in criminality in our country, young people have contributed more than their fair share to the rise. The evidence tells us that among juveniles, learning disabled or not, the crime rate has increased faster than in any other segment of the population. It is the sad truth that the group among whom violent crimes are growing fastest is our children.

One large medical center in Washington, D.C. reports that there has been a 1,740 percent rise in the number of children and teenagers treated for knife and gunshot wounds since 1986.[24] Not long ago in Chicago, an 11 year old suspected murderer was being sought by the police. His record showed a string of felonies including armed robbery and auto theft that began around his eighth birthday. The public was spared a trial, because three days later, the boy was found executed with two bullets in the back of his head. Allegedly, he was killed by a 14 year old who was acting on orders from older gang members who were concerned that the secret workings of their group would come to light in any investigation. Dyslexia don't mean nothin' if your dead.

Given this frightening perspective, we can return to an examination of the relationship between learning disability and juvenile delinquency. At the outset, there are two things about this relationship that must be stressed. First, the large majority of students who are learning disabled do not violate the law. For most, engaging in criminal activity is not something they do as they attempt to adjust to the difficult aspects of their adolescent development. But second, the prevalence of learning disabilities is substantially greater (some studies say twice as high) in juvenile delinquents than it is in non-delinquents. Clearly, there is a connection between the two problems, and therefore, there is legitimate reason to be concerned.

It isn't easy to unravel and understand the connection between learning disability and juvenile delinquency. Once again, it may help to begin with what is known with certainty. With hardly an exception, studies have shown that adolescents with learning disabilities have more problems with the law than their classmates who are not learning disabled. It has been reported that as many as half of all juvenile offenders had previously been diagnosed as learning disabled in school. Furthermore, follow-up studies of delinquents have shown that among those who are learning disabled, there is a higher rate of recidivism and parole violation. Studies yielding these statistics have been replicated more than a few times; what remains, however, is the problem of correctly interpreting what they mean.

Nowhere have I read or heard the suggestion of a direct cause and effect relationship between learning disability and juvenile delinquency. A more logical explanation is that these are two problems which grow from a common core of characteristics. One does not cause the other; they are related because they share some of the same predisposing factors. Poor impulse control, short attention span, low frustration tolerance, hyperactivity, problems in perceiving relevant social cues, academic failure in school—all of these characteristics are prevalent in both groups; therefore, their memberships overlap.

---

[24]All crime statistics from: Greene, Bob. *Chicago Tribune* 5-9-94, Tempo section, p.1.

It is also true that certain variables related to family disorganization are part of the picture. Both learning disability and juvenile delinquency increase when financial problems, divorce, alcoholism, child abuse, and criminality are present in the home. But, what confuses the issue is that even when these variables are held constant; that is, when they are present to an equal degree in both learning disabled and non-learning disabled groups, the incidence of juvenile delinquency is higher in the LD group. This would suggest that factors associated with learning disability itself may predispose LD adolescents to become involved in delinquent activities. The question is: what are those factors?

It is very likely that students who are learning disabled, with all their academic, social, and emotional failures in school, will be more prone to embrace delinquency as a result of their desperate attempts to gain acceptance from a group in any way they can. As limited as they see themselves in their ability to gain approval in more traditional ways, they are driven to seek acceptance, no matter how risky it may be, in what they perceive as the only way open to them. With the powerful need for recognition during adolescence, having a few bad friends is considered better than having no friends at all.

Another factor to consider is that, apart from any consideration of academic failure, there is the possibility that some of the characteristics commonly associated with learning disability create a greater susceptibility to delinquent behavior. To better understand this susceptibility, let's design another research study to see how the link between learning disability and juvenile delinquency may be established.

We'll have two groups of high school students, and in each group there will be 100 individuals. Both groups will consist of students who are equally intelligent, the same age, go to the same schools, and have similar backgrounds. Furthermore, the number and kinds of family problems in both groups will not be significantly different. The only difference between groups is that the students in one have learning disabilities and the students in the other do not.

All other things equal, if the students who are learning disabled in our research are typical, they would be more impulsive, less socially perceptive, more easily swayed by peer pressure, less able to delay personal gratification and engage in cooperative problem solving, less skilled at anticipating consequences of behavior, less able to deal with anger and frustration, less able to see things from the viewpoint of others, and less mature in the development of judgments regarding the rights of others and the rules of society. So, even though it is true that learning disabilities do not *cause* juvenile delinquency, it is feasible to suggest that the above characteristics would increase the susceptibility of those adolescents who are learning disabled to commit delinquent acts.

It may also be that those who work in the juvenile court system, police officers and judges, are not entirely even handed when disposing of cases in which a learning disabled defendant is involved compared to those in which learning disability is not present. This is not to say that a deliberate bias exists, but rather to suggest that without knowledge of the characteristics associated with learning disability, there will be a greater probability for those involved in the determination of guilt or innocence to find against a learning disabled offender.

For example, let's say it were possible to find two teenagers who had committed precisely the same criminal act. One of these adolescents is learning disabled and the other is not. In their initial encounters with the police, and later, in front of the judge, it is likely that the learning disabled offender, with his or her greater problems in verbal expression, relative inability at presenting oneself in a positive light, or tendency to be impulsive and blurt things out when it might be best to clam up, will have less chance for leniency. This differential rather than preferential treatment ultimately contributes to the alarming statistics that suggest a link between learning disability and juvenile delinquency.

Whew! At this point, you may wish to take a break. Anything to interrupt this continuing flow of depressing news. Have a cup of coffee, take a kleenex to your rose colored glasses, rent a movie, or hug your child. Or, with all the bad tidings, perhaps you are thinking about hugging a movie and renting your child.

There is no denying the fact that the research findings do not come together to make a pretty picture. On the other hand, it's not entirely bleak either. The picture is not carved in stone. There are some places to turn and some things to do that can increase the chances that your child's adolescence will be a healthy and productive time; a time that will lay the foundation for a successful transition to independent adult living.

It's almost time to look at the brighter side. We will begin to do so in the next chapter after examining some of the things that have been learned about adults who are learning disabled. In the meantime, it would be a good idea to review the major ideas that have been presented in this chapter:

- For a growing minority of children in our country, societal and cultural changes have essentially eliminated childhood as a protected period of time.

- The majority of children face issues of independence, physical changes, sexuality, peer pressure, and career choice as they make a good transition to adolescence.

- Along with changes within themselves, the transition to adolescence is complicated by changes in schools. Less tolerance of learning problems, more teachers, and higher expectations for independent academic functioning characterize the high school.

- Adolescents with learning disabilities have a more difficult adjustment due to continuing delays in academic achievement, lingering problems with prerequisites for learning, social skills deficits, and emotional disturbance.
- Adolescents who are learning disabled are more susceptible to juvenile delinquency than those who progress through school with less difficulty.

# Chapter 8

## *Adults at Last*

Many groups participate in initiation ceremonies that signify the end of adolescence and the beginning of adulthood. In some Italian families, for example, there will be a large, festive dinner to mark the passage for a young person. At the end of the meal, one of the elders smashes a plate. This symbolizes the breaking of the dependency relationship associated with childhood. In essence, it means that with the exception of emergencies, "You're on your own Buster".

For others, a religious ritual is involved. Jewish people have the Bar Mitzvah ceremony. After several years of preparation under the tutelage of a Rabbi, the initiate reads a selection from the Torah, a holy book. Proud parents, other relatives and friends attend the service at a synagogue. Later, there will be a family party, gifts, and the expectation that the young person will begin to assume adult responsibilities.

Other rituals associated with the onset of adulthood are practiced all over the world. People from cultures very different than ours commemorate the occasion. Among the Maasai of Kenya and Tanzania, adolescent boys and girls are circumcised as they enter the adult phase of their lives. The ritual is an important part of tribal custom. Much planning precedes the event, and it is followed by days and nights of joyous celebration.

The ceremony begins at dawn. Because of the exalted status associated with their future roles as warriors, boys are expected to endure the process without crying out in pain, flinching, or even blinking. Failure to exhibit such control results in much ridicule for them and their families. Completing the ritual is proof that they are prepared to endure the challenges of adult life with courage and dignity. Most of us would agree that successful initiates have been admirably courageous and dignified, particularly since novocaine and surgical scalpels have not yet found their way into the tribal medicine chest. All things considered, we would choose to break a plate, study with a Rabbi, or do just about anything else to demonstrate our readiness for adulthood.

Despite clear differences in the kinds of initiation ceremonies practiced by different groups, there is general agreement regarding the behaviors that are associated with adult status. No matter where adults live, they are expected: 1) to support themselves, 2) to function independently with no need for supervision, and 3) to behave in ways that are not threatening or unacceptable to others in the community.

Here, in our society, the schools play an important role. It is assumed that products of our educational system will move into the adult segment of the life cycle with the ability to do the three things listed above. For some adults who are learning disabled, however, adjustment has been difficult. Evidence from follow-up studies shows that academic, vocational, and social outcomes do not, as a rule, compare favorably to those attained by the general population of adults. Some of the results of these studies are presented below.

Almost all of the research on adults with learning disabilities points to continuing deficiencies in reading, spelling, mathematics, and written expression. Despite early identification in school, comprehensive diagnostic work-ups, and years of remedial attempts by conscientious, well-trained teaching specialists, the fact is that academic retardation remains. Although there will be some variation, most of the time achievement in these areas tops out at around the fifth or sixth grade level.

With this level of achievement, it follows that the percentage of adults with learning disabilities who drop out before graduation from high school has been much higher than in the general population. And, although the number is increasing, compared to the rest of the adult population, those who have gone on to pursue any type of post secondary education at a junior college, technical training school, or university, are relatively few.

Deficiencies in academic achievement are made even worse, because adults who are learning disabled have their greatest difficulty with the *application* of basic academic skills in the workplace and in everyday living situations. For example, even if an adult has finally memorized the multiplication tables and can do problems involving fractions, decimals, and percentages, these skills will be of limited value if that person can't transfer and apply them when handling money, making a budget, or conducting routine banking operations. Similarly, adults' abilities to read and write will be of little value to an employer unless those abilities can be used to comprehend, analyze, and solve work related problems. Furthermore, if those solutions aren't communicated in clear and effective ways to fellow workers and supervisors, the grade level that one has attained becomes largely irrelevant.

Low levels of academic achievement along with problems in applying those skills which have been learned have limited the potential for vocational adjustment among adults who are learning disabled. Most of the follow-up studies have shown higher rates of unemployment and underemployment. Typically, the largest percentage of adults with learning disabilities who are working at all are employed in low level service, fast food, laborer, production, or helper jobs. While it is true that these kinds of jobs continue to be available to provide entry level opportunities for young people coming into the work force, it is also true that most of them do not provide the level of salary required to live independently. The fact that many of these positions are part time and therefore do not provide medical and health benefits makes it even harder to attain independent adult status.

The negative effects of academic deficiencies and difficulties with vocational adjustment are accompanied by continuing delays in social adjustment in many adults who are learning disabled. The social imperception present during adolescence remains in evidence. Adults may continue to be unaware, or, at least, misread the moods, body language, facial expressions, and other subtle, but socially relevant, cues expressed by other people. Or, they may hesitate to socialize, because relating with other people will bring scrutiny. They may avoid social interactions for fear their learning disabilities will be exposed. The secret they have worked so hard at keeping will be laid bare, out in the open. So, they have fewer close friends, and they don't participate as often in leisure time, recreational activities. Compared to adults of the same age who are not learning disabled, they are less likely to be married and more likely to be living in the homes of their parents or relatives.

When adults with learning disabilities are asked to comment on their own adjustment problems and the areas in which they feel they need the most help, they mention things like shyness, dating problems, and lack of self-confidence. Overall, they are much more concerned about shortcomings in the social sphere of their lives than they are with academic weaknesses or job related problems. Giving priority to social skills deficits is certainly appropriate, because finding and keeping a job and advancing in one's career are often more dependent upon interpersonal skills like getting along with others, sharing responsibility, negotiating, and resolving conflict than they are upon the actual vocational or academic skills necessary to do a job.

In summary, the results of follow-up studies of adults who had been classified as learning disabled in school suggest that the transition to adulthood is very difficult. Many adults who are learning disabled are not leading satisfactory, meaningful lives. The majority are not able to support themselves and do not live independently. As the author of one study concluded: "former special education students do not appear to be partaking of the fruits of our society".[25]

---

Yes, I know. You're probably depressed and getting worse. The consequences of learning disability seem to merge into a gloom and doom scenario that just won't go away. This is a tedious, three act play that begins in early childhood, proceeds through adolescence, and continues its long, melancholy run into adulthood. It's easy to succumb to that kind of negative thinking; after all, the research findings are so clear and consistent. They indicate that in every important area of adjustment—academic, social, emotional, vocational, and independent living—learning disability causes persistent problems that ultimately diminish the quality of life for all those who are close to it.

But, there is a brighter side. Be reminded that research does nothing more than suggest what may be true for groups in general. It usually neglects to tell us about those individuals who are exceptions to the rule. The truth is there are exceptions, plenty of people with really serious learning and physical disabilities who are able to deviate from the general pattern and go on to achieve at very high levels. We need to turn to these people, not just because they provide a ray of optimism, but because there is much they can teach us. They are surely the minority, but their stories provide both inspiration and concrete suggestions for helping families cope with disability and ultimately maximize their children's potential for success. The play may have a happy ending yet.

I met an amazing woman at a convention attended by teachers of children with disabilities. Her name is Bonnie Consolo, and she spoke to us about overcoming adversity. A few years later I saw her in a film about her life and on Sixty Minutes on television. At the time, she was married and had two children. She lived with her family in a nice home in Kentucky. She referred to this home as her heaven; it was the place she liked to be the most. She got a lot of pleasure from cooking and baking, shopping and puttering in her garden. She dressed herself, put on her jewelry and cosmetics, and drove her car. She cut her young sons' hair and their food, tied their shoestrings, wrote checks to pay the bills, and played horseshoes with her husband in the back yard. People who lived nearby said she was a good neighbor who was happy to share her recipes for sourdough bread and canned preserves. She said she liked to do difficult things, but when questioned, she had a hard time thinking of anything that was difficult for her.

---

[25]Edgar, E. "Secondary programs in special education: Are many of them justifiable? *Exceptional Children*, Vol. 53, 1986, p. 556.

You're probably wondering what's so amazing about her. What's the big deal? So what if she did the same common, everyday things that millions of people do as they go about managing their daily routines. Most of the time, there is nothing remarkable about going shopping except the prices.

You would change your mind very quickly, though, if you were to see Bonnie Consolo in action. You would see that she has no arms. She was born with nothing below her shoulders. You would no longer consider the things that she does routine and everyday after you watched her do them with her feet and toes. To see her is indeed marvelous, for she is a vivid reminder of how tremendously adaptable humans can be. She proves that there is almost no limit to the things that people can do, even in the face of what would seem to be huge barriers, given that they are motivated and persistent enough.

When Bonnie Consolo is asked about how she developed her incredible dexterity, she attributes it to two things. She believes that being born with her disability, rather than losing her arms later in life was actually an advantage. It forced what she calls "an early and automatic takeover" in her brain. Cells which normally would have been responsible for movements of arms, hands, and fingers were quickly replaced by others that controlled legs, feet, and toes. She maintains that learning to move her lower extremities was just as natural for her as learning to control our upper extremities is for the rest of us.

She also credits her parents for the degree to which she has coped with her disability. Early in her life, she learned important lessons from them. In place of self-pity, her parents taught her to think of herself as unique. They taught her that there was no one else like her in the world (or at least in Kentucky), and that she could succeed at anything she wanted if she tried. She tells us that they adamantly refused to do things for her when they believed she could learn to do them herself.

Intuitively, Bonnie Consolo's parents must have understood the difference between the words "disability" and "handicap". They knew that a disability is an inability to do something, a diminished capacity to perform in a specific way. Without arms, there is no question that their daughter was a disabled person. But, they also knew that a handicap is a disadvantage imposed upon a person. Parents can impose handicaps on disabled children by not giving them opportunities to do things they would be able to do for themselves.

In their wisdom, Bonnie Consolo's parents stubbornly refused to deprive her of those opportunities. Despite the fact that it would have been much easier and quicker for them to dress and feed her, to bathe and groom her, and to write and turn pages for her, they required that she learn to do these things and everything else on her own. So, while her armless condition is a permanent disability, it never became a handicap. She does everything the rest of us do. She had wise parents. They insisted that she be independent. They did nothing to suggest that she was incapable. They allowed her to **take control** of her life. So must you, for the benefit of your child.

On the surface, there would seem to be very little that Bonnie Consolo and her parents would have in common with Indochinese refugee families. Sometimes, however, looking a little deeper leads to a different conclusion. Let's take a look.

For a period of about six years between 1977 and 1983, difficult economic and political events forced many Vietnamese, Chinese-Vietnamese, and Laotian people to flee their homes and seek refuge in the United States. Their escape from Southeast Asia had not been easy. The uprooting was a serious disruption in their lives that often had traumatic effects. In some cases, the process of resettlement took many months or even years. During this time, families lived in relocation camps where the children had no formal education. Many of the children didn't know English when they arrived; they had not been exposed to Western ideas or culture; and their possessions were often limited to the clothes they were wearing when they got here.

Shortly after resettlement, the children began attending schools in this country. One research study describes the academic achievement of these young children.[26] The authors of the study looked at a sample of 200 refugee families who had 536 children of school age. At the time of the research, these families had been in this country an average of three and a half years. Parents and children were interviewed in their native language, and the children's records were gathered and analyzed.

The children were going to elementary and secondary schools in low income, urban areas, cities including Chicago where the school districts have consistently been criticized for the very poor academic achievement of students. Given the emotional trauma associated with their uprooting, the long interruption in their formal education during the resettlement process, their relative lack of proficiency with the English language and exposure to Western culture, their poverty and limited access to what many consider the stimulation and enrichment that come with affluence, and their attendance at schools not noted for superior academics, it would have been logical to assume that these refugee children were not doing well in school, In fact, just the opposite was the case.

Based upon analyses of grades given by their teachers and performance on nationally standardized tests of school achievement, the academic progress of

---

[26]Caplan, C., Choy, M., & Whitmore, J. "Indochinese refugee families and academic achievement". *Scientific American.* Vol. 266 (2) 1992. pp. 36-42

these children was remarkable. Their overall performance in school was at the 54th percentile, slightly better than half of all the children in this country. In mathematics, a subject which requires less language facility, their performance was even better. More than half of these students placed in the top 25 percent in math, and more than a quarter of them were in the top 10 percent, a level of achievement almost three times higher than the national norms. Moreover, the data indicate that this high level of academic achievement had been attained by the large majority of the children, not just a few isolated geniuses who had pulled up the group average.

The kinds of adversities faced by these refugee children are obviously quite different from those in Bonnie Consolo's life. What is clear, however, is that these children had learned and were applying the same kinds of dogged determination and persistence that were required to overcome their own problems and become successful. Of course, these traits were learned from their parents. It turns out that despite a very different set of problems, the children of Vietnamese boat people and the girl with no arms from Kentucky had parents with a lot in common.

A strong sense of family that is guided by mutual respect, cooperation, and harmony between generations was a common characteristic found in many of the Asian families interviewed in this research. Parents were very supportive of their children's educational endeavors, and, at the same time, they had very high expectations. Without much formal education themselves, and with very limited proficiency in English, they still managed to set high standards for their children. These standards were communicated to the children on a regular, daily basis as parents set aside other chores and made a place and time available for their children to complete their assignments from school. Just like Bonnie Consolo's parents, they did not do the work for their children; instead, they created an environment that made it possible for them to do it on their own.

One of the most important characteristics noted in these families was the belief that individual effort is more important than anything else in the attainment of goals. The authors of the research state: "The refugees did not trust fate or luck as the determinant of educational outcome; they believed in their potential to master the factors that could influence their destiny". Again, just like Bonnie Consolo's parents, these people believed that encouraging their children to rely on their own abilities and requiring them to assume control over their lives would ultimately help them become independent and successful people.

You may be one of those stubborn parents, not easy to convince, not yet ready to assume a more optimistic stance. After all, despite their achievements, neither Bonnie Consolo or the children of Indochinese refugee families are learning disabled. There is no reason to believe that the kinds of neurological dysfunction that have been suggested to cause learning disability in your child were factors that were present in their lives. So, to diminish your doubts, we need to look at some information about people with precisely the same kinds of learning disabilities you're seeing in your family.

We know there are adults with learning disabilities who have nevertheless managed to become highly successful. They are people who have achieved to the highest levels imaginable despite growing up in the constant company of their learning disabilities. If we could interview these people, get to know them, and, at the same time, talk with other, less successful adults who are learning disabled, it might be possible to isolate the ingredients of success. We could look back at the lives of both groups and identify, with more precision, those factors that separated the ones who did really well from the ones who didn't. Then parents could have access to that information, apply that which pertains to their own family situations, and increase the probability of successful adjustment for their children.

Fortunately, in the last few years, there has been much more interest in studying learning disability in us older folks. In fact, precisely the type of investigation proposed above has already been done. A very enlightening report of this study appears in a recent article published in the Journal of Learning Disabilities.[27] We'll examine the report of this study in some detail, because there is much that parents can learn from it that relates to the levels of adjustment their children might ultimately attain as they get older.

The authors of the article, Drs. Paul Gerber, Rick Ginsburg, and Henry Reiff, believe they have identified a number of factors that influence success in people who are learning disabled. Their contention is that these factors are not rigid, inborn things; instead, they are convinced they are subject to change and can be taught. If they are correct and these factors can really be taught, it would be extremely important; it would mean that parents would indeed by able to do specific things to help their children and adolescents adjust more acceptably as they move into their adult years. Parents would have more ammunition, a larger number of effective ways of dealing with the problem early that might make for a better adjustment, despite learning disability, later.

The study began by finding a group of successful adults with learning disabilities. These people were identified as the result of a search that covered all of North America. Nominations came from several organizations including The National Network of Learning Disabled Adults, The Orton Dyslexia Society, and The Learning Disabilities Association of America. Other nominations came from people teaching in colleges of education and from other institutions or individu-

---

[27]Gerber, P. et al. "Identifying alterable patterns in employment success for highly successful adults with learning disabilities." *Journal of Learning Disabilities*, Vol. 25 (8), 1992, pp. 475-487.

als who had contact with people who were learning disabled. This search resulted in an initial group of 181 people. Understand that all of these individuals were contacted, because, in the opinions of those who were conducting the investigation, they were successful, although learning disabled, adults.

Each of these people participated in an initial telephone interview that lasted about 40 to 50 minutes. Their age, race, gender, educational history, current employment, and annual income were noted. They gave information about their degree of job satisfaction, recognition they had achieved in their fields, and their parents' occupational levels. They also responded to questions about the severity of their learning disabilities, their type of learning disability (reading, writing, math, speaking, hyperactivity, attention deficit, etc.), when and how they were initially diagnosed as learning disabled, and whether they had any other disabilities such as defective eyesight, hearing, or movement problems.

The information gathered during these initial phone conversations was used to place candidates for further participation in the project into either of two groups: 1) a *high* success group, or 2) a *moderate* success group. Determining the degrees to which different people are successful will always be somewhat subjective, but such a determination can be made more precise by relating success to specific criteria. In this study, the authors chose five criteria to use as measures of success. These were: 1) level of education, 2) job status, 3) income level, 4) prominence in one's field, and 5) job satisfaction. Objective standards were set so a panel of five experts could rate each of the 181 candidates as either *high, medium,* or *low* on each of these five criteria. Then, to be placed in Group 1, the high success group, a candidate had to have a *high* rating on at least four of the five criteria and no rating of *low*. Candidates were placed in Group 2, the moderate success group, if the panel of experts gave them a majority of *moderate* ratings on the five criteria and no more than one *low* rating.

This time consuming effort was necessary in order to establish groups of adults between whom a reliable distinction could be made with some confidence. Now, as a result of the detailed rating system they used, the authors of the study could be reasonably certain in contending they had identified two groups of people who were really different. One of these groups was made up of highly successful adults with learning disabilities and the second consisted of adults with learning disabilities who had attained more moderate degrees of success.

The number of people in the study was reduced by only including individuals in the high success group who could be matched on age, gender, race, severity of learning disability, type of learning disability, parental occupation, and socio-economic status with individuals in the moderate success group. This matching process is common in research studies. The purpose of it is to be as certain as possible that individuals in both groups are the same on all important dimensions except the one variable being investigated. In the study, that one thing was the degree of success (either high or moderate) achieved by adults with learning disabilities.

The matching process reduced the number of participants to a final total of 71 people. Of these, 46 were highly successful and 25 were moderately successful. Having almost twice as many highly successful adults was something the authors of the study had planned for, since they were most interested in determining those factors that characterized people who, notwithstanding their learning disabilities, had really "made it big" compared to those who were doing OK but not setting the world on fire.

The 71 participants came from 24 states and Canada. The following information applies to the adults in the high success group: In this group, there were 32 men and 14 women who ranged in age from 29 to 67 and had reached an average age of 45 years. They were employed in 26 different occupations, and their annual incomes ranged from $30,000 to over $100,000. Almost half (21) of these people were earning more than $100,000 a year. With respect to educational levels, 2 had graduated high school, 3 had some college, 9 earned bachelor's degrees, 2 had some graduate credits, 2 had master's degrees, 2 had some credits beyond the master's, and 26 had Ph.Ds or M.Ds. (Not too shabby for LD, wouldn't you say?)

In the moderate success group, there were 16 men and 9 women spanning an age range of 34 to 59. Their average age was 44 years. Their range of annual income was $10,000 to over $100,000 with half earning between $40,000 and $50,000. One had graduated high school, 1 graduated high school and had some college credits, 1 earned a degree from a junior college, 4 earned bachelor's degrees, 15 had their master's, and 3 had either a Ph.D. or M.D.

With the completion of this preliminary phase of the study, the main thrust of the investigation began. Interviewers were carefully trained, and they traveled to participants' home towns to conduct their interviews. Each of the 71 participants responded to a series of 130 open ended questions during audio-taped sessions that lasted anywhere from 3 hours to nearly 8 hours. The average amount of time required for an interview was 4 and 1/2 hours. As a way of reducing possible effects of bias stemming from preconceived opinions or expectations, neither the interviewers or the participants knew who was in the high success or moderate success groups.

Participants were asked questions relating to nine general categories: 1) reasons for their success, 2) their jobs, 3) education, 4) family, 5) social adjustment issues, 6) emotional disturbance, 7) feelings about their own disabilities, 8) problems they had encountered in daily living, and 9) recommendations they would make to parents, teachers, and employers of people with learning disabilities. The responses (researchers call this information "raw data") of the 71 participants to the 130 questions across these 9 general categories were analyzed in order to: 1) identify factors that lead to successful adjustment in adults with learning disabilities, and 2) isolate factors that distinguished between those who were highly successful adults and those who were moderately successful.

Now we come to the good part, the results. What did the authors of the study learn about factors influencing success in adults with learning disabilities? And, most importantly, what are the implications of what they learned for parents of children who are learning disabled?

Remember that at the start of the study, the investigators suspected that high success in adults with learning disabilities might be the result of a separate set of factors than those that are responsible for moderate success. This did *not* prove to be the case. Results of the study showed that there was only one set of factors relating to the successful adjustment of adults with learning disabilities. It turned out that those adults who had managed to become highly successful hadn't done *different* things than those who were moderately successful; instead what they had done was more of the *same* things, only better. With only one set of factors to consider, the results of the study are less complicated and the implications for parents become more obvious. Now, we can specify what those factors are.

One factor was always present in the lives of successful adults with learning disabilities. More than anything else, the thing that is key to their success is **control.** These people grabbed experience by the throat and stubbornly took responsibility for their own adjustments. (Just like Bonnie Consolo and Vietnamese refugee children.) In place of passively waiting for life to happen and yielding to the obstacles that learning disability creates, they were able to overcome them by actively controlling their own destinies.

The authors of the study define control as "making conscious decisions to take charge of one's life and adapting and shaping oneself to move ahead." Success does not just happen as a result of a lucky combination of chance events. On the contrary, successful adults who are learning disabled decide to confront their disabilities head on, they are tenacious in their desire to overcome them, and they formulate a clear plan to do so.

One of the participants in the study worked as the chief executive officer for a bank. He commented on the kind of desire that is required. "I'm a real believer in determination", he said. "It is three fourths of the battle. There are tons of geniuses in the world who never make it and there are lots of people with personality who don't either. The difference between making it and not is determination . . . you absolutely have to stick with it."

Often, we hear the words "burning desire" in descriptions of people who seem driven to get ahead. And interestingly, several of the very successful adults in this study alluded to fire when describing their motivations to succeed. "I've always had a kind of burning feeling . . . kind of like being on fire to be successful", one said. Another said, "If the fires of your drive go out, you will lose your self-respect". A third said, "You fight until you can't fight anymore, and then you fight some more . . . you take the hurt and turn it inward and it becomes part of the burn . . . it has to burn."

Here we see clear evidence of the power of motivation. A strong drive to succeed may not always be reflected in superior results on IQ tests, nor does it necessarily relate to high levels of academic achievement. Instead, these people tell us that the process of becoming successful starts by making a choice. What turned out to be most important for adults with learning disabilities was their firm decision to take responsibility for their lives. They "got after it" without making excuses, whimpering, or learning to be helpless. Their message is clear: To ultimately become successful, one begins by choosing to be.

Knowing where they wanted to go and how to get there was part of their stubborn motivation to get ahead. Setting goals, both long and short-term, was a strategy that was consistently applied by the successful adults in this study. Often, they had set their goals in a sequence that became progressively more difficult; that is, achieving their goals had been gradually more challenging. Being successful on minimal goals in the near term provided the foundation for the more challenging goals they had set for themselves later on. With each success, they grew more confident that their long term goals were realistic and attainable. And, as it turned out, they were correct.

What they practiced is a very practical approach to achievement. It's good to have a vision for yourself in the future, even a lofty aspiration is OK; but then sit down and specify the steps to be taken in the present and immediate near term. One man in the study explained, "Successful people have a plan, goals, strategy, otherwise you are flying thorough a cloud and then you hit a mountain". A similar idea was expressed by another participant who happened to be a psychologist. He said, "You should link efforts to outcomes . . . stay in your areas of strength".

The authors of the study go on to tell us that adults with learning disabilities did what they called "reframing" along the way to becoming successful. Reframing refers to" . . . reinterpreting a learning disability experience in a more productive and positive manner". It is a process during which people change perspective about their problem and make the absolute best out of a bad situation. In reframing, people with learning disabilities come to understand that the disability is only one part of their personalities, and by itself, will not be the basic difficulty they encounter. Instead, what can become the real problem is an inability to confront and overcome the challenges they face as they learn to live with it. In short, they did not allow their disabilities to become handicaps.

Those adults who were able to reframe their learning disabilities passed through a number of stages, and in some instances, the process was very difficult and took them a long time. Early in the process, they had to recognize and accept their disabilities. They realized that they learned in a different way, did things differently than other people, and that it was quite all right to be different. One successful adult summed it up this way: " . . . You are not going to succeed out there if you can't look at yourself in the mirror. If you can't deal with who you are and recognize your gifts and disadvantages, you are not going to make it".

It seems clear that until people come to grips with the fact that their disabilities are real and are something they are likely to be faced with forever, moving ahead may be very difficult, if not impossible. With this acceptance comes a better understanding of strengths and weaknesses. For example, an attorney who was learning disabled said, "As a dyslexic, you have to accept the degree to which you will and won't succeed in life. The biggest advantage is that once you realize you can't do all these things, you become good at finding alternative solutions and at making the most of what you have. . . . I think the anger, sense of injustice, and wisdom that situation has given me has helped me. . . . "

Think of reframing as an enabling process. It only goes as far as to put people in a position to take action. Subsequently, though, it remains up to them to take it. Appropriate levels of recognition and self-acceptance will be of no use whatever unless a person actively takes steps toward the attainment of goals. The adults in this study all chose to **do** things in order to get what they wanted. To gain control of their lives, these successful people took their newly reframed attitudes and put them into action in the form of some very concrete behaviors. We'll examine those behaviors next.

It was quite obvious that successful adjustment for these adults with learning disabilities had not come easily. There were many frustrations and failures along the way, but these did not deter them from pursuing their goals in a resilient and determined way. Pick whichever of the following terms you prefer: persistent, stubborn, willful, headstrong, unyielding, hard working, pigheaded. They all mean about the same, and they certainly apply to the people in this study. What came through in their interviews was the fact that their success came from their willingness to do whatever it took to get what they wanted and their ability to work harder than anyone else they knew. Statements like: "I overcame my problem with sheer grit and determination", I made accomplishments by working harder than others and gutting it out", and "I never stop trying. . . . I have an incredible amount of persistence" were very common.

Reread the three preceding quotes and you'll see the word "I" in each of them. Consistent reference to oneself could be interpreted to mean that these hard driving, success oriented adults were somewhat selfish and egocentric, or at least unwilling to get help from other people. It might seem as if they pursued their goals with a degree of singlemindedness that effectively shut out everyone else. Actually, this was not the case at all. One of the things these successful adults did was surround themselves with other people. They relied upon their parents, spouses, other family members, and friends for help and support. Often, they searched for specific people to function as mentors for them and reinforce the skills and knowledge they needed for advancement in their fields. So, in contrast to being loners, the quality of their personal relationships was one of the important elements of their success.

The incredible amount of persistence referred to above was not applied by these adults in an indiscriminate way. They were clever about it. They practiced what could be called "selective persistence"; that is, they channeled their energies and efforts into only those areas for which they felt the likelihood of success was greatest. As the old song goes, they chose to "accentuate the positive and eliminate the negative".

The authors of the study refer to this selective persistence as "goodness of fit". Adults who were learning disabled and successful had fit themselves into environments that maximized their skills and abilities. In short, they capitalized on their strengths. And by doing things they were good at, they eventually found themselves in careers they loved. Levels of job satisfaction were extremely high; in fact, the highly successful adults, almost without exception, revealed a strong passion for their work. This should not be surprising, since we all like to do the things we're good at.

Part of capitalizing on one's strengths requires that people adapt to their weaknesses. Some flexibility is needed in order to avoid tasks that are difficult and upon which efforts would be wasted. Another very important thing that successful adults with learning disabilities do is go about things their own way. Early in their lives they learn that techniques that work for other people are not useful for them. Then, they are very creative in coping with their problems by using strategies which serve as detours. So, they do not bang their heads on the wall; they walk around it.

A good analogy here would be people, blind since birth, who have learned to use their other senses more efficiently. Their hearing and touch become more acute; they become areas of strength as they go about the business of learning in school and getting around in their communities despite their continuing inability to see. Similarly, those adults with learning disabilities who become successful learn there is more than one way to solve problems and that original solutions to them can be found even in the continued presence of their disabilities. A dyslexic entrepreneur learns to use a word processor that has spell and grammar checks as she writes her business letters. A salesman with a memory problem draws caricatures of his clients that trigger their names in his mind. A lawyer, still deficient in organizational skills, develops a color code for his files to help him distinguish at a glance the type and priority of each of his cases. These people use a large variety of very imaginative coping mechanisms on the way toward achieving their goals and successes.

The authors of this study conclude their report with a sobering comment about the participants' feelings toward school. With near unanimity, these adults believed that school had not been useful for them. They felt it had little value, did not relate to their later success, and, in many cases, was actually a destructive element in their lives.

Negative feelings about education are certainly not limited to those people with learning disabilities who participated in this study. Almost everyone who has asked adults who are learning disabled about their earlier years in school has noted similar attitudes. For example, a college graduate who was working as a congressional aide despite his learning disability said, "Junior high school was wretched. I was made to feel that I was dumb. In elementary school and junior high, I had a really rotten self-image." Another young woman commented as follows: "I get very defensive still . . . and am afraid to ask questions in fear that I will be wrong. Every teacher should remember their worst class when they were in school and realize that that's how LD kids feel all of the time." Finally, a 33 year old woman with a college degree who works as a stock broker said, "I think of my whole school experience as being bad. Horrifying. Someone at school knocked all the confidence out of me when I was little. I'm still always working on that. It still hurts me. I think about it a lot."[28]

It's apparently true that many adults with learning disabilities had very hurtful experiences when they were in school. However, it is also true that these adults are old enough to have gone to school during the years before learning disabilities were recognized and included as a part of special education. Now, for the current generation of children with learning disabilities, those who are in fact participating in special programs, the hope is that more will view their schooling in a positive light and as an experience that contributed to better levels of adjustment as adults.

Drs. Gerber, Ginsburg, and Reiff, the principal investigators in this study, have made an important contribution to our understanding of learning disabilities, the long term effects they have on people, and what it takes to achieve success despite them. They learned so much because they reversed the procedure that is usually followed in research studies. Instead of starting at the beginning with young children who were learning disabled, stating hypotheses, applying different treatments to those children, and waiting years to determine which treat-

---

[28]Polloway, E.A., et al. "Learning disabilities in adulthood: Personal perspectives". *Journal of Learning Disabilities*, Vol. 25 (8) 1992, p. 522.

ment, if any, might have had an influence on later degrees of success, they started at the end. Theirs' was a retrospective study, because they immediately went to older people who would know the most about coping with learning disability and looked back at their earlier development. There can be no better way to discover factors necessary to succeed than to go directly to a group of adults who are learning disabled and already successful and ask them how they did it.

Three success stories have been presented. The characters were an armless woman, Indochinese refugee children, and adults with learning disabilities. Regarding their backgrounds, the nature of their disabilities, and the kinds of adversities they faced, the people in these stories are as different as people can be. And yet, in at least six ways, they had important things in common. These things are summarized below:

1. They learned that success came from their own efforts and that taking control of their lives by assuming responsibility for achievement was the key.

2. They had parents who were insightful and tough enough to see beyond their children's problems and demand effort from them.

3. They set clear goals, and they implemented specific strategies to attain them.

4. They capitalized on their strengths and devised effective ways to compensate for their weaknesses.

5. They had other people who were positive influences for them; people who were supportive and functioned as mentors.

6. They worked harder than anyone else; they persisted; they never gave up!

You may wish to reread these six things. Taken together, they represent a general formula for success. They are a good place to start. Now, be as objective, careful, and honest as you can as you assess how much they apply to you and your child at the present time. If you see some discrepancies after comparing them to the situation that currently prevails in your family, all of you have some work to do. Some changes are in order.

While the formula may be a good beginning, what is still required is a distillation of this general information about success into a series of more specific suggestions you could apply in your own family. We begin at that point in the next chapter.

# Chapter 9

# *Bringing It All Home*

You have read about a number of people with very different backgrounds who were able to compensate for a wide variety of disabilities and problems, overcome the adversities they created, and reach successful levels of adjustment. So, at this point, it would not be unreasonable to expect you to be feeling at least a little more optimistic about the effects of learning disability on your child's future. However, any renewed sense of optimism you may now have is likely to diminish rather quickly unless you can move beyond generalities about success, formulate a more specific plan of action, and implement it. This may be a problem, because change is difficult, particularly when habits, attitudes, and methods that you have practiced for a long time are involved.

We began learning how to be parents a long time ago, when we were children. Didn't you ever catch yourself saying exactly the same things to your children that your parents said to you when you were a child? Words that you heard so often, and which were so irritating that you vowed you would never say them to your own children. But now, maybe in the midst of some stressful family episode, you hear them again, only this time they're coming out of *your* mouth. You repeat them almost verbatim and with the same nauseating inflection your parents used. How about: "Stop that whining before I *really* give you something to cry about". Or perhaps, "We don't care what *other* parents let their kids do; as long as you're living under this roof, you'll live by *our* rules". And the inevitable: "Wait 'til your father gets home from work; then you'll *really* be in trouble".

Beyond parroting their words, we relate to our children in other ways that are usually quite similar to what we experienced, years ago, growing up with our own parents. The methods of discipline we are comfortable with, our ways of showing affection, the amount of protection we provide, the kinds of standards we set and expectations we have; indeed, it is likely that much of what we do as parents in general is influenced and patterned after what we encountered as children ourselves.

If it is true that the origin of parental attitudes and child rearing practices can be traced to childhood, it would follow that these same attitudes and practices might be difficult for you to change now, many years later, as adults. If you think of yourself as an "old dog" and therefore inflexible and resistant to learning new tricks, some of the suggestions that follow may seem hard to apply. It will be easier to overcome any resistance, though, if you remember that you're asking your children to cope and compensate for some very real disabilities. To require that much effort and flexibility from them without demonstrating similar willingness to change yourself would be unreasonable and would probably delay any significant growth. Assuming, then, that there is some potential for change in the old dog yet, let's begin to consider some specific suggestions.

First, telling the truth about learning disability is essential. There will be little progress unless **everybody** at home; that is, both parents, brothers and sisters, and the child with the disability can stand up, face it directly and say, in so many words, "We have some learning disability at our house". In too many families, everyone knows that learning disability is present, but nobody is willing to acknowledge it. It sits there like a big pink elephant on the middle of the living room rug while people tiptoe around it pretending it's invisible and hoping not to disturb it.

It's not likely to vacate the premises, so instead of denying that it's there, it will be much more productive to talk about learning disability. Bring it to the surface, point out what is unique about each member of the family, and stress that it's OK, even good, to be different. Methods and materials are readily available that will help stimulate discussions. Go to your local public library and get some books about learning disability that explain the problem in language that is suitable for children.[29] If you haven't already done so, join a parent organization, attend meetings regularly to hear guest speakers and talk with other parents, and subscribe to monthly periodicals that publish articles about learning disabilities.

Simulations are another excellent way to encourage talking about the problem. They are fun and provide at least a brief approximation of what it might be like to be learning disabled for family members who aren't. Have older children or adolescents try the reading disability exercise and other simulations in this book. Or, give everyone a hand mirror, felt tipped marking pen, and a piece of paper upon which a continuous design of curved and angled lines has been drawn. Place the paper flat on a table and hold the mirror upright, behind it. Look at the design in the mirror and try to move the marker along the lines without straying from them. This will be very difficult to do, because it requires correcting for the reversed images created by looking in the mirror. It is a task which shows the

---

[29]See: 1. Roby, C. *When learning is tough: kids talk about . . .* A. Whitman & Co. Morton Grove, Il. 1994.
2. Fisher, G. et al. *The survival guide for kids with LD.* Free Spirit Pub. Co., Minneapolis, 1994.

kinds of frustrating perceptual problems that are commonly associated with learning disability.

What you're trying to do is bring everyone to the point of feeling easy and open about learning disability so that the child most directly affected can admit its presence, begin recognizing areas of strength, and move on from there. After facing up to the problem, moving on is likely to require working on personality traits like self-confidence and persistence.

Discussing how to modify personality traits associated with learning disability requires returning to the notion of "learned helplessness". This idea suggests that children who consistently face failure and frustration come to believe that continued efforts will be futile. They blame their failure on factors within themselves such as lack of intelligence, and they attribute whatever few successes they have things outside of them like luck.

In lieu of dogged persistence, they are quick to give up. They have no goals, because they think continued failure is inevitable. They are not able to see anything positive or productive about their learning disabilities. They do not develop creative ways to work around obstacles, because those obstacles have overwhelmed them. They do not capitalize on their strengths, probably because they aren't confident enough to feel they have any. They take no responsibility for their own progress; instead, they embrace what is essentially a fatalistic, "whatever will be will be" attitude toward school and every other aspect of their lives. They careen through their days making no decisions to take charge of their lives. Thus, they do not adapt or shape themselves in order to move ahead. They are not in control. What is clear is that they exhibit characteristics that are exact **opposites** of those that adults with learning disabilities consider vital to their own success. Sadly, even with their arms, they turn out to be much more handicapped than Bonnie Consolo.

It is important to note that the kind of helplessness described above is *learned* behavior. This behavior is not predetermined by fate. Neither is it fixed by heredity at the moment of conception. On the contrary, it develops gradually over time, in response to repeated and numerous environmental events. So, if children can learn to be helpless, it follows that they can also learn to be competent.

In contrast to people with learning disabilities who learn to be helpless and fail, people who are in control learn to help themselves and succeed. They begin learning to cope and compensate for their disabilities from parents who know how to foster **self-esteem** and **independence** in their children. These are two behavioral characteristics that can be nurtured in young people. With self-esteem and independence, children and adolescents are able to begin making conscious decisions to take charge of their lives; they can shape and adjust themselves in order to cope and make progress.

Much has been written about self-esteem. Entire shelves in the library tell us that we're both OK, how to like ourselves, and how to be assertive. The core of the message in all these "how to" books is essentially the same. Self-esteem means feeling good about yourself. It is a sense of competence we attain as a result of being successful at things and getting the recognition and respect of other people. We take personal credit for our accomplishments, and we can tolerate some failure. With self-esteem, we grow confident and more willing to try new things. We grow into capable adults. Without it, even at old age, we may still be babies.

Self-esteem is a fragile thing. It is easily influenced by our experiences and can be enhanced or diminished depending upon our judgments of how we do on everyday activities compared to others around us. The passage that follows was written by a person with a learning disability who grew into a well-adjusted adult:

> I have experienced first-hand the anguish, anger, despair and utter frustration of the child who cannot tell the literate person that literacy is not the *only* level on which he exists; that he is a whole person with many ways of giving and receiving information other than by reading and writing; and that the social environment's demand for functional literacy tends to overshadow all the other potentials an individual may possess. Functional literacy is not the only measure of an individual and never was. My argument is with the world of education which tends sometimes to forget the relative narrowness of its focus and thereby does many of us a disservice. . . . It is possible to achieve a successful, fulfilling life even without the ability to read. . . . The educational system could deal with the dyslexic child by working with the strengths and talents of that individual child instead of concentrating on his or her inability to read and thus destroying the child's faith in him/herself. I successfully completed high school and obtained a college degree even though I am functionally illiterate. I learned with my heart, my hands, my mind, and my will, and not through literacy . . . everyone has skills and talents, even if they are not those which our society and its educational machinery traditionally values. . . . There is a person inside the person the school and society is trying to teach. We must learn to respect and re-value that person. It is only because the system's view of literacy is so inflexible that dyslexia is regarded as a "learning disability" at all. What an incredibly narrow view of learning this is, and what an incredibly limiting view of human potential![30]

---

[30]Smith, C.R. *Learning disabilities: The interaction of learner, task, and setting.* pp. 319-320.

The author of the above passage, Richard Devine, works as a goldsmith and still has a severe reading disability. With unusual eloquence, his words are both a condemnation of the educational system and a testament to his ability to achieve despite his academic weaknesses.

In Mr. Devine's writing, there is an important reminder for parents of children with learning disabilities. He tells us that within every child, there is untapped talent and creativity. There are interests and capabilities. All of these are potential strengths. It is imperative that you find them and help your child capitalize on them as soon as possible.

School, with its emphasis upon academic achievement, may not be a place where your child has experiences that regularly enhance self-esteem. Self-devaluation is more likely. However, students with learning disabilities who discover they have abilities in areas other than academics are less likely to be devastated by school failure. Billy, you may recall, turned to swimming and wrestling. For others, it may be art or music. Read what one mother had to say about her son who was learning disabled and his drums:

> We would watch our son carefully, always amazed at his inability to be perfectly still. Even when we forced him to sit up straight with his hands on the table and his feet on the floor, it wasn't a minute before he would start his tapping. First his fingers, then his hands, his legs, and sometimes, believe it or not, he'd bounce his butt up and down too. One evening, my husband came home with a set of drums. He felt that if our son was going to do all that incessant tapping, at least some good might come from it by learning an instrument. We got him a few lessons, and he took off! The drums became the center of his life. When he got to high school, he tried out for the marching band and was quickly accepted. Then, he was approached to participate in the school's jazz combo, and after their first "gig", every one of his classmates knew him. Can you imagine what a two minute, frenzied drum solo in front of 500 adolescent peers did for his ego? Today, our son makes his living as a musician. He is a percussionist in the local symphony orchestra, plays in two jazz bands, and teaches young children how to drum. Recently, I asked him how he felt in school with all the academic problems he had. He said, "I knew all along that most of the other kids could do things that I couldn't, but I also knew I was the best in that whole school at what I did".[31]

---

[31] Personal correspondence, May, 1994.

It's beautiful, isn't it. Here is a person with a learning disability who actually feels he was better than anyone else at something! Of course, all children may not be as talented as this one; they may not be the best in the whole school; but all children have strengths, interests, and potentials that can be cultivated and nourished to the extent that they gain a measure of recognition and healthy self-esteem.

The possibilities are almost limitless. Drama, scouting, collecting, skiing, martial arts, model building, photography, cooking, jogging, painting, ham radio, carving, cartooning, film making, skating, body building, aerobics—all of these and many other activities are available to serve as buffers between your children's academic difficulties and their self-esteem. Find one or more and watch them take off!

As self-esteem develops, so will self-reliance. Children and adolescents who begin to feel good about themselves are building the foundation necessary to function as independent people. As they contemplate their children's futures, parents will indeed say, "We want our children to grow up to be self-supporting, healthy and happy, independent adults." It's what we all want for our children, but sometimes, particularly when a disability is present, we get off the track and do precisely what we shouldn't.

Here is an example of the wrong approach involving an adolescent who was going to school at her community college. She was attractive, a good athlete, and popular with her classmates. She was bright enough; her performance on intelligence tests placed her in the above average range, and talking with her indicated that her interests and knowledge of general information were appropriate for her age.

Her grades through grammar school had been good, but in high school, they had been only average, even a little below. During much of the time she was in elementary and high school, she got help in a resource room for students with learning disabilities. Now, in college, writing was still a problem for her, especially compositions beyond one or two pages. One day, during the fall of her freshman year, she brought home an assignment from her English class. Her project for the semester was a 15-20 page term paper about capital punishment. She was required to do some research on the topic and write a paper that would present both sides of the issue and conclude with a statement of her own opinion.

Instead of feeling anxious and insecure at the thought of writing a long term paper, this student, who had never written one before, felt confident it would get done. You see, her father was a sociologist; in fact, he was a professor at the same college she was attending. He knew all about capital punishment; he talked about it in his classes, and he had presented several scholarly papers on the topic at professional conventions. She just knew daddy would help her; he would never let her down; after all, he loved her.

And how he helped her! He loved her so darned much that he wrote the paper for her. Oh, she typed it all right, but he wrote it. Two weeks later, when her teacher returned the term paper with a big red A on the title page, it was hard to tell who was more elated, father or daughter.

Of course, neither one of them should have been the least bit happy or proud. Consider what this father, a man who vividly demonstrates that holding advanced degrees has little to do with being an intelligent parent, had really said to his daughter. He told her that he did not yet have confidence in her ability to function as a mature person. He told her she was not yet capable and whole, and the best way to mask her incompetence was to have him assume responsibilities for her. The clear message he had conveyed to his daughter was that she was still inadequate; and, by his happy reaction to "her" grade, he let her know that continuing to be dependent upon him in the future would be just fine. (Or, at least until she got married, at which point her husband might be expected to take over.)

Think about it. Without denying his love, this father's relationship with his daughter was contaminated. Those with a tendency to psychoanalyze might be tempted to attribute his kind of misguided parental overindulgence to unresolved guilt associated with her learning disability. Kind of like, "I must have done this to you, so I'll make it up to you". Others, less psychologically oriented and therefore not so bent upon seeking subtle and underlying motivations, would probably feel that he was just taking the easy way out. It required less time and effort for him to complete her assignment for her than to arrange things which would have enabled her to write the paper herself. So he got an A when a C, earned independently by her, would have been so much better.

Whatever the reason for dad's behavior, by loving his daughter the way he did, he was doing his bit to create a handicapped person. To do things for our children that they could do for themselves is ultimately one of the most destructive things we can do to them. Reflect back to Bonnie Consolo's parents next time you feel guilty or are tempted to take the easy way out. They were tough enough to love their daughter the right way.

Knowing what *not to do* is important during the process of helping children who are learning disabled become self-reliant. However, the level of independence they will ultimately need to take full control of their lives and become capable, resourceful, and successful people requires that you get active and *do* some things too. Begin with a careful analysis of the overall way that you relate to your children. Try not to focus on isolated or specific events; instead, look at the big picture, what might be considered your general manner of parenting.

A number of interesting and instructive research studies have been done that examine the relationship between parenting styles and children's development. One of these studies identified three different styles—authoritative, authoritarian, and permissive—and looked at their respective effects upon children's behavior.[32]

In this study, authoritative parents maintained a tight grip on parental reins. They were controlling and demanding. They were quick to reward their children for responsible behavior and equally speedy in applying punishment for deviations they considered unacceptable. Punishment, however, was never applied without explanations and suggestions for improvement. These parents left no doubt about their expectations for obedience, satisfactory performance in school, and sharing of chores around the house. At the same time, however, they were affectionate and willing to discuss their children's opposing viewpoints with them. It was obvious that they valued independent thinking and behavior in their children, and they responded favorably to it.

Authoritarian parents also had high standards for behavior. But in place of explanations and discussions with their children over disagreements, they were uncommunicative and rejecting. These parents placed a premium upon absolute compliance for its own sake, and there was little verbal exchange with their children when conflicts arose. Power struggles, with no attempt to reason or work through problems, were common in their homes. Since adults are usually bigger and more powerful than their children, they usually prevail in these struggles. It's not a fair fight, but when your opponent and the referee are the same person, that's how it goes.

Permissive parents, as you may have already figured out, had a very different style than the others. They tolerated all of their children's impulses. There were no rules or standards of behavior that were consistently applied in their homes. With none present, there was nothing to enforce. Children were essentially free to conduct themselves as they wished, both with respect to their behavior at home and their achievement in school. They just sort of floated along. Outwardly, they may have seemed to enjoy the freedom, but inside, at least on occasion, I'd bet they were hoping for someone to spell out a rule or two and set some limits.

From this study, we learn that very different patterns of children's behavior developed in response to the three styles of parenting. It turned out that children of permissive parents had the most problems controlling their impulses and developing self-reliance. Apparently, parents who are permissive, who place no demands on their children, and who utilize what is essentially a free floating, unstructured style, run the risk of increasing the degree to which their children remain dependent, long after such dependency is appropriate. At the other ex-

---

[32]Baumrind, D. "The contributions of the family to the development of competence in children". *Schizophrenia Bulletin*, Vol.14, 1975, pp. 12-37.

treme, those children with strict and rigid, authoritarian parents tended to be withdrawn, unhappy, and distrustful. They were more guarded in their relationships with others and had difficulty interacting in social situations.

Authoritative parents are OK. In fact, the may even be excellent. In many cases they may be just what children with learning disabilities need. In this study, the children of authoritative parents turned out to be the most independent, purposeful, cooperative, socially adept, dominant, and achievement oriented.

The implications are obvious. Children, who naturally imitate the behavior of their parents, learn to be self-reliant from affectionate, supportive parents who are themselves independent and secure in maintaining positions of authority in their homes. Authoritative parents who have high expectations for their children, who convey clear standards of behavior, who reward compliance to those standards but are willing to discuss deviations, and who are consistent as they discharge their parental responsibilities provide the best environment for the development of the kind of independence their children need to assume control of their lives, help themselves deal with their disabilities, and succeed despite them.

Authoritative parents help their children develop in other important ways, too. For example, they can do much to improve deficiencies in organization and time management. "His days seem totally disjointed, without order or harmony"; "She just can't seem to get her act together and get started on anything"; or, "He never finishes a task when he's supposed to, because he loses all track of time". If your child is at all typical, chances are you have said one or more of the above sentences more often than you would like.

Children with learning disabilities frequently have the information and skills needed to complete a task, but gathering the necessary tools, getting down to work, and using them in the correct sequence until the task is finished seem beyond them. Their perceptual problems, spatial distortions, impulsiveness, attention deficits, and related characteristics place them at the mercy of a confusing mess of overwhelming stimulation. They may spend so much time and energy just keeping the lid on this pot of bubbling disarray that they have too little left over to get organized. Consistent maintenance of high standards of behavior and firm expectations for task completion by authoritative parents will certainly not eliminate the perceptual problems and attention deficits etc., but, very importantly, they will never allow for their being used as excuses either.

It's easy to forget, particularly if we view ourselves as well-organized, temporally responsible adults, that we didn't start out that way. We didn't come into the world with the ability to systematically manage our affairs and proceed through a sequence of interrelated activities in a thoughtful, carefully organized, and timely way. A lot of experience and a long process of learning were required. You can accelerate that learning process in your child by doing specific things to help improve organizational and time management skills. Consider some suggestions below:

One space at home for your child that everyone understands is exclusively for work is crucial. This work station, study carrel, private office, business room, or whatever you wish to call it must be free of materials and equipment that relate to play, leisure time activities, or anything else other than work. Things like a television and VCR, stereo equipment, telephone, any toys and games, pictures of "significant others", and similar objects of distraction will have to be located elsewhere. The message is clear: this is the place you go to work; nothing else happens here.

In your son or daughter's work space, a desk drawer or shelf that is compartmentalized will help too. With one slot designated for pencils, another for paper, a third for reference books, and others for paper clips, rubber bands, the stapler, and ruler etc., getting one's act together becomes easier. After a few trials with help from you, older children and adolescents should be responsible for maintaining an adequate quantity of supplies and keeping their work place sufficiently neat and clean by themselves. You will have to be flexible enough to accept some latitude when applying *your* standards for neatness and cleanliness. Being authoritative does not equate with rigidity, and to get into major struggles over minor differences is to waste your big ammunition on small battles.

Show children how easy and helpful it is to make lists and schedules, not just for school assignments but for all of their daily, routine activities. A calendar for listing "things to do" and when to do them is one of the least expensive and best investments there is. As they list their responsibilities and check them off in order of completion, they learn to prioritize and approach tasks in a logical, step by step sequence. They will be learning important organizational skills. The calendar, a concrete and constant reminder of the passage of time, will build and reinforce their temporal skills. They will actually be able to see deadlines approaching instead of just thinking (or not thinking) about them. Most importantly, they will be deriving the additional satisfaction associated with being independent people who are beginning to take responsibility for their own development.

"C'mon, get with it", you may be saying. "My child is dyslexic. He can't write entries in a calendar, and even if that were possible, he couldn't read them back." If you are indeed saying or even thinking that, I would say to you: "C'mon get with it, think back to what you have learned about adults with learning disabilities who make it. Remember the general formula for success".

One part of the formula stressed the fact that these successful people had learned to capitalize on their strengths and devised effective ways of compensating for their weaknesses. So, if your child's reading and writing are still delayed to the extent that the traditional methods of recording entries on lists and schedules are impossible, all that is needed to compensate is a small, hand-held tape recorder.

The idea is to cope, to work around disabilities that may always be there. Learning to rely on a tape recorder makes coping very easy and provides practice with a device that will be invaluable in school and in the future. Recording class assignments, lecture notes, dates and times of business meetings, travel directions, items to bring home from the grocery, dates of wedding anniversaries and children's birthdays—all of these everyday requirements and many others can be handled in an organized and timely way. A tape recorder is at least as important in your child's book bag as pencils and paper.

Personal computers have become much more affordable. Consider buying one; in fact, make it a priority. The cost will be more than offset by the advantages they have for your child and the rest of the family. They are highly efficient electronic organizers that operate at the speed of light. They provide a place for everything in neatly arranged files. Information is at one's fingertips and can be retrieved quickly and simply by depressing a key or clicking a mouse.

Children who develop some elementary computer skills and are motivated to write computer programs of their own will be practicing the type of logical and sequential thinking that can't help but develop better organizational skills. Even older people who have been flexible enough to move out of the stone age and learn the basics of computing will attest to how much easier it is to get things done in an organized and time efficient manner.

Computers provide some other extremely useful ways for coping with learning disabilities that were impossible just a few years ago. They are infinitely patient tutors that can give immediate feedback as they drill and reinforce basic academic skills in novel and interactive ways. Their colorful and game like modes of presentation are attractive and often highly motivating. They make no judgments; they never get angry or tired, and they never ground us or send us to our rooms.

We forget that reading is just one of a number of tools for gathering information. It enables us to share the thoughts of another person. For people who are good at reading, it is an efficient way to learn about things. However, reading is not the only way to learn; there are other tools. For children who are not such good readers, computers are capable of getting information into their heads through other channels. CD Rom makes entire encyclopedia available, and with multimedia presentation formats, children with reading disabilities have much easier access to this information. Blind children read and learn with their fingers; children who are learning disabled can read, learn, and share others' thoughts by seeing and hearing.

Anyone who is engaged in written expression, from six year old children composing their first stories to the most accomplished authors, has the same two essential tasks. There is the creative task that requires formulating a sequence of ideas in one's brain, and there is the mechanical task of getting those ideas down on paper. Computers, at least not yet, do not help with the creativity. But, they are immensely helpful with the mechanics; that is, they can help with problems in legibility, spelling, punctuation, grammar, and vocabulary.

Problems with fine motor coordination that used to result in illegible handwriting and unreadable papers become irrelevant when children learn the keyboard and type their work. Problems with visual memory that underlie persistent spelling problems are quickly circumvented with a word processing program that has a built in spell-check. Newer word processing programs have grammar and punctuation checks that monitor those kinds of errors and suggest corrections. Even a limited vocabulary can be expanded by using a program with a thesaurus. Don't stifle your children's creativity by forcing them to get bogged down and exhausted over relatively trivial things like poor spelling, grammar, and handwriting.

If you're still wavering on the potential value of a computer, perhaps the words of a person with a learning disability who benefitted will convince you:

> I faked my way through school because I was very bright. I resent most that no one picked up my weaknesses. . . . I was afraid to know myself. A blow to my self-esteem when I was in school was that I could not write a poem or story. I could not write with a pen or pencil. The computer has changed my life. I do everything on my computer. It acts as my memory. I use it to structure my life and for all of my writing since my handwriting and written expression have always been poor.[33]

Advanced technology is here to stay. Use it. Buy a computer. Your child will benefit. Later on, if things work out as you hope they will, your successful and grown up child's secretary will take over.

As your child improves at organizational and temporal skills, you can begin to help with the development and use of more advanced strategies. Goal setting, for example, is another part of the general formula for success. Adults with learn-

---

[33] Polloway, E.A., et al. "Learning disabilities in adulthood: Personal perspectives". *Journal of Learning Disabilities*, Vol. 25 (8) 1992, p. 521.

ing disabilities consistently mentioned how important it had been for them to be as precise as they could in identifying what they wanted in the future. Then, they devised a plan and followed the steps necessary to reach their goals. The parents of Indochinese refugee children were also sticklers for goal setting. The objective was that their children would do well in school, and subsequently, everyone followed a meticulous plan to achieve it.

Now, it's your turn. At the beginning, aim low. You might start by agreeing with your child on short term, easily attainable goals. As examples: By tomorrow night, I will have washed, dried, and folded my clothes. By the end of the week, I will have finished my math packet for homework. In two weeks, I will have enough money to buy my sister a birthday present. By next month, I will have applied for three after school jobs. Obviously, there are countless other possibilities.

Goals should be written and displayed in a visible place. Posting them on a bulletin board in the work area and checking them off as they are met is a good idea. When children can look back at a series of prior accomplishments it's very useful, because it gives them an obvious reminder of how capable they are. They come to learn that there are people around to help, but ultimately it is their own efforts that determine how successful they are. It's called growing up.

There is no reason that goal setting should be an activity restricted to a child who is learning disabled. Make it part of the whole family's routine. When children see older siblings and parents managing their affairs competently and helping themselves get what they want, the process of setting goals becomes a natural way of combating learned helplessness. What is important is establishing a truly ingrained habit of setting goals, planning, and following through. This must become as natural as brushing one's teeth in the morning.

Equally important will be your providing consistent and immediate reinforcement for trying. Should your child, after a conscientious attempt, fail to reach what seemed like a simple goal, reward the effort, nevertheless. You might want to briefly discuss and explain what went wrong and try to *elicit* an alternative plan. Resist any temptation to do the planning yourself despite the fact that it might be quicker and easier. The plan must come from your child; you can make suggestions and even refine the plan, but the best chance for attaining a goal comes when the person responsible feels a sense of ownership. Let them take control. It's what successful people do.

Practice the goal setting habit consistently with your child. Work to gradually increase the challenge and the time that it takes to attain them. Whether the objective is modest like pleasing a sister with a birthday present or huge like pleasing oneself with a college degree or a fulfilling career, the process involved is the same: set goals, plan strategies, and follow through. Each success adds to a backlog that will make it easier to persist until the next goal is achieved.

It's true. Billy's mom was right; there are no guarantees. The business of rearing children is so complex and influenced by so many factors outside of our control that we can never know for certain how it will all turn out. The contention here, however, is that you can shorten the odds. One more time, consider the general formula for success. It talks about parents who were tough enough to demand effort, but, at the same time, were supportive, positive influences in their children's lives.

Perhaps longer than other parents, you will have to be there as a staunch advocate, mentor, and consistent source of support. Almost without exception, successful adults who are learning disabled point to particular members of their families as sources of inspiration, motivation, and persistence. These are some of their words: "My parents never said anything degrading about my disability. Mom was an advocate for me. School knees still quake when she comes around. Mom went to schools and insisted that I get the education I needed". And from another, who said, "My mother was an incredible help. She helped me with diagnosing my problem. She got me help when I needed it, then advocated for my mainstreaming when I was ready. The biggest influence in my positive attitude was my mother". And from still another, "I have an extremely supportive family who has helped me through my educational goals . . . my parents made me feel that I could learn in a different way. Dad pointed out that other people had faults. He had had school problems too, but he is a very successful business man".[34]

Finally, it is also true that no matter the degree to which you read and further your knowledge about learning disabilities, join and actively participate in parent support groups, objectively evaluate the pros and cons of various treatment regimens, and try your absolute best to foster your child's self-esteem and independence, there will still be bad days. There will be days when you have tiring conferences at school, trying episodes at home, and feel just plain frustrated and discouraged. At those times, it may help to remember a few sentences written by Dr. Barbara Cardoni, a Professor at Southern Illinois University and founder and director of their program for college students with learning disabilities. "Never tell children that they are bad or evil. Tell them you hate the act or the behavior but never the person. You can never say 'I love you' too often, to anyone."[35] Remember, too, that the victory is sweetest when the odds are longest.

---

[34]Polloway, E.A., et al. "Learning disabilities in adulthood: Personal perspectives". *Journal of Learning Disabilities*, Vol. 25 (8) 1992, p. 521.

[35]Cardoni, Barbara. *Living with a learning disability.* p. 116.

# Epilogue

Billy is a sophomore in high school now. Not long ago, he came home from school and informed his mom that his friends didn't call him Billy anymore. He told her that "B" was the shortened version he chose to go by. She said, "Bill" was as short as it would get at home, at least for her, and that his dad would have to make up his own mind.

Bill still struggles academically, but his grades are good. He's not an official participant in special education anymore, but he does have permission to go to the LD resource room teacher whenever he feels he needs some help. Those visits have decreased this year. Bill is proud of his work at school, and especially so when he completes it entirely on his own.

He is quite an expert on his computer, and he uses it for most of his written assignments. Apart from that, he has learned some computer language and written a few programs of his own. Math and science continue to be his best subjects, and although he hasn't decided for sure, he says he wants to go to college and work as a veterinarian or computer scientist when he gets older.

Bill is active in extracurricular activities at his school. He's on the varsity swim team and junior varsity wrestling team. As one of the younger members of the letterman's club, his letter sweater is one of the most cherished items in his wardrobe. Unlike his dad, who keeps his in the back of the closet and only takes it out on rare occasions, Bill wears his almost every day.

He spends time each day body building. He won't admit it, but the word among some of the more aggressive freshman and sophomore girls is that he's' become quite a "hunk". Several unsolicited phone calls each night are evidence of their feelings.

Like every other teenage boy, he looks forward to getting his driver's license next year and his own "wheels". He bags groceries at the neighborhood supermarket and is saving some of his wages each week to help pay for a used car. He has shown a recent interest in learning to play the guitar. He pursues this new hobby with much enthusiasm, loudness, and persistence, if not a lot of talent.

Bill has done well. There are residuals of his attention deficit and impulsivity, but he has been able to manage them without drugs for several years. Of course, he remembers his early years in school, his medication every morning, and his participation in special education. His parents know that drug abuse is a problem in every high school. They have talked with Bill about it, and he is sensitive to their concerns. He has told them not to worry, because "I got my drugs out of the way in grade school".

Now, there is a little brother at home, six years younger than the twins. Once in a while, Bobby will be restless and difficult to get to sleep. Bill suggested to his mom that maybe he would quiet down if they took him for a ride in the car. She wondered if he could have possibly remembered.

Billy's parents have done well too. They continue to be active in the parents' group for children with learning disabilities. Very often they will speak with "new" parents; that is, people who are in the same position they were 10 or 12 years back. They think about those early days often, read the journal at least once a year, and give thanks that their son has done so well. They know that in the future, Billy's learning disability is likely to "rear its ugly head" occasionally, but they are confident that their boy will cope. I think he will cope too, in large part, because of them. Now it's your turn.

# References

Bateman, B. (1992). "Learning disabilities: The changing landscape." *Journal of Learning Disabilities*, 25, 29-36.

Baumeister, A., et al. (1989). "New morbidity: Implications for prevention of children's diseases." *Exceptionality*, 1, 1-16.

Baumrind, D. (1975). "The contributions of the family to the development of competence in children." *Schizophrenia Bulletin*, 14, 12-37.

Bennett, William J. (1994). *The Index of Leading Cultural Indicators*. New York: Simon and Schuster.

Blaskey, P. et al. (1990). "The effectiveness of Irlen filters for improving reading performance". *Journal of Learning Disabilities* 23, 10: 604-611.

Bryan, T. (1983). In C. Collin (Ed.) *Keys to Success*. Monograph of the Michigan ACLD Conference.

Caplan, C., Choy, M., & Whitmore, J. (1992). "Indochinese refugee families and academic achievement." *Scientific American*, 266 (2), 36-42.

Cardoni, Barbara. (1987). *Living with a Learning Disability*. Carbondale, Illinois: Southern Illinois University Press.

Chalfant, J.C. (1985). "Identifying learning disabled students: A summary of the National Task Force Report". *Learning Disabilities Focus*, 1, 9-20.

*Chicago Tribune.* 4-15-93, Section I, p. 18.

Cobb, R.M. and Crump, W.D. (1984). *Post School Adjustment of Young Adults Identified as Learning Disabled While Enrolled in Public Schools*. (Final Report) Washington, D.C. ERIC Document 253029.

Cohen, A. (1988). "The efficacy of optometric vision therapy." *Journal of American Optometric Assoc.*, 59, 95-105.

Edgar, E. (1986). "Secondary programs in special education: Are many of them justifiable?" *Exceptional Children*, 53, 555-561.

Gadow, K.D. (1986). *Children on Medication: Vol. I, Hyperactivity, Learning Disabilities, and Mental Retardation*. San Diego: College-Hill.

Gerber, P.J., Ginsberg, R., and Reiff, H.B. (1992). "Identifying alterable patterns in employment success for highly successful adults with learning disabilities." *Journal of Learning Disabilities*, 25, 475-487.

Greene, Bob. *Chicago Tribune*, 5-9-94, Tempo section, p.1.

Hughes, R., and Brewin, R. (1979). *The Tranquilizing of America.* Chicago: Harcourt & Brace, Jovanovich.

Irlin, H. (1983). "Successful treatment of learning disabilities." Report to the American Psychological Association.

Kavale, K.A., and Forness, S.R. (1983). "Hyperactivity and diet treatment: A meta-analysis of the Feingold hypothesis." *Journal of Learning Disabilities,* 16, 324-330.

Myers, P. and Hammill, D. (1982). *Learning Disabilities.* Austin, Texas: PRO-ED.

Nutrition Foundation. (1980). Report of the National Advisory Council on hyperkinesis and food additives. New York.

Polloway, E., Schewel, R., and Patton, J. (1992). "Learning disabilities in adulthood: Personal perspectives". *Journal of Learning Disabilities,* 25, 520-522.

Rie, H.E., Rie, E.D., Stewart, S., and Ambuel, JP. (1976). "Effects of ritalin on underachieving children". *American Journal of Orthopsychiatry,* 46, 313-322.

Robinson, G. and Conway, R. (1990). "The effects of Irlin colored lenses on students' specific reading skills and their perception of ability: A twelve month study". *Journal of Learning Disabilities,* 23, 589-596.

Ross, D. and Ross, S. (1982). *Hyperactivity.* New York: John Wiley and Sons.

Schmidt, Randolph, E. *Chicago Sun-Times*, 4-8-94, p. 30.

Smith, C.R. (1994). *Learning Disabilities: The Interaction of Learner, Task, and Setting.* Boston: Allyn & Bacon.

Sylvan Learning Center, (1991). Advertising Brochure, Front insert.

Walker, S., III. (1974). "Drugging the American child: We're too cavalier about hyperactivity." *Psychology Today,* 8, 43-48.

Wender, P. (1971). *Minimal Brain Dysfunction in Children.* New York: Wiley Interscience.

# Appendix I

*Individualized Educational Plan*

MDC/IEP Page 1 of _____

## MULTIDISCIPLINARY/IEP CONFERENCE SUMMARY REPORT

### ☐ MDC

PURPOSE OF CONFERENCE

☐ a. Initial Evaluation/Eligibility Determination

☐ b. Reevaluation

☐ c. Determine Relationship of Disabling Condition(s) to Disciplinary Code Violation(s)

☐ d. Other _____

### ☐ IEP

PURPOSE OF MEETING (Check appropriate boxes)
☐ Initial IEP
☐ Annual Review
☐ Educational Setting Change
☐ Program Services Change
☐ Interim Review
☐ Graduation
☐ Other (specify) _____

DISABILITY REQUIRING SPECIAL EDUCATION
(See MDC Sec. 11)
Primary _____
Primary _____
Secondary _____
Secondary _____
Secondary _____

**CURRENT STUDENT DATA FOR THE 199___ - 199___ SCHOOL YEAR**

Conference Date(s) _____

1. **Name of Student** [Last, First, Middle]

   School/District Now Attending _____
   Current Grade _____

   Birth Date ___/___/___   I.D. # _____   Sex ___   Home District/School _____
   Home Phone _____

   Student's Address [Street, City, Zip Code]

   Parent/Guardian/Surrogate Parent
   (Name) _____ (Relationship) _____
   Home Phone _____
   Work Phone _____
   Address _____   ☐ Same as above

   Parent/Guardian/Surrogate Parent
   (Name) _____ (Relationship) _____
   Home Phone _____
   Work Phone _____
   Address _____   ☐ Same as above

   Primary Language/Communication Mode
   Student's _____   Parent's _____

### PARTICIPANTS

| District Director/Designée | LEA Representative | Parent/Guardian |
|---|---|---|
| Principal | Teacher | Parent/Guardian |
| Teacher | Teacher | School Psychologist |
| School Social Worker | Counselor | Speech/Language Pathologist |
| Other (specify title) | Student | Other (specify title) |
| I have received a copy of this report. (Parent signature) | Date copy sent to parents (if parent is not in attendance) | Person who prepared this summary |

NSSED 9/92   cc: Student File-white ● LEA Coordinator-yellow ● Parent-pink ● Teacher/Service Provider-goldenrod   A

Student's Name _____   Date _____   MDC/IEP Page _____ of _____

2. REASONS FOR REFERRAL AND REFERRAL SOURCE
   _____
   _____

3. REGULAR EDUCATION INTERVENTIONS PRIOR TO INITIAL REFERRAL
   _____
   _____

4. PARENT INPUT
   _____
   _____
   _____
   _____

5. CASE STUDY INVENTORY

| Case Study Components | Completed by: Name/Title | Case Study Components | Completed by: Name/Title |
|---|---|---|---|
| a. Interview with Child | | g. Learning Processes and Educational Achievement Level Evaluation | |
| b. Parent Consultation | | h. Learning Environment Assessment | |
| c. Social Developmental Study (Include assessment of adaptive behavior and cultural background) | | i. Specialized Evaluations ☐ Psychological | |
| | | ☐ Medical | |
| d. Academic History and Current Educational Functioning | | ☐ Speech/Language | |
| | | ☐ Other (specify) | |
| e. Vision and Hearing Screening Date: _____ | | j. Observation of Student | |
| f. Medical History and Current Health Status | | k. Independent Evaluation (if applicable) | |

6. STUDENT PERFORMANCE ANALYSIS

   Using data obtained from the case studies, record the multidisciplinary team's analyses of the student's physical, social, emotional, intellectual, health, and academic functioning levels which may indicate the existence of a disability for which special education may be required. Describe in quantitative and qualitative terms the student's functioning in the following categories:

   a. Health           c. Hearing                    e. General Intelligence      g. Communicative Status
   b. Vision           d. Social/Emotional Status    f. Academic Performance      h. Motor/Orthopedic Status

   FUNCTIONING LEVELS: State findings and conclusions regarding deficits in the student's ability to function based on the case study evaluations. Identify the special evaluation methods/instruments used and results which support findings and conclusions.

   | Category |
   |---|
   | |

Student's Name _____ Date _____ MDC/IEP Page _____ of _____

6. Categories of Student Functioning:

   a. Health
   b. Vision
   c. Hearing
   d. Social/Emotional Status
   e. General Intelligence
   f. Academic Performance
   g. Communicative Status
   h. Motor/Orthopedic Status

   | Category |
   |---|

   | Category |
   |---|

   | Category |
   |---|

   | Category |
   |---|

Student's Name _____  Date _____  MDC/IEP Page _____ of _____

7. SPECIFIC LEARNING DISABILITY DETERMINATION

   a. Does a severe discrepancy exist between the student's achievement and academic potential with regard to oral expression, listening comprehension, written expression, basic reading skills, reading comprehension, mathematics calculation, or mathematics reasoning which requires the consideration of special education and related services?

   ☐ Yes    ☐ No    (If "yes," complete 7b-g. If "no," proceed to Section 8.)

   b. If 7a. is answered "yes," describe the discrepancy(ies) and the basis for determination.

   c. Describe relevant behaviors noted during observations by a person other than the child's teacher and the relationship of that behavior to academic functioning.

   d. Describe any educationally relevant medical findings.

   e. Is the severe discrepancy between potential and achievement primarily the result of:
      1. Visual, hearing, or motor disability?  ☐ Yes  ☐ No    3. Emotional Disturbance?                          ☐ Yes  ☐ No
      2. Mental retardation?                   ☐ Yes  ☐ No    4. Environmental, cultural, or economic disadvantage?  ☐ Yes  ☐ No

   f. Does the student have a specific learning disability for which special education and related services are required?    ☐ Yes  ☐ No

   If the answer is "yes," record the SLD eligibility in Section 11.

   g. PARTICIPANTS    If the determination for placement is LD, agreeing participants must initial next to name in Section 1 certifying that the report reflects their conclusion. Any school district personnel disagreeing with these recommendations must submit a separate minority report indicating which areas of the report they disagree with and the reasons for their disagreement.

8. OPTIMAL LEARNING STYLE. Identify student's optimal learning style and areas of strengths.

9. DISABILITY DETERMINATION                          EDUCATIONAL INTERFERENCE

   _____ affects _____
   _____ affects _____
   _____ affects _____
   _____ affects _____
   _____ affects _____

NSSED 9/92        cc: Student File-white • LEA Coordinator-yellow • Parent-pink • Teacher/Service Provider-goldenrod        D

Student's Name _____ Date _____ MDC/IEP Page _____ of _____

10. **EDUCATIONAL NEEDS.** If applicable, identify the unique programming needed to address those areas in which disabilities interfere with educational performance.

11. **ELIGIBILITY** ☐ Yes ☐ No

| Primary | Secondary | |
|---|---|---|
| ☐ | ☐ | Specific Learning Disability (D) |
| ☐ | ☐ | Autism (O) |
| ☐ | ☐ | Brain Injury (P) |
| ☐ | ☐ | Speech and/or Language Impairment (I) |
| ☐ | ☐ | Mental Impairment (B or A or M) _____ |
| ☐ | ☐ | Behavior Disorder/Emotional Disorder (K) |
| ☐ | ☐ | Visual Impairment (E or H) _____ |
| ☐ | ☐ | Hearing Impairment (F or G) _____ |
| ☐ | ☐ | Physical Disability (C) |
| ☐ | ☐ | Other Health Impairment (L) |
| ☐ | ☐ | Developmentally Delayed (N) |

12. **DISCIPLINARY CODE CONSIDERATIONS.** Does this student's disability interfere with his/her ability to abide by the school district's disciplinary code?

    ☐ Yes ☐ No

    If yes, explain rationale and behavior management plan which may be considered for inclusion in the students's IEP.

    _____
    _____
    _____

    If no, explain rationale: _____
    _____
    _____
    _____
    _____
    _____
    _____

13. **TRANSITION PLAN FOR STUDENTS 14½ YEARS AND OLDER**

    _____
    _____
    _____
    _____
    _____

    COMMENTS

Student's Name _____ Date _____ IEP Page _____ of _____

AREA OF EDUCATIONAL INTERFERENCE _____

CASE MANAGER _____ SERVICE PROVIDER(S) _____

PERFORMANCE LEVEL _____

| GOAL TYPE | ☐ Annual<br>☐ Transition Plan | GOAL NUMBER | GOAL STATEMENT |
|---|---|---|---|

| SHORT-TERM OBJECTIVES | INITIAL PERFORMANCE LEVEL | MONITORING SCHEDULE | EVALUATION PROCEDURES | CRITERIA FOR MASTERY | DATE(S) PROGRESS REVIEWED | EXTENT OBJECTIVES MET |
|---|---|---|---|---|---|---|
| | | ☐ Daily<br>☐ Weekly<br>☐ Monthly<br>☐ Quarterly<br>☐ Grade Period<br>Other ____ | ☐ Tests<br>☐ Charting<br>☐ Observations<br>☐ CBM<br>Other ____ | ☐ ____ Accuracy<br>____ of ____ Trials<br>Other ____ | | |
| | | ☐ Daily<br>☐ Weekly<br>☐ Monthly<br>☐ Quarterly<br>☐ Grade Period<br>Other ____ | ☐ Tests<br>☐ Charting<br>☐ Observations<br>☐ CBM<br>Other ____ | ☐ ____ Accuracy<br>____ of ____ Trials<br>Other ____ | | |
| | | ☐ Daily<br>☐ Weekly<br>☐ Monthly<br>☐ Quarterly<br>☐ Grade Period<br>Other ____ | ☐ Tests<br>☐ Charting<br>☐ Observations<br>☐ CBM<br>Other ____ | ☐ ____ Accuracy<br>____ of ____ Trials<br>Other ____ | | |

cc: Student File-white • LEA Coordinator-yellow • Parent-pink • Teacher/Service Provider-goldenrod

Student's Name _____  Date _____  IEP Page _____ of _____

| RELATED SERVICES (Type) | Projected Date of Initiation | Projected Minutes Per Week | Anticipated Duration |
|---|---|---|---|
| | | | |
| | | | |
| | | | |
| | | | |

OTHER CONSIDERATIONS (Describe, as applicable, considerations regarding LRE, summer school, graduation, discipline, the need for additional evaluation, transition plan, etc.) _____
_____
_____
_____

EDUCATIONAL PLACEMENT OPTIONS

A. List placement options considered and reasons each was rejected based on the goals developed to address student educational needs identified in the MDC:
_____
_____
_____
_____
_____
_____

B. Placement Determinations
   1. Setting in which student will receive special education and related services.

   _____  Program  _____
   Projected Date of Initiation     Projected Minutes Per Week      Anticipated Duration

   2. Regular education classes and activities in which student will participate and any required modifications.
   _____
   _____
   _____

C. If placement is to be in a separate class or facility:
   1. What is the nature or severity of the student's disability that precludes placement in a regular class or facility?
   _____
   _____

   2. Explain why supplementary aids and services cannot be used to educate the student in a regular education class or facility.
   _____
   _____

TRANSPORTATION

☐ Walk      ☐ Daily on vehicle with regular education students
☐ Parent    ☐ Daily on vehicle with special education students

Vehicle Adaptation (specify) _____
Other _____

NSSED 9/92      cc: Student File-white • LEA Coordinator-yellow • Parent-pink • Teacher/Service Provider-goldenrod      G

# Appendix II

# Addresses of Organizations

Attention Deficit Disorder Assoc., 8091 S. Ireland Way, Aurora, Colorado, 80016

CHADD (Children with Attention Deficit Disorder) 499 N. W. 70th Ave., Plantation, Florida, 33317

Council for Exceptional Children, 1920 Association Dr., Reston, Virginia, 22091

Division for Children with Learning Disabilities (A branch of the Council for Exceptional Children), 1920 Association Dr., Reston, Virginia, 22091

Council for Learning Disabilities, P.O. Box 40303, Overland Park, Kansas, 66204

Disability Law Center, 11 Beacon St., Suite 925, Boston, Massachusetts, 02108

Disability Rights Center, 1616 P. Street, N.W., Suite 435, Washington, D.C., 20036

Family Resource Center on Disabilities, 20 East Jackson Blvd., Room 900, Chicago, Illinois, 60604

Learning Disabilities Association of America, 4156 Library Road, Pittsburgh, Pennsylvania, 15234

National Center for Learning Disabilities, 99 Park Ave., Sixth Floor, New York, New York, 10016

National Network of Learning Disabled Adults, 800 N. 82nd St., Suite F2, Scottsdale, Arizona, 85257

Orton Dyslexia Society, 727 York Road, Baltimore, Maryland, 21204

M8130-TN
29